Couple Burnout

Couple Burnout

Causes and Cures

Ayala Malach Pines

Routledge • New York and London

Published in 1996 by
Routledge
29 West 35th Street
New York, NY 10001

Published in Great Britain by
Routledge
11 New Fetter Lane
London EC4P 4EE

Library of Congress Cataloging-in-Publication Data is available from the Library of Congress.

For my parents,
Zev and Judith Malach,
the most loving couple I have ever known

Contents

Acknowledgments

One of the greatest pleasures in finishing a book is the writing of acknowledgments. It marks the end of a process, and enables a sentimental reflection on the whole of it. My work on the subject of couple burnout, and this book, have benefited from the contributions of many people. I discussed the ideas expressed in this book with Patrick Taffe and gained greatly from his breadth of knowledge, intelligence, and love. My dearest friend, Lynn Freed, painstakingly read successive drafts of the manuscript, very much improving it with her amazing talent for words. Lillian B. Rubin, who is a wonderful friend and role model, provided valuable criticism of many of the ideas expressed in the book.

Other close friends, in and out of psychology, have read earlier drafts of the book and made thoughtful comments that helped improve it both in content and in style. I would like to express my appreciation to Charles Alexander, Ruth Dieches, Yehuda Handelsman, Dennis Jaffe, Barbara Jonas, Lynne Kaufman, Ellen Kirschman, Anya Lane, Rafi Malach, Uzi Nitsan, Cynthia D. Scott, Israel Segal, and Lil Tulp. Linda Hermelin was helpful in editing the manuscript.

While conducting the research on which the book is based, I learned from valuable discussions with several brilliant colleagues, whom I am also lucky to have as close friends; these include Elliot Aronson, Dalia Etzion, Arie Kruglanski, Christina Maslach, Baruch Nevo, and Ofra Nevo.

x

Ayala Malach Pines

My agent, Judith Weber, of Sobel Weber Associates, deserves special thanks for her continuous guidance and support. Nancy Coffey of St. Martin's Press, the publisher of the trade version of the book, will always have my gratitude for her belief in the book. Philip Rappaport, my editor on this revision for couple therapists, and the rest of the editorial staff at Routledge were great to work with. Thank you!

Most important, however, I would like to express my deep affection and gratitude to all the individuals and couples who took part in my research, workshops, and clinical work, who opened their hearts, minds, and lives to me, and on whose experiences this book is based.

Introduction

This book was written primarily for professionals who work with couples. Its purpose is to describe the phenomenon of couple burnout—its causes, danger signs, and symptoms—and to suggest the most effective strategies for coping with it.

The book is based on extensive research and clinical work with individuals and couples. The research included analysis of several thousand questionnaires (using the Couple Burnout Measure, see Appendix 1) and interviews with hundreds of individuals and couples, both burned out and happily married. The couples included in the interviews were in traditional as well as nontraditional marriages, both heterosexual and homosexual, in the United States and abroad. Quotes from the interviews are interspersed throughout the book. The clinical work included many years of work with burned-out individuals and couples as well as hundreds of couple burnout workshops across the United States and abroad.

One of the most important conclusions I have reached based on the clinical work is that understanding the process of burnout is the first step in learning to cope with it. Again and again I have seen in my work with individuals, couples, and groups that merely identifying burnout for what it is can have a healing effect. A typical reaction has been: "So it's burnout! And I thought there was something seriously wrong with us!" (or "with me"). Guilt and blame are replaced by renewed energy for coping simply by labeling the problem as "burnout."

The conceptual framework of couple burnout is an integrated approach that combines the advantages of the psychodynamic, systemic, and behavioral approaches, with the less recognized and less acknowledged advantages of the existential and social psychological perspectives. Rather than focus on couple or individual pathology, the conceptual framework of couple burnout focuses on the normal process of attrition that long-term intimate relationships undergo as a result of stresses from within and without the relationship, especially when people are trying to derive a sense of existential significance from their intimate relationships.

The first chapter in this book explains the historical and philosophical context for the emergence of burnout, and presents its definition and danger signs. The second chapter gives the burnout model, which details the process of burnout from the birth of love until its death. It also describes the antithesis of burnout—"roots and wings." The third chapter discusses burnout within the context of clinical approaches to couples.

The burnout perspective is helpful in noting the similarity in people's choices of a career and a romantic partner and the consequences of this similarity for coping with burnout in both spheres. Chapter 4 addresses the issue of balancing an intimate relationship with an important career. Other chapters address gender differences in couple burnout (chapter 5) and burnout in sex (chapter 6).

Is burnout inevitable? This question, asked by many people, is addressed in chapter 7. Chapter 8 presents research findings of comparisons between burned-out and happily married couples. The results of the comparison are presented, as are recommendations on how to avoid couple burnout.

In addition to a theoretical perspective, the book offers detailed instructions for professionals interested in applying the conceptual framework of couple burnout in their work with individuals, couples, and couple groups. Chapter 9 presents a step-by-step description of a couple burnout workshop, including detailed descriptions of several experiential exercises as well as ideas for using these exercises in the context of couple counseling.

As noted earlier, among the individuals and couples who participated in the studies of couple burnout there were both heterosexual and homosexual individuals and couples. Since the responses of the homosexual individuals and couples were not significantly different from those of the heterosexual ones, they were combined in the tables and the discussions. As we will see in the examples presented throughout the book, the problems related to burnout are rather similar in gay and straight couples.

Note

The names and all other identifying characteristics of the people who are quoted throughout the book have been changed to protect their anonymity.

1

Couple Burnout: Definition, Causes, and Symptoms

How we loved in the fashion of all lovers, and strove not to let the little things of existence destroy us. How they did, and how we forgot. Just like everyone else.
            —Han Suyin, *A Many Splendoured Thing*

"Love at first sight." "Made for each other." "Happily ever after." For most people growing up in a western culture, the expectations for love and marriage are extremely high. These expectations set the stage for burnout. Even if they should know better, when they fall in love, most people hope that their love will last forever. This hope has the power to blot out awareness of obvious faults, reduce common sense, and obliterate foresight. Burnout occurs when, maintaining these idealistic notions about love, people run into the stark reality of everyday living. It is the psychological price many idealistic people pay for having expected too much from their relationships, for having poured in more than they have gotten back—or believing they have done so. Burnout is caused by too great a discrepancy between expectations and reality. With the accumulation of disappointments, with the stress of day-to-day living, comes a gradual erosion of spirit and eventually burnout.

Dona is a tall, striking woman and a successful architect in her early forties. After fourteen stormy years of marriage, Dona is burned out:

> I feel hollow in this relationship. There is nothing between us: no bond, no communication, no sharing, no contact, no feelings, nothing. We have no plans together, no interests together. The tensions are making me tired and sad. There is no hope for us. There is nothing that he does that enhances my life in any way, emotionally, intellectually, physically. I don't feel like a couple; I feel emotionally deprived. I feel resentful and irritated. I have to close myself off emotionally to stop feeling that way. I can't give myself sexually or emotionally any more. I don't believe life has anything to give me. I would do anything to be free of him. I have no feelings for him except irritation and sometimes pity. When I come home and he's there I get all uptight. I wouldn't stay with him for anything.

Dona's husband, Andrew, a dark, good-looking man in his mid-forties, is an accountant. Describing life in a burned-out marriage he says:

> It's awful. I mean, it really is almost like living with a stranger. That's how bad it gets. Once there's no more interaction it's just poof, it's gone. I'm really living a life of quiet desperation.

Andrew and Dona's feelings of emotional depletion, their hopelessness about their future together and helplessness to make things better, are the hallmarks of burnout, a painful denouement for many marriages. While marital problems are as old as the institution of marriage, burnout is a modern phenomenon. It has to do with the importance of romantic love to our generation, and the fact that love has become a highly valued foundation for marriage and most other couple relationships.

There are few adults growing up in this culture who do not know what "romantic love" is and who have not experienced it at one time or another in their lives. Scholars, such as Elaine Walster, who have studied romantic love define it as "a state of intense absorption in another," and of "intense physiological arousal." At times it involves only "longing for complete fulfillment." For the lucky it involves the "ecstasy in finally attaining the partner's love" (Walster and Walster 1978, 9).[1]

While romantic love has reigned supreme among other forms of love since time immemorial, only in recent years has it been promoted as the basis for mate selection. There is a universally shared desire to believe that the emotional bond of love is enough to sustain a long-term couple relationship. The voice of reason, which would be welcomed in any other human endeavor, is scorned when applied to mate selection. Consider, for example, a scathing description of today's young urban professionals that appeared in a *New York Times* article. The author of the article dubbed the Yuppies "unromantics." The reason: they are considering each other's assets (country house, income potential, schooling, family) before deciding that they could make suitable marriage partners. The Yuppie approach to marriage fits the description of a famous sociologist, Erving Goffman:

> A proposal of marriage in our society tends to be a way in which a man sums up his social attributes and suggests to a woman that hers are not so much better as to preclude a merger or partnership. (Goffman 1952)

To a romantic society such as ours, this kind of a steely-eyed materialism about marriage seems cold and cynical, if not entirely inaccurate. There is a shared resistance to viewing an intimate relationship as a business proposition. As a matter of fact, very few businesspeople get into a lifelong partnership with the scant information most couples have about each other. But love and marriage are viewed as affairs of the heart, and love is seen as an experience that defies reason and is meant to defy reason.

Love is seen as an act of freedom and self-determination. Romantic love has an appeal on several scores. It carries individualism to its furthest extreme. The beloved is unique and irreplaceable. In a country that considers the pursuit of happiness a birthright, it is a pure expression of this pursuit, pulling with it intimacy, family, and hopes for the future. It is even an expression of equality—differences in background do not matter to lovers. Since they are glorified in each other's eyes, there is a sort of star-crossed equality between them.

All this is part of the ideology of romantic love. In fact, the ideology does not always match the way people actually select their mates. In reality, class, ethnic, and racial differences do matter, but there is a belief on the part of lovers (a belief shared and reinforced by society at large) that love will overcome these differences. There is a desire to believe that love can conquer all.

While everyone is exposed to information about the failure of romantic love, and some people have a firsthand experience with its
fragility as the foundation of couple relationships, most people still
want to continue believing in it—probably because they see no
immediate or better alternative. The high divorce rates do not deter;
most divorced people cannot wait to remarry and give love another
chance. In fact, more people are marrying and cohabiting today than
ever before in history.[2] As Ingrid Bengis concluded, "The only permanent thing about love is the persistence with which we seek it"
(Bengis 1972).

Love. Why are so many people today obsessed with love? The
answer, I will argue, has to do with people's need to give meaning to
their lives. Romantic love is an interpersonal experience in which we
make a connection with something larger than ourselves. For people
who are not religious and who do not have another ideology they
strongly believe in, love can be the only such enlarging experience.
As Otto Rank so aptly noted, people are looking for romantic love to
serve the function that religion served for their predecessors—giving
life a sense of meaning and purpose (Rank 1945).

The ultimate existential concerns about the meaning of life are
universal. They include, according to Irving Yalom, the terror of our
inevitable death, the dread of groundlessness in the vast universe, the
total isolation with which we enter life and with which we depart
from it, and the meaninglessness of our own self-created mortal life
(Yalom 1980).

The tremendous sense of isolation and fright attached to these
concerns result from the unique duality of human beings, which
Kierkegaard described 150 years ago as a "synthesis of the soulish and
the bodily" (Kierkegaard 1957, 39)—the paradox of the spiritual self
that can transcend life imprisoned in a mortal body that cannot
escape death. From time immemorial people have attempted to deal
with their feelings of existential isolation and fright by giving meaning to their lives. This can account in part for the importance of
romantic love to Americans. Ever since its founding by people escap-
ing religious persecution, America has struggled to remain secular.
Since a secular society does not provide ready answers to the existential dilemma, "love," as Erich Fromm put it, becomes "the answer to
the problem of human existence" (Fromm 1956, 7).

In his Pulitzer Prize–winning *The Denial of Death*, Ernest Becker
expands on this idea. Becker discusses the universal need to feel "he-

roic," to know that one's life matters in the larger "cosmic" scheme of things, the need to merge with something higher than oneself and totally absorbing. For modern people who reject the religious solution to the existential dilemma, one of the first alternatives has been "the romantic solution." The "urge to cosmic heroism" is fixed on the lover, who becomes the divine ideal within which life can be fulfilled, the one person in whom all spiritual needs become focused (Becker 1973, 160).

But even people who believe in romantic love may find it difficult to admit that through it they are seeking a solution to the existential dilemma. First, this admission implies that they need another human being to make their lives matter—which can be construed as weakness of character. Second, to admit that romantic love is the vehicle for finding ultimate meaning in life is to agree that the quest for love is a religious quest. This is probably unacceptable to most people, since the substitution of romantic love for God would seem positively sacrilegious to the faithful, and unseemly to the rest.

Nevertheless, it seems to be exactly that for people who do not feel a personal connection to God and who seek a connection with something larger than themselves in romantic love. Love promises to fill the void in their lives, to eliminate their loneliness, to justify their existence, to provide security and everlasting happiness. The promise of love is attached to a specific image of a person or a relationship. When people meet a person who fits their romantic image, they fall in love. They then expect their relationship with that person to make all the promises of love come true. When the person or the relationship fails them, they burn out.

Western culture would have people believe, then, that love can answer the question of human existence, provide the best basis for marriage, and celebrate democracy, equality, freedom of choice, and the pursuit of happiness. These expectations are transmitted via popular songs, books, television, and the movies, which preach that love is the most important thing in life. Love, we are told, is what "makes the world go 'round." We are also told that true love lasts forever. A couple can live "happily ever after," "till death do us part."

People's ideals determine expectations and the understanding they bring to bear on relationships. Those who uncritically internalize the ideals expect a relationship to solve their problems and give meaning to their life. When these expectations are not met, they are not only disappointed in their mate, but their world has no meaning.

In fact, some romantic expectations can be achieved in a couple relationship, but other expectations are totally unrealistic. People who want to live "happily ever after," who expect the simple act of marriage to give focus and meaning to their lives and to answer all of life's basic questions, are very likely to be disappointed. Hanging on to those notions almost guarantees burnout. Yet we are actually socialized to believe in them.

Culturally shared expectations are often expressed in truisms and proverbs. In one of my studies of marriage burnout I asked a hundred married couples to what extent they believed in ten romantic truisms such as "love at first sight" and "a match made in heaven." (The ten are presented in the box on page 7.) I discovered that belief in such romantic truisms was correlated with marriage burnout.[3] This can mean that the level of burnout (which reflects people's experiences) influences their belief in certain truisms. Alternatively, it can mean that the belief in the truisms (by creating unrealistic expectations) influences their level of burnout.

Because we have, as a society, continually raised our expectations as to what constitutes a romantic success story, today people are more ready than ever to abandon a relationship if it fails to fulfill their expectations. The high divorce rates (the United States has the highest in the world) are one testimony to that.[4] There is no longer a requirement to prove moral incertitude or "breach of contract" to end a marriage. Incompatibility—the failure of love to meet our expectations—is often grounds enough.

The expectations we have today of love are not built into human nature. As Nathaniel Branden noted in *The Psychology of Romantic Love*, throughout most of human history this notion of love being required for marriage was unknown:

> Young people growing up in twentieth century North America take for granted certain assumptions . . . that are by no means shared by every other culture. These include that the two people who will share their lives will choose each other, freely and voluntarily, and that no one, neither family nor friends, church or state, can or should make that choice for them; that they will choose on the basis of love, rather than on the basis of social, family, or financial considerations; that it very much matters which human being they choose and, in this connection, that the differences between one human being and another are

To what extent do you believe the following ten truisms, using the scale:

1	2	3	4	5	6	7
Do not believe at all			Believe to a certain extent			Believe totally

___ Love at first sight
___ A match made in heaven
___ Living happily ever after
___ Marriage kills love
___ True love is possible only after the infatuation is over
___ Love, like a good wine, can get better with time
___ One should not marry for love
___ People who wait for the perfect mate remain single
___ A matchmaker is the best way to ensure a happy marriage
___ True love is forever

Couples are asked to respond to the ten truisms, guess each other's answers, and then compare notes.

immensely important; that they can hope and expect to derive happiness from the relationship with the person of their choice and that the pursuit of such happiness is entirely normal, indeed is a human birthright; and that the person they choose to share their life with and the person they hope and expect to find sexual fulfillment with are one and the same. Throughout most of human history, all of these views would have been regarded as extraordinary, even incredible. (Branden 1983, 56)

Denis de Rougemont made similar observations about the un-paralleled importance given to love in modern times:

No other civilization, in the 7,000 years that one civilization has been succeeding another, has bestowed on love known as ROMANCE anything like the same amount of daily publicity. . . . No other civilization has embarked with anything like the same ingenious assurance upon the perilous enterprise of making marriage coincide with love

thus understood, and of making the first depend on the
second. (de Rougemont 1940, 291–92)

Ironically, the celebration of love, the "daily publicity" bestowed on
it, and the importance and glory attributed to it have produced an
apparent scarcity rather than an abundance. Never before in history
have so many people been disappointed in the promise of romantic
love. Could the importance attributed to love make people more susceptible to burnout, or is this insidious process of love's erosion
indigenous to all long-term intimate relationships? My interest in
such questions was the original impetus for studying couple burnout.
My goal was to understand burnout, its causes and consequences, and
how best to cope with it.

What Is Couple Burnout?

Burnout is a painful state that afflicts people who expect romantic
love to give meaning to their lives. It occurs when they realize that
despite all their efforts, their relationship does not and will not do
that. Marriages can be disappointing and unhappy without being
burned out. When a mate is sloppy or inconsiderate, one can decide
to live and let live, but when one looks for the relationship to give
meaning to one's life, such annoyances can be unbearable.

Couple burnout is caused by a combination of unrealistic expectations and the vicissitudes of life. It is not caused—as most clinical
approaches to couple therapy believe—by a pathology in one mate,
in both mates, or in the relationship.

The burnout of love is a gradual process. Its onset is rarely sudden.
Instead, there is a slow fading of intimacy and love accompanied by a
general malaise. In its extreme form, burnout marks the breaking
point of a relationship. The burned-out person is saying in one way
or another: "This is it! I've had it with this relationship. I can't take
this anymore."

Burnout is formally defined (and subjectively experienced) as a
state of physical, emotional, and mental exhaustion caused by a
chronic discrepancy between expectations and reality.

Physical Exhaustion

The physical exhaustion of burnout, unlike that caused by running a
marathon or spending the day raking leaves, appears as chronic fatigue

that is unrelieved by sleep. Typically, burnout victims wake up exhausted on Monday morning after spending a whole weekend in bed. After dragging their feet all day, when night finally arrives, they cannot fall asleep. Their stomach churns as they remember every unkind word, every inconsiderate act of their mate. Each "crime" on their long list becomes magnified in the twilight of sleep. They are furious. They toss and turn. When they finally manage to fall asleep, they are haunted by nightmares (their home struck by an earthquake, etc).

Some people take sleeping pills or drink alcohol to help themselves fall asleep, but the next morning they awake fatigued, groggy, and with a splitting headache. The typical burnout victim feels more and more weary. Occasionally people have chronic headaches, stomachaches, or back pains. They become susceptible to illness, catching every cold or flu around. Some people don't feel like eating ("I have a gigantic lump in my throat"). Others eat compulsively ("At least I can get this enjoyment out of life").

Emotional Exhaustion

Burnout victims feel emotionally drained, disillusioned, and resentful. They don't feel like explaining anything, and they don't want to "work through" problems. They are convinced that there is no hope for them or the relationship. They grow more and more unhappy. Every day seems worse than the last. Life feels empty and meaningless. Nothing seems to matter anymore. Frequently depressed, they need what little energy they have left for work and the children. There is no light at the end of the tunnel. As bad as things are, they feel helpless to bring about change. They have given up on the idea that they can change their mate, and they don't have the energy or the inclination to try to change themselves. Since they see no hope for change, they feel trapped. In extreme cases, the feelings of futility and despair can lead to an emotional breakdown or to serious thoughts of suicide.[5]

Mental Exhaustion

The mental exhaustion of burnout manifests itself most clearly in a lowered self-concept and in a negative attitude toward everything about the relationship, particularly the mate. When couples are first in love, they not only adore each other, they also feel pretty good about themselves. This, in turn, makes them feel good about the rest of their life. It is as if the magic of love touches everything. Through the rose-colored glasses of love, both partners look handsome, charming, and sexy. Life makes sense and is all promise.

When burnout starts, things are no longer wonderful. Both partners are painfully aware of all the little (or not so little) things that the other one is doing that make them want to jump our of their skin and scream ("the way he coughs," "the way she drives," "the sight of his back," "her unshaved legs"). Their endurance for these and other behaviors is severely hampered.

The feelings of disenchantment are not limited to the mate. There is a terrible feeling of personal failure, of having failed in the most important relationship in one's life (even if it was not your fault and even if you did everything in your power to prevent it from happening). Looking at themselves in the mirror, burnout victims see a person they do not like. They discover some nasty streaks in themselves they never knew existed. The sense of disappointment, like the love before it, transcends the couple. It affects the way they feel about other people, about their life, about the future, and about their ability to love.

Emotionally Demanding Situations

Living with another person is always demanding. It requires adaptation and compromise because, by definition, people are different, see things differently, and have different values, needs, and expectations. One has to accommodate the other person in one's emotional, as well as physical, space. That accommodation is never easy. It is especially hard when one cares deeply about the other person. In the same way, a long visit by a close family member can be more stressful than a long visit by a casual acquaintance.

What makes the accommodation to a mate so hard is the realization that it is supposed to go on forever, and forever is a very long time. It is one thing to have a wild affair on a cruise ship, knowing it will be over when the ship reaches shore. In such a situation it is relatively easy to overlook or disregard annoying habits, even irreconcilable differences. It is far more difficult to look the other way when your mate throws a wet towel on the bed for the hundredth time, and you know this is going to go on for a lifetime.

The stresses inherent in living with another person "until death do us part" are amplified by the very romantic notions that often lead to marriage. If you believe that love conquers all—even wet towels on the bed—yet find yourself blowing up at your mate over a wet towel, you either have to conclude that love doesn't conquer all or that love does conquer all but you don't love your mate enough.

People in an arranged marriage who discover that their mate is not a paragon of virtue are no doubt disappointed. But people who married for love are likely to be devastated. Burnout afflicts most people who enter marriage "starry eyed" and infatuated, who idealize their mate and think they have found their Prince/Princess Charming. The stresses that they find most unbearable are the daily drudgery, the hassles and pressures of everyday life. Burnout is far less likely to happen to those who enter marriage with a practical, or even cynical, outlook and who view marriage as a business arrangement. In short, *in order to burn out one must, by definition, have once been "on fire."*

Although being "on fire" involves the danger of burnout, being too cautious about an emotional commitment carries its own dangers. A relationship that starts as a practical arrangement is not necessarily going to succeed—quite the contrary. Planning for the end of a relationship seems to be one of the surest ways to end it. A well-known palimony lawyer says that most marriage contracts with a divorce clause end up in court.

The Onset and Afterlife of Burnout

Romantic love is not an eternal flame. If fuel is not added to it, sooner or later the flame is going to burn out. The onset of burnout is rarely sudden. It is insidious. It seldom results from a single traumatic event or even several traumas.

When people hear about a friend or a neighbor divorcing and try to figure out what led to the schism, they quickly seize upon concrete, traumatic, and dramatic events: the husband gets drunk and beats his wife; the wife has a lover. These things occasionally do cause the breakup of a marriage, but they are not the causes of burnout.

Burnout results from disappointment in love as an answer to the existential dilemma. It is aided by an accumulation of love-eroding stresses, a gradual increase in boredom, and a build-up of petty annoyances. It is virtually impossible to single out one precipitating factor.

Like the camel's back, love is squashed by the accumulated weight of trivial "straws":"she would straighten my desk and I could never find anything I was looking for"; "he never put the toilet seat down."

Burnout starts with a growing awareness that things are not quite as good as they used to be, that the mate is not quite as exciting and wonderful as he or she used to be—reminders of the reality so effortlessly denied during infatuation. There is an irritating conviction that one mate is not giving to the relationship as much as one does, that one's most important needs are not being met. If nothing is done at this stage to stop the process, things are bound to go from bad to worse. The infrequent periods of discontent become more and more frequent. The mild feelings of dissatisfaction grow into a smoldering fury. After reaching a crisis point, couples have a choice between staying in a dead relationship, or breaking up.

Dona describes the "causes" of her burnout:

> There were many incidents. Every morning something would happen. Like he'd bang a door shut that I hadn't shut. I often leave doors open. Instead of saying, "What a charming thing—here's a person with an open personality" (I think it's very symbolic)—he'd bang this thing shut. And it immediately caused tension. And my immediate thought was: another nail in your coffin. That's what I kept thinking every time he'd do something. . . . Every day cemented my feelings. . . . I like to have things around and Andrew doesn't like things. He was always clearing things and putting them in the garage. He wouldn't even ask me. Like he'd take all of our daughter's mugs—leave her only one— and put the rest in the garage. It would just infuriate me. . . . His smoking cigars drove me up the wall, too. Every night he would smoke one cigar. I just hated the smell and the staleness of it.

Andrew used to clear things out and smoke cigars even when he and Dona first met, but Dona was in love with him then. Now there is no love to balance out the irritations.

Is it possible to turn a burned-out relationship into a living and loving one? Yes! But that does not mean that all burned-out relationships can or should be saved, that the spark should be rekindled no matter how small and at any cost. There are couples whose love for each other is long gone, couples who nevertheless cling to the marriage. On the other hand, there are couples who give up too quickly. As soon as the first blush of love is gone, as soon as they experience a few problems, they split up—even when there is a great deal of affection and caring between them.

The decision as to whether a relationship is dead or still has a spark that can be rekindled should be made only by the two people involved, and made jointly. It is rarely possible for just one person in a couple to rekindle the spark.

In most cases, where the spark is gone completely for both partners, it is best to part amicably and give each other a chance to start a new life with another person. Burnout can be a positive turning point not only when conquered, but also when it is a signal to leave a long-dead relationship behind and move on to a new, perhaps very different relationship.

In saying that in order to burn out one needs to be first on fire, and that burnout can be a positive experience, I of course do not mean to imply that burnout is a prerequisite to having a good relationship. There are couples who have figured out from the start what is necessary in order to keep the spark alive in their relationships. Studying these loving (as opposed to burned-out) couples was one of the most rewarding parts of my research.

For a relationship to be truly alive, the romantic flame does not have to be raging in full force all the time. Sometimes the flame dies down. Other times it flickers. For secure couples, neither event is perceived as a serious threat. Actually, couples in relationships that are loving and alive tend not to worry too much about the spark. "One of the best things about my relationship with Colleen is that we can let things die down once in a while," says George, who has been living with Colleen for eleven years. "We even go as far as talk about breaking up, and about me moving out of the house. Then, when we calm ourselves with the knowledge that we could live alone if we wanted to, we enjoy starting the romance again."

Romantic ideals notwithstanding, it is hard to imagine actually living in a relationship in which the romantic flame is at full intensity all the time. It would be too all-consuming and exhausting. And, in real life, couples do not "live happily ever after" unless they take steps to protect the romantic spark. If these steps are not taken, burnout is inevitable.

Burnout as a Hallmark of Times

While burnout has been a "dictionary word" for many years, its introduction as a psychological concept is fairly recent. It was only in the mid-seventies that the first articles dealing with career burnout appeared in scientific journals. Soon there were books, newspaper and magazine articles, and television talk shows dedicated to the problem. Scholars started doing research on burnout and developing theories to predict when it would happen and why. Today there are many books and hundreds of articles on burnout. It is interesting that despite its obvious relevance to areas outside of work and despite several calls to expand it to other spheres of life, heretofore nothing has been written on the subject of couple burnout.

As one of the pioneers in the research on career burnout, I witnessed firsthand people's tremendous excitement and relief when introduced to it. I have the sense that, while burnout is not a new phenomenon, its ubiquity is a statement about our time. It has less to do with the people involved, and more to do with existential concerns and our culture's answer to them (Pines 1993).

In order to fully understand burnout, we need to expand from a focus on the individual (who experiences it) to a focus on the culture. Several cultural trends, over the past century, have radically changed the institution of marriage and thereby increased the stress on modern marriages.

One such trend has been the breakup of the extended family and the loss of many family functions to formal institutions and agencies. (Care for children, for example, is often transferred to child-care centers, care for the elderly to homes for the aged.) This trend has removed some of the traditional reasons for keeping marriage intact.

In the past, marriage involved two extended families and was forever, regardless of how the couple felt about each other. Mothers told their daughters, "You're not just marrying him, you're marrying his family." Two families joined by marriage had a vested interest in keeping couples together. When a problem arose, it was treated as natural and normal. ("I had the same trouble with your father. That's just the way men are.") Unhappiness alone was rarely seen as a justification for breaking the marital bond. ("He doesn't drink, doesn't beat you, and brings home all the money he makes. What else do you want?") Many modern couples, on the other hand (especially what are called DINKs—Double Income, No Kids) consider happiness as the sine qua non of matrimony. When happiness vanishes, so does the reason for staying married (Dyer 1983).

Today extended families are rare. Young couples often move away from home and sever ties with relatives and childhood friends. When their work demands it, they move again. The absence of close friends and family makes modern couples need, expect, and demand more from each other.

Being without an extended family is not all bad. According to Robert Bellah and the other authors of *Habits of the Heart,* it gives couples the advantage of greater personal freedom to define their roles, their expectations, and the nature of their relationship (Bellah, et al. 1985). Modern couples have greater freedom to create the kind of life they want for themselves. This freedom, combined with the greater demands couples make on each other, is manifested in yet another cultural trend that has influenced modern marriage—the high rate of divorce.

The renowned family therapist James L. Framo writes:

> Husbands and wives are capable of creating a whole range
> of miseries for each other, ranging from loneliness in mar-
> riage, bitter frustration, cruelty, degrading conflicts . . . or
> waiting for each other to die. (Framo 1981, 133)[6]

For people who base their marriage on love, living in a loveless marriage is unacceptable. The alternative they often opt for is divorce. People today are less concerned with the stigma associated with divorce, and there has been, in recent years, a growing acceptance of the idea that divorce is a reasonable alternative to an unhappy marriage. Even the law in some states now recognizes incompatibility as grounds for divorce: in the eyes of the law it is possible for two people to discover, after many years of living together, that they were not made for each other.

Breaking up isn't so hard to do either. In the 1970s, most states expanded the grounds for divorce to include some form of no-fault divorce, with the result that it has become much easier to end a marriage. In addition, the stigma associated with obtaining a divorce isn't as harsh as it used to be (Norton and Glick 1976); in 1980 and again in 1984, the people of the United States elected Ronald Reagan, a divorced and remarried man, president. At no time did Reagan lose, as a result of the divorce, his position as representative of traditional, conservative values.

Changing roles of men and women are yet another cultural trend that has put a stress on relationships. According to one view, the changing role of women is often the cause of couples' problems. Marriage therapists James and Janice Prochaska report, for example, that "the most common reason for couples coming into marital therapy is that the marriage is being shaken by the wife's struggle for equality" (Prochaska and Prochaska 1978, 3). Similarly, Philip Blumstein and Pepper Schwartz, in their survey of 12,000 American couples, report that "women who can support themselves can afford to have higher expectations for their marriages beyond financial security, and because they are more self-sufficient, they can leave if these expectations are not met" (Blumstein and Schwartz 1983, 309).

According to another view, changes in the roles of men most often precipitate marital problems. Barbara Ehrenreich argues that the collapse of traditional marriage was caused by "men's revolt" against their breadwinner role (Ehrenreich 1983).

Our Fallacy of Uniqueness

Most people are aware of the changed social norms regarding love, marriage, divorce, and the roles of men and women. Many find it is easy to talk about trends and demographics. They can discuss them in the abstract with great articulation, yet (consciously or unconsciously) they assume that they themselves are immune to such generalizations. Social psychologists call this our "fallacy of uniqueness." One of the best literary descriptions of this fallacy can be found in the preface to Han Suyin's *A Many Splendoured Thing*:

> "Do you really think, then, that other people get as much pleasure and happiness out of their bodies as we do? Do you really think this love will not last for ever? I do not believe it." And he looked round him for confirmation. But there was only myrtle and long grass and bracken, hill slope and sea, and ourselves all golden with lying in the sun. "Dear love, even the paunchy, ugly people of this world believe they love as much as we do and forever. It is the illusion for all lovers to think themselves unique and their words immortal." (Suyin 1960, xii)

When people fall in love they are sure that no one has ever loved as they do. When they are in pain they are convinced that no one has ever suffered as much. And when they burn out, they rarely place the blame where it belongs. They seldom think, for example, how cultural forces have shaped their unrealistic expectations of a love relationship. Instead, they blame their mates. They think about all the things their mate does that are so painful or aggravating. "He is a narcissist, he can only think about his own needs." "She is demanding, nagging, and manipulative."

People do not acknowledge that they have fallen for the romantic ideals promoted by our culture. What is even more surprising is that they do not acknowledge the effect of outside stresses and pressures on their relationship: work stresses, problems with in-laws, having young children at home, illness, or, for gay couples (especially when one or both of the mates is not openly gay), having to conceal the true nature of their relationship. The struggle to make it to the top of a career ladder can be draining. So is the tedium of caring for young children day in and day out. And so is also the need to hide from family and colleagues the fact that you and your mate are a couple. Pressures and stresses like these are part and parcel of life. It is very hard to be romantic when you are exhausted from office work, physical labor, tending children; it is very hard to feel butterflies of love when your stomach is churning with anxiety over money. Stresses such as these, which have nothing to do with a couple's love for each other, can erode a relationship as much as a woman's demands or a man's narcissism.

While couples may understand (in their heads) that such stresses affect their relationship, in their hearts they still blame each other for not making it right. Or else they blame themselves for things beyond their control (like unemployment or like society's attitudes toward homosexuality), which is just as wrong. Both kinds of blame are part of the price we pay for believing in our own uniqueness.

Why Couples Need to Know About Burnout

In working on the problem of burnout, my focus has been on the shared expectations and stresses common to relationships and the shared cultural values contributing to these stresses. I believe that it is fiendishly difficult for couples to stay together in a society in which love is exalted yet breaking up is the norm. It is a society in which the informing wisdom is "get the most out of life," "look out for number one," and "do your own thing"; there is no extended family to help couples in trouble and no reminder of how much the partners mean to each other.

The pressures and stresses built into a couple sharing a life together are enormous. It is almost inevitable that, with time, these stresses will become intense and at times even unbearable. With all the erosive tendencies indigenous to love relationships, instead of being surprised by the high levels of burnout among couples, we should marvel at the fact that some relationships, even after many years, are still exciting and mutually supportive, that the spark in them is still alive.

Identifying the negative effect of unrealistic expectations and outside stresses on the erosion of love is essential for combating burnout. Knowing that these kinds of stresses can lead to burnout in any relationship helps break the fallacy of uniqueness. Realizing that burnout is a common response of romantic couples to stressful situations can free such couples to direct their efforts toward changing those situations, rather than trying in vain to change each other.

While burnout can be an extraordinarily painful experience, it can be conquered. As with most other difficult emotional experiences, if properly dealt with, burnout can provide a chance for a couple to reevaluate their relationship and to nurture its growth. Couples who burn out, and who learn to cope with it effectively, often emerge with better, fuller, more exciting relationships.

A Note to Therapists

For therapists, especially those psychodynamically oriented, the discussion of burnout as a failure in people's existential quest for meaning may seem too abstract and removed from the realities of their work with individuals and couples. For them, such concepts as unconscious mate selection and projective identification may seem more relevant to the couple issues they see in their office. Indeed, unconscious forces undoubtedly play an important role both in mate selection and in the issues that later become burnout-causing stresses in relationships. I address these issues in chapter 2, while discussing internal romantic images, in chapter 3 during the presentation of the psychodynamic approach to couple therapy, and in chapter 10 in the discussion of couple burnout workshops. The value of starting this book (as well as work with couples) by presenting the existential perspective of burnout is that this perspective avoids the pathologizing so common in the clinical approaches to couples' therapy. More on that in chapter 3.

Furthermore, the conceptual framework of burnout helps individuals and couples to break away from their fallacy of uniqueness and to view their problems as normal and normative. This frees energy that was previously used to defend against blame of self and of the partner, energy that can then be used for improved coping. Removing the "blame frame" is one of the greatest advantages of using the conceptual framework of couple burnout.

2

The Couple Burnout Model:
Falling In and Out of Love

For love is strong as death, passion deep as the grave; it blazes up like blazing fire, fiercer than any flame. Many waters can not quench love, no flood can sweep it away.

—Song of Songs

Falling in Love

Romantic relationships start with falling in love. If you don't initially have passion, obviously you can't lose it later. Thus, those people who enter relationships for reasons other than romantic love—as well as people who do not believe in love or who are forever seeking but never able to find the "right" person—cannot burn out in a love relationship.

Falling in love, whether it is love at first sight or a slowly developing passion, is the ideal stage against which the rest of the relationship is judged—most often unfavorably. This is the stage that lovers want to preserve or go back to. A woman in her late thirties describes it:

> The night we met (we were both invited to a dinner party at a mutual friend's house) I was so excited I couldn't sleep. I kept going over every word he said, wondering whether he was experiencing some of the excitement I was feeling.

When we became lovers I was happier than I had ever been.
I felt I was floating on air. I was so excited I couldn't eat. He
occupied my mind every single moment. I thought he was
the smartest, most handsome, most sexy man I had ever
met. Life had an incredible intensity. The world was in
bright colors. Our sex was fantastic! I felt alive. Now I
notice all those little obnoxious things I was totally
unaware of before, like the way he eats, the way he talks,
how infantile he can be. He doesn't seem so good-looking
to me any more. I realize now that the great sex at the
beginning had more to do with my infatuation than with
his skill as a lover. But oh, how I miss the excitement and
the romance. I would happily exchange all of my grownup
insights for the blindness and passion I had.

Infatuation, blindness, passion. Lovers want to believe that their
love is unique, magical, something best left to poets. They want to
believe that the attraction between lovers is a mystical coming
together of souls—what Victor Herbert described as "the sweet mystery of life."

Psychologists, however, are not willing to leave love to poets,
romantic dreamers, and lovers. They want to find out what attracts
two lovers to each other, to explain how someone falls in love with a
particular person and why.

When people are asked why they fell in love with their mate, typically their answers include a list of attractive attributes such as looks,
personality, achievements, and values (similar to theirs and hence
"right"). They rarely list the ways in which the beloved satisfied cultural norms ("She's from the right kind of a family, with the proper
schooling"). Nor do they usually mention the emotional state in
which they were (as a result of something that happened in their
work or personal life) when they fell in love.

When people fall in love they tend to assume that the magic was
created exclusively by the endearing attributes of their beloved.
Somehow they feel that if they were to admit how much outside
forces affected them, it would diminish the magic of love (or the
magic of the loved one). They prefer to think that they are independent, different, that their love is capable of breaking formulas. But
studies show that the circumstances under which we meet someone
are extremely important.

Situational Variables

The two situational variables that have received the greatest research attention are proximity and emotional arousal.

Proximity

Studies show that people do, at least figuratively, marry the person next door.[1] In one classic study (Bossard 1932), 5,000 marriage licenses were examined. Findings showed that 33 percent of the couples lived within five blocks of each other. The percentage of marriages decreased steadily and markedly as the geographical distance between residences increased. Apparently, two people must not only have a chance to meet before they can fall in love, but they also have a higher probability of falling in love if they see each other frequently.

Robert Zajonc believes this phenomenon is due to the effect of "repeated exposure." In one of his studies, Zajonc arranged a series of very brief meetings (not more than 35 seconds) for the subjects and limited them in terms of the possibility of interaction (no conversation was allowed). Nevertheless, as the frequency of these meetings increased, the level of affection expressed by the subjects toward the strangers with whom they interacted increased (Zajonc 1968). The reason, argues Zajonc, is that we are programmed to evaluate negatively and avoid things that are unfamiliar to us. An unfamiliar person or thing can be dangerous. Repeated exposure gives us confidence that the other is not dangerous, so we can relax and respond positively.

Emotional Arousal

When we are excited, we are much more likely to fall in love—also when we are angry, frightened, jealous, euphoric, or feeling rejected. Anyone, in fact, who experiences the physical arousal that goes along with strong emotions is potentially a romantic person. If a man should meet an unusually desirable woman while he is agitated, he is more likely to be intensely drawn to her than he would be under normal circumstances. So concluded social psychologists Elaine Walster and Ellen Berscheid, in their two-factor theory of love:

> To love passionately, a person must first be physically
> aroused, a condition manifested by palpitations of the heart,
> nervous tremor, flushing, and accelerated breathing. Once

he is so aroused, all that remains is for him to identify this complex of feelings as passionate love, and he will have experienced authentic love. Even if the initial physical arousal is the result of an irrelevant experience ... once he has met the person, been drawn to the person, and identified the experience as love, it is love. (Walster and Berscheid 1971, 47)

According to Walster and Berscheid (who base their theory on the pioneering work of Stanley Schachter), it takes two things to fall in love: arousal and a romantic interpretation. A man suffering from the pain of rejection is ripe for a rebound love affair. Wartime lovers find passion in the shadow of death. A woman who is recovering from the loss of her father is ripe for falling in love, and so are people who are involved in a traumatic event or who are about to leave a place forever. Happy occasions, too, lead to love. Examples are couples who meet at weddings, on vacation, at parties, and on the first warm day of spring.

Studies demonstrate the effect of physical and emotional arousal on romantic attraction.[2] Researchers tested the theory that arousal makes people more likely to fall in love by telling subjects that they were going to get a "pretty stiff" electric shock, by making them walk across a very deep river on a shaky rope bridge, by having them be rejected by a young woman who was previously warm and accepting, and by actually giving them an injection of adrenaline. In all cases the aroused subjects, when presented with an attractive person of the opposite sex, were more likely to interpret their physical arousal as a romantic attraction than were unaroused subjects. All this research lent support to Walster and Berscheid's tongue-in-cheek conclusion that "adrenaline makes the heart grow fonder."

An important part of the emotional arousal of infatuation comes from the challenge and risks involved in falling in love. While falling in love is wonderful, it is also dangerous and risky. It means being vulnerable. It means the possibility of hurt and disappointment. Just as rock climbing is more exciting than hill climbing—because it involves greater risks—falling in love is more exciting than falling in like. This kind of emotional arousal is recreated later in the life of a couple whenever the relationship faces a threat (for example, as a result of the involvement of one of the mates with another person).

Physical and emotional arousal alone are not enough to make people fall in love. The next prerequisite is meeting someone who fits their romantic image.

Ayala Malach Pines

Romantic Images

Romantic images develop very early in life and are powerful because they are based on memory of experiences that occurred before the development of language. Parents pass on romantic images to their children in two ways: by the way they express (or do not express) love toward the child, and by the way they express (or do not express) love for each other. Since their parents' relationship is, for most people, the relationship they observe first, most closely, and over the longest period of time, it has the strongest influence on their image of love. People who grew up in families filled with tension and conflict develop concepts of love and relationships very different from those of people who grew up in warm and affectionate families.

Romantic images are then strongly influenced by our first personal experiences of love. We internalize the image of the person who taught us the meaning of love by satisfying (or not satisfying) our physical and emotional needs during the first days of life. As adults we look for a lover who will fit that internalized image. Some people look for a physical fit (a woman is attracted to men who like her father are short, dark, and tough but good-looking). Some people yearn for an emotional fit (a man is attracted to women who are like his mother: bright, articulate, vivacious). Some people look for the exact opposite of their parents (a man whose mother was intrusive, emotional, heavy set, and dark is attracted to aloof, emotionally reserved, skinny blonds).

When people are emotionally aroused and meet a person who fits this internalized image in some important way, they project their image onto him or her. This is why when they fall in love people often say, "I feel as if I've known him all my life." This is also why they are so often surprised and disappointed to discover, when the infatuation is over, that their lover has some nasty personal characteristics they had overlooked and does not possess all of the wonderful qualities their love-struck eyes beheld. It is as if they could not see the actual person—only the projection of their internalized romantic image.

Marilyn French describes the disappointing discovery of the person behind the projected romantic image in *The Women's Room*:

> Then one day, the unthinkable happens. You are sitting
> together at the breakfast table and you're a little hung over,
> and you look across at beloved, beautiful golden beloved,
> and beloved opens his lovely rosebud mouth showing his

glistening white teeth, and beloved says something stupid.
Your whole body stops midstream: your temperature drops.
Beloved has never said anything stupid before. You turn
and you look at him; you're sure you misheard. You ask
him to repeat. And he does. He says, "It's raining out." And
you look outside and it is perfectly clear. And you say, "No,
it isn't raining out. Perhaps you'd better get your eyes
checked. Or your ears." You begin to doubt all his senses. It
could only be a flaw in his sensory equipment that would
make him say a thing like that. But even that flaw isn't
important. Love can't be stopped by locksmiths, contact
lenses, or hearing aids. It was just that you were hung over.

But that's only the start. Because he keeps on, after that,
saying stupid things. And you keep turning around and
looking at him strangely, and my God, do you know what,
you suddenly see that he's skinny! Or flabby! Or fat! His
teeth are crooked, and his toenails are dirty. You suddenly
realize he farts in bed. He doesn't, he really doesn't understand Henry James! All this while, he's been saying he
doesn't understand Henry James, and you've thought his
odd, cast-off, remarks about James showed brilliant perception, but suddenly you realize he missed the point entirely.
(French 1977, 365–66)

Romantic images have a powerful influence on our choice of a
romantic partner. The subject of unconscious mate selection has been
addressed by many psychodynamically oriented writers.[3] According
to one version of this view, people marry their worst nightmare: those
who fear rejection and abandonment, for example, marry those who
fear intrusion and engulfment. As one mate seeks closeness, the other
mate seeks distance. One suggested explanation for this seemingly
unreasonable selection has to do with "repetition compulsion," which
compels people to repeat their childhood traumas. People fear rejection and abandonment because they experienced it as children, so
they are compelled to repeat that trauma as adults. And who is more
appropriate for this repetition compulsion than a mate who repeats a
trauma of intrusion and engulfment?

According to the second psychodynamic version, unconscious mate
selection is motivated by people's urge to heal childhood wounds.
While the relationship may appear a living hell, it actually offers both

mates the best possible opportunity to heal these wounds. Marcy, a lesbian woman in her early forties, provides an example.

Marcy is cut off from her family of origin. As a child she adored her successful, emotionally distant father and dreamed of following in his footsteps. When she grew up, she joined his business and labored in it hoping to get his approval. She left the business and cut herself off from him and her mother (who sided with him) after years of painful disappointments.

Marcy was forty when she fell in love, for the first time in her life, with a gorgeous redhead named Marie. Marie, who was a successful business executive, was very attached to her family, especially to her daughter. While Marie was the one who first initiated their relationship, Marcy quickly became the pursuer and Marie the distancer. Her frustration with the pursuer/distancer dynamic was the reason Marcy first came to therapy. It was the holiday season and Marie's daughter was home from college. Marcy felt rejected and hurt because Marie, who at that time was trying to keep their relationship a secret, spent "all" her time with her daughter.

In addition to working with Marcy on her family of origin issues— the issues that made her cut herself off from her parents and become the pursuer in her intimate relationship—I also suggested that she enlarge her circle of friends to make her less dependent on Marie to fill all her emotional needs.

Since she was lonely and desperate, Marcy went to a lesbian club in town. It was the first time she visited the place. As luck may have it, the woman who picked her up was "the exact replica of Marie"— same red hair, same dark green eyes, same delicate figure. But unlike Marie, this redhead was a pursuer and she pursued Marcy with great vim and vigor. Was Marcy thrilled and delighted to find a woman who looked like the woman of her dreams, but unlike Marie wanted to spend every moment with her? Hardly. Marcy complained that the "other woman" was "too much." She was "too pushy" and was in her face all the time.

In order to work on her unresolved childhood issue of a distant and unresponsive father, Marcy needed a lover—like Marie—who was distant and unavailable and thus enabled her to reenact her childhood trauma of rejection. A woman like the second redhead, who was a pursuer and looked exactly like Marie, simply did not match her romantic image. This is why, despite all Marcy's declarations of how much she wants someone who will be responsive and loving, she was not attracted to the other woman.

Needless to say, the relationship with a pursuer like Marcy enabled Marie to work on her own unresolved childhood issue, which resulted from growing up with an engulfing and undifferentiated family.

Some romantic images include parts of the self that people deny. As a result, people may choose a mate who represents that denied part. For example, one woman learned as a child to suppress her hostility and aggression. She suppressed these feelings so well that she was not even consciously aware of her current hostile and angry feelings. Now she is irresistibly attracted to aggressive, even violent men, recently falling in love and marrying one. Through her interactions with her husband (in which she plays the role of the sweet and gentle woman tormented by an aggressive and hostile man) she is able to confront her own hostility without needing to admit to it in herself. Needless to say, her husband can at the same time experience, through his interactions with her, his denied gentle and sweet side.

At times, internalized images can be very negative. When the first love-models a child experiences are withdrawn, cold, and punitive, these will be the dominant characteristics of the internalized romantic image that the child will carry as an adult. Such adults tend to fall in love repeatedly with people who are withdrawn, cold, and punitive, who are sure not to return their affection. They may complain bitterly about their partner's coldness, but when offered a chance for a relationship with a warm, giving, and loving person, they reject it: such a person does not fit their romantic image and therefore does not ignite in them a romantic spark.

In extreme cases, romantic images can be self-destructive, compelling the individual to repeat a childhood trauma of abuse. A woman who was beaten and sexually abused by her father as a young girl, was married three times—each time to a violent man who beat and raped her. After she managed to escape from the third husband and was recuperating at a shelter for abused women, she met a sweet man who was her social worker. He was warm and loving to her and offered to take care of her. She refused his advances because, she said, he was "boring," and "there's no spark." In effect, she was saying that the only way there could be a spark for her was if the man was a potential abuser like her father. Unless a woman like this deals with the unresolved childhood trauma that created her destructive romantic images through long-term psychotherapy, or else decides to avoid men with whom she feels "the spark," she is practically guaranteed to continue repeating the trauma by getting involved with abusive men.

The more severe the childhood trauma, the more urgent is the need to overcome it, and the more obsessive the love through which the person attempts to overcome the trauma.

Because romantic images are imprinted at a very young age, they are resistant to change. Even after therapy, and after making the connection between childhood trauma and attraction to abusive men, such a woman is still likely to feel this attraction. The insights she gains will only serve to help her resist getting involved with them.

Even when people's childhoods do not involve a history of abuse, they may have unresolved issues that they work through in their relationships. Their romantic image helps them identify the person who is most appropriate for the task. Dona (the architect who burned out after fourteen years of marriage) came from a broken home where she never had a chance to observe love between her mother and father. Consciously, her image of love was one of total sharing, but her unconscious romantic image made her choose a man who struggles to get away from exactly this kind of closeness:

> My image has always been of total sharing. To me the idea
> of perfect love is an incestuous brother-sister who love
> each other, look alike, and who have similar interests, simi-
> lar backgrounds, who are like the male and female of the
> same person—it's total sharing. All your images are locked
> up in what you think, and Andrew does not match my
> images. There is no bonding between us. And that word
> bonding has become very important to me. I really want a
> friend in a man. I want someone I can share everything
> with. I have a lot of friends and know how to share with
> friends. But Andrew doesn't. He doesn't have a lot of
> friends, and he doesn't know how to share with anybody.

Andrew came from a large, close-knit family, a family he perceived as "too close" and engulfing. Consciously, the most important characteristics of a love relationship for him are freedom and independence, but unconsciously his romantic image made him choose Dona, who is looking for exactly the kind of relationship he is trying to escape:

> The fact is that I, sort of, like things to be unstructured. I
> like the freedom it gives me. Freedom to do my own thing,

I guess. . . . We all need emotional relationships. That's for
sure. Or at least I do. I can't get emotionally involved with
someone unless I have some respect for them on a professional level. It is important to me that the woman I am
with have some self-sufficiency. What absolutely turns me
off is a dependent woman. I like to get some response from
the other person, some feedback. . . . I hate being manipu-
lated. I like to live and let live. . . . Dona was trying too
much to make me do what she wanted me to do. She was
too pushy, too manipulative. . . . A pretty good definition
of tyranny is when one party says to the other, "Look, you
gotta do this, and I don't care whether you get anything
out of it or not, because that's what I want. . . ." She always
wanted security, security, security. It became oppressive.

Dona's and Andrew's romantic images directed each of them to a
person with whom they had the best opportunity to repeat or heal
their childhood trauma—for Dona a trauma of separation and abandonment, for Andrew a trauma of engulfment and intrusion. If they
could have seen their frustrations with each other as opportunities
for personal growth, they would have been able to give each other
what they both needed most: for Dona that would have been some
measure of closeness, for Andrew some measure of freedom. Unfortunately, they were both stuck in their different (both conscious and
unconscious) scripts, which generated very different expectations. As
a result, they both felt frustrated in the relationship and eventually
burned out.

When people's romantic images do not include such serious issues
as abandonment or engulfment, they have less to work through in
the adult love relationship. When they choose a mate, the choice
seems to "make more sense" than do those made by people who are
working through childhood traumas: the expectations of each other
are easier to fulfill. Ellen and Anthony are an example of such a couple. This is a second marriage for each, and they have been together
five years. They talk about their dreams and expectations:

When I was still married to my former husband, during the
time our marriage was beginning to fall apart, I used to
have a recurrent daydream in which I saw myself in bed
with a man I love. His face wasn't clear. What was clear,

however, was that it was morning. (My husband and I never made love in the morning, so that became an important part of my fantasy.) But what was even more important in my fantasy was the knowledge that this man was someone who loved me, who loved touching me (something my husband rarely did), and with whom I could talk about everything. Someone with whom I could be totally honest. That's what was most important to me: good talk and good sex. My relationship with Anthony is the realization of these fantasies.

Anthony's romantic ideal seems very compatible with Ellen's:

I always had an aversion to concretizing romantic ideals or images, in part because I felt that an important part of the magic of love is that it is not specified in advance. So, on the one hand, all my life I had the desire to keep my options open to all exotic possibilities, and on the other hand, my personal experience has shown me that the odds are very small of a relationship lasting any length of time without a similarity in background, culture, and world view. In my relationship with Ellen I was able to have my cake and eat it too. Because there is something very exotic about the fact that she spent her childhood in the Far East, and yet our world views and romantic ideals are very similar. I want the person I am with to be able to defend themselves verbally and talk openly about feelings. That sex has to be good is obvious.

In working with individuals and couples on issues related to couple burnout it is important to ask such questions as: What attracted you to your mate and your mate to you when you first met? What is your ideal relationship? What is your mate's ideal relationship? When you were growing up, how did your parents treat you? How did they treat each other? Is there any similarity between your mother and your mate? Between your father and your mate? Is your mate the complete opposite of either parent? Are you yourself similar or different from either one of your parents? Addressing these kinds of questions can help identify couples' romantic images. (In chapter 9 I describe in detail how these questions can be addressed in the context of a couple burnout workshop.)

A humorous example of how differences in romantic imagery can be the source of many repeated conflicts appeared in a cartoon showing a bride and groom exchanging vows. There are balloons over their heads to show what each is thinking. In the balloon over the groom's head there is a vision of the bride serving him breakfast in bed. In the bride's balloon there is an image of the groom serving her breakfast in bed. . . .

As noted in the previous chapter, we are socialized to believe that finding our "match made in heaven" (the person who fits our internal romantic image) will guarantee the kind of happiness only love can provide, total bliss and contentment, where all our questions and doubts about ourselves and about life will be answered. That is why when love fails us, it is such a traumatic experience.

For a woman like Dona, who came from a broken home and never experienced the warmth and security of a loving family, the image of "perfect love" was associated with "total sharing." Yet she fell in love with Andrew because he was "very romantic. . . very handsome . . . the strong silent type." She felt that total sharing with a man like that ("strong and silent," which is to say unavailable like her father, who left the family when she was a child) would compensate her for her childhood loneliness, alleviate all her insecurities, and answer all her dreams. When it became clear that Andrew could not, or would not (as Dona perceived it), do that, she felt disappointed not only in him but also in her entire life.

Some couples think they share romantic ideals even when in fact the two of them have very different images of the perfect relationship. A colleague of mine, who is a brilliant couple therapist, told me that only after seventeen years of marriage, and after couple therapy, did it dawn on him that his wife *really* meant it when she said that gifts of expensive jewelry were to her a sign of love.

Sonya's father died when she was five, and her romantic image was a daddy substitute. Gary grew up in a Middle Eastern family in which his father was "the ruler of the roost" and his mother was weak yet very warm and nurturing. When they first met at work, both Gary and Sonya were in a period of transition. Sonya had moved from the West Coast, where she had lived all her life; Gary had just taken a new job after working for the same company for many years. Gary's and Sonya's looks matched each other's romantic image: like their opposite-sex parents they were both tall, dark, and attractive and took care to enhance their appearance with fashionable clothes.

Since they worked at the same place and interacted with each other daily, it did not take long before they fell in love. Gary loved the way Sonya looked up to him, yielding and demure. Being in control made him feel good. Sonya loved the fact that Gary was taking care of her and acting fatherly. In short, both found in each other the materialization of their romantic image.

Later, of course, as is always the case, the things that they found most attractive about each other turned out to be the most stressful: Sonya had temper tantrums whenever she didn't get from Gary something important she wanted. These tantrums were extremely stressful for Gary, and his response to them was to withdraw. Sonya fell in love with Gary because he was like a father. Yet her greatest stress was when he was like her father—which is to say, "not there." Gary fell in love with Sonya because she was like a little girl, and his greatest stress was when she acted like a little girl. Their childhood issues influenced their romantic images. Their matched romantic images made them fall in love with each other but later became their major source of stress.

Even when two people are emotionally aroused, interacting frequently, and their romantic images match, further screening is necessary before they choose to commit to each other.

Love Filters

Love filters help people screen out "unsuitables" and establish among potential candidates the one with whom they can "let themselves" fall in love, the one to whom marriage seems plausible. Say a conventional woman notices a man at a very dramatic moment during a bank holdup. He is dark and handsome, just like her father, and seems in command of himself. She is quite clearly emotionally aroused, because of the danger. Will she fall in love with him? It is not likely if he is the bank robber. Her love filters tell her he is not a suitable candidate for a happy marriage.

Psychologists have focused a great deal of research effort on studying love filters—who falls in love with whom and who marries whom. One of the filters that has received the greatest research attention (probably because it is easy to study) is similarity.[4]

In a classic study of engaged couples, similarities were found in family background, education, income, and social status of parents, religious affiliation, types of family relationship (happiness of parents' marriage, attitude toward parents, and sex of siblings), sociability (being a "lone wolf" or socially gregarious), leisure-time preference ("stay at home" vs. "on the go"), drinking and smoking habits, number of same-sex as well as opposite-sex friends, and courtship behavior (including number of previous engagements and steady dates, and attitudes toward marriage) (Burgess and Wallin 1953).

In addition, other studies discovered that similarities in such things as intelligence, physical attributes and attractiveness, mental health, psychological maturity, developmental failures, and even genetic make-up were part of the picture. The bulk of the research, however, focused on similarities in attitudes and personality. The conclusion: happy couples are more alike than are unhappy ones.[5]

This research documents what folk wisdom has known all along, that "birds of a feather flock together." However, there is clearly more to failing in love than simply finding the person who is most like oneself in every way possible. (Most people would not fall in love with an exact replica of themselves.) As is so often the case, folk wisdom has a contradictory law: "Opposites attract." Which "law" should we trust? The obvious answer is that both laws operate, but at different times. Only after a potential candidate has passed the initial screening of similarity does complementarity come into play. When two people have similar intelligence, values, and world views, they can get close enough to discover that one of them needs to be in charge and the other needs to be taken care of.

Theodore Reik observed in *The Need to Be Loved* that people fall in love for selfish reasons. They sense something lacking in themselves and seek the missing quality (or qualities) in a mate (Reik 1964). This is why a compulsively logical man is attracted to an excessively emotional woman. Each supplies part of the qualities needed for a complete joint personality, and each benefits from the part provided by the other.

Robert Winch, in his theory of complementary needs in mate selection, explains the rationale behind complementarity. Love, argues Winch, is the experience of two people jointly deriving maximum gratification for important psychological needs with minimal pain (Winch 1958).

Carol, an attractive woman in her midtwenties married to a wealthy man much older than herself, explains:

> My father left my mother and the four children when I was
> just a baby. My mother had great difficulty making ends
> meet, and I grew up feeling very insecure about money. I
> used to dream that my father returned and made every-

thing all right. My husband gives me the fathering and
economic security I so much longed for.

Bernard Murstein elaborates on the theory of complementarity
by adding exchange theory (Murstein 1976). Murstein believes that
attraction depends on the fairest exchange value of the personal assets
and liabilities that each partner brings. He views people as rational
beings who screen potential lovers and form relationships that are
likely to provide them with maximum potential gratification at the
lowest cost. Like any good business executive, he says, people choose
to marry the person who provides them with the best all-around
package deal.

A forty-two-year-old man explains his decision to marry his wife
by saying:

> Maybe she wasn't the hottest romance of my life, but she
> was a beautiful woman, warm, kind, and sensitive, and she
> said she loved me. Even then I knew she was going to be a
> wonderful mother. I was sure we could build a home
> together and that was the most important thing to me, cer-
> tainly more important than the intensity of sexual infatua-
> tion, which I knew never lasts anyway.

Love, according to Murstein's theory, is the feeling of mutual satisfaction two partners derive from knowing that they got the best
"exchange value" for their relationship. In other words, love happens
when both partners feel they made the best possible deal.

In order to make such a good deal, candidates need to pass through
more than a single screen. The funnel of screens people use when
selecting a mate is encompassed by the "filter theory," which
describes the process of mate selection from falling in love until marriage. Social background, values, interests, and complementary needs
all come into play, but at different stages. Different filters operate
during infatuation, courtship, and marriage. When people meet,
background and place of residence limit the field of eligibles. Only
after passing this initial screen can couples discover that they have
shared values and interests. A disagreement on important values
makes further development of the relationship unlikely. A deepening
involvement enables the discovery of complementary psychological
needs. Most people need to feel a certain degree of security in a rela-

tionship before they let their guard down and admit to emotional needs such as a need to be mothered or fathered. Obviously, the needs to be mothered and fathered are not compatible—both imply a desire to be taken care of. A more reciprocal or compatible arrangement is between a man who likes to be mothered and a woman who enjoys mothering, or between a woman who wants to be fathered and a man who enjoys fathering his mate.[6]

More "primitive" prerequisites for romantic attraction include smell, touch, and taste (Fisher, 1992).[7] A woman who finds a man's smell offensive is not likely to agree to go on a date with him, even if he fulfills all her other selection criteria. Similarly, a man is not going to pursue a relationship with a woman whose touch he finds repugnant. On the other hand, if two people touch hands, or lips, and "electricity" passes between them, they are likely to be drawn to each other despite differences in background and social objectives. The best literary example is, of course, Romeo and Juliet. After being attracted to each other's looks across the dance hall, after their first words, the first touch, the first kiss, not even the longstanding feud between their families can stop them from falling in love.

The sensual responses of sight, smell, touch, and taste continue to play an important role throughout a relationship. A woman describes how her senses told her that her marriage was over: "As I looked at his pimpled back, I felt a wave of nausea. I couldn't bear the thought of him touching me. At that moment I knew I had to get out of the marriage, and fast."

Even couples in love who come from a similar background, share similar values, have complementary needs, and are attracted to each other's sight, touch, and smell are never matched in all areas. In the early stages of the relationship there is a tendency to downplay differences, to assume that love can overcome them. In fact, experience shows that time tends to exacerbate them—consider a two-pack-a-day smoker husband and a nonsmoker wife. During courtship the woman dismissed smoking as an issue. She said that smoke doesn't bother her—but then again, she has never lived with a smoker, and no one in her family smokes. After two years of living with foul-smelling ashtrays around the house, a stale-smelling bedroom, and cigarette smoke trailing through the bathroom and kitchen first thing in the morning, it begins to grate on her. So she starts nagging him to quit, claiming she can't breathe when he smokes in the same room. She demands that he open the windows even when it is freezing outside. He resents her change in attitude, saying: "You knew I smoked. You never complained about it before."

The issue of smoking becomes like the proverbial cap left off the toothpaste tube—a cause for perpetual arguments and fights. The issue remains a sore point between them, especially when the wife points out the health risks involved for both of them. The wife now insists that if she had to do it all over again, she would be sure to marry a nonsmoker. The husband, likewise, says he wishes he had chosen a smoker. These kinds of trivial issues—windows open at night, windows closed, pets on the bed, pets off the bed, TV on during dinner, TV off during dinner—slowly erode goodwill and intimacy.

The filters I mentioned are, obviously, not the only ones. Some women would not marry a man who was not successful and some men would not marry a woman unless she was willing to have a big family. All filters operate in different degrees for different people and during different stages of a love relationship.

Love filters, romantic images, and situational variables work together. Love filters help emotionally aroused people select from the candidates that match their romantic image the one to fall in love with.

It is important to remember that, while love filters are rather stable, and romantic images are engraved at a very early stage and are thus resistant to change, emotional arousal is by its very nature temporary. When emotional arousal ends, infatuation ends and love begins (Tennov 1979). When emotional arousal diminishes, the risk of burnout increases. The negative correlation between emotional arousal and burnout has important implications for coping with burnout.

Therapists can help individuals and couples discover their love filters by using a simple exercise. The first step is to think about all the people they have ever been in love with and choose from them the two with whom they were most passionately in love (or whom they married). The next step is to recall as many details about these two people as possible: their looks, personality, behavior, attitudes, background. Next they should consider everything and anything these two have in common. Are they both warm? Cold? Good in bed? Intelligent? Able to get close? Religious? Well educated? Exotic looking? Whatever the people they have loved most passionately have in common represents something in themselves—their filters for selecting an appropriate lover and mate.

The Effect of the Environment

When two people fall in love, they want nothing more than to continue being in love forever. However, fortunately for some and unfortunately for others, they do not live in a vacuum, and one's environment determines to a large extent what happens to relationships. Much as they would like to remain immersed in the magic of their love, sooner or later all couples—no matter what their personalities, and no matter how many or how few unconscious, unresolved conflicts they bring with them into the relationship—have to deal with the world around them. Lucky lovers live in a supportive environment where challenge, encouragement, rewards, and opportunities for growth are abundant. Unlucky lovers live in an environment dominated by pressures and stresses. Because environments are different, the passage of time has a different impact on different relationships—enhancing some and eroding others. Time, in and of itself, does not cause burnout; this is an important point I will return to later.

By emphasizing the role of the environment I do not mean to disregard the importance of personality. Obviously, mates' personalities are significant, especially in the initial stage of mutual selection. Even if certain characteristics eventually cause enormous stress in a relationship, they were not enough of a hindrance during the infatuation stage and could even have been an attraction.

People interact with their environment in individual ways. Some people are robust, others are frail. Some are bold and aggressive, others shy. Some people can handle anything and others fall apart at the slightest provocation. These characteristic ways of dealing with the world seem to hold true even in different situations. While people can change their behavior and modify their way of relating to the world when conditions demand it, they cannot change their personality. In fact, it is usually easier to change the environment than it is to change people's basic personality. Since the environment affects relationships so strongly, it is important for couples—and for people working with couples who are interested in preventing burnout—to know what it is in the environment that causes burnout, and what prevents it.

Finding these things out was one of the goals in my research on couple's burnout.[8] I will discuss briefly three features in the environment that were found to most enhance burnout and three features that were found to best buffer against it. It is noteworthy that one of the most significant differences between gay and straight couples is the greater stress from the social environment experienced by those in gay relationships.

Variables That Enhance Burnout

Overload. "How often do you experience overload in your couple relationship, which is to say, a feeling that you have gone beyond the point of endurance, because the tasks imposed on you are either too many or too hard?" This was the first question presented to the couples.

Results show that the higher the frequency of overload, the higher the level of burnout.[9] This was true for the two kinds of overload addressed in the question—quantitative and qualitative. Quantitative overload happens when people feel that they have more tasks than they can perform well or too many tasks to perform in the time allotted. It can happen, for example, when a couple decides to fix up an old house and spends every minute plastering, wiring, and painting. Qualitative overload—a feeling that the required task is beyond one's capabilities—can happen when a couple needs to discipline an unruly teenager who was found using drugs. Over time, such problems can eat away at a good marriage. Steve describes it:

> I spend too many hours at work, and the work is too intense and too high pressured. The sheer number of hours I am working with people there is creating an intensity that diminishes the intensity of my relationship with Susan. I don't have enough emotional resources to come home and be anything more than perfunctory. It is perfectly obvious to me that I have to change the way I am working. But, on the other hand, if I really want to succeed in this business I can't afford to pull back in any area that I can think of. So I am in a classic Catch-22 situation.

Conflicting Demands. "How often do you feel caught by conflicting demands caused, at least in part, by your spouse?" The more frequent such conflict, the higher the burnout.[10] The wife feels caught between the demands for attention, time, and nurturing of her children and those of her husband; the husband feels caught between the demands of his wife for financial security and her demands for his time and attention. Such demands—legitimate or not, real or imagined, impossible to satisfy all altogether, or impossible to satisfy at the same time—are extremely stressful. Susan says:

> I feel torn between the people in my life who, as dear to me as they are, seem to just want and want. If I would respond to all their requests they could fill my days, leaving time for nothing else. The worst are the "little favors." So little that I feel embarrassed to object or refuse, but so many that they drown me. They all feel they have the right to ask me because they love me, or because they are family, or friends. And I agree with them. So I do it. But at the end of the day I am exhausted and furious, especially at Steve, who is never home to help.

Family Commitments. "How often do you feel pressured by family commitments?" The more frequent such pressure is, the higher the level of burnout.[11] Overload, conflicting demands, and family commitments have an important thing in common: all three reflect a failure to perform according to some expectation, standard, or "should." These expectations can be imposed by an external force, by one's own standards of excellence, or by one's romantic ideals. Failure, or the fear of failure, causes the overload, the pressure, and the conflict.

Another similarity is that all three drain energy. People who experience overload believe the things expected of them are more than they can handle. Conflicting demands make them feel that no matter how hard they try, they cannot satisfy everyone's demands. Family commitments (even those taken on voluntarily) make them feel they are out of their emotional and physical depths. In all three cases, the overwhelming sensation is exhaustion. The feelings of failure and exhaustion deplete romantic love. Since the stress is coming from the outside, it is not surprising that people often focus their blame for the erosion of love outward. Yet all too often that blame is not directed at the stressful environment but instead (unfairly) at the mate. Gus and Lana are an example of such misattribution.

Gus and Lana always came to my office late in the evening. That was the only time both of them could get away from their respective jobs—he as an organizational consultant, she as the mother of five young children. Both described themselves as physically, emotionally, and mentally exhausted, and they looked the way they felt. They defined their problem as burnout. Their sex life was practically nonexistent. Their communication was limited to the details involved in sharing a household, such as who would pick up a half-gallon of milk from the supermarket and who would drive the eldest child to a piano lesson.

Gus and Lana both had demanding work schedules. After many years with a large corporation, Gus had decided to start his own consulting firm. While his former job had been very well paid and secure, his new job was neither. He spent a lot of time convincing companies to give him contracts. In addition to the actual work those contracts demanded, he had to take care of all the administrative details. The financial pressures had been wearing him down. Lana's work was stressful in a different way; with five children in the house (two still in diapers), she could not remember when she had last slept an entire night. In addition, she felt isolated and unsupported, and overwhelmed by the endless tasks involved in caring for a big house and five little children.

The reality of their daily life explained Gus and Lana's physical exhaustion quite well. The fact that both of them cared very much about what they did, and felt they weren't achieving their aspirations, explained their emotional and mental exhaustion far better than their own assumption that they had fallen out of love with each other.

Variables That Prevent Burnout

Variety. "How much variety is there in your intimate relationship?" The greater the variety, the lower the burnout.[12] Variety can be found somewhere in the happy middle ground between overload and boredom. People function best at their own optimal level of variety. Extremely high levels of variety can be experienced on overload and create anxiety and stress, while extremely low levels can be experienced as boredom and create annoyance. The optimal level is different for each person, and it requires continuous stimulation (Duffy 1962). This is why no matter how exciting a marriage is initially, in the absence of variety, boredom and monotony can wear it down.[13]

The ways couples introduce variety into their relationships are as different as couples are. For some, variety means travel—anything from a hike in the woods to a drive to a beautiful sea resort to traveling in Europe. For some, variety is people related; they like to meet new people and to introduce them to each other. For some, it means learning new skills, taking classes, learning a craft. For some it involves physical activities—sailing, playing tennis on sunlit courts, skiing on snow-covered mountains, or jogging around the neighborhood. For others it involves playing bridge, giving parties, going to concerts, participating in sports events, or supporting political causes. For some, it means making certain times or dates special. One couple has lunch together every Wednesday at a different restaurant each time, which they alternate responsibility for choosing. Another couple reserves Sunday mornings for leisurely breakfast in bed with fresh muffins, coffee, and a newspaper.

Variety is in the eye of the beholder. For some couples, "lunch on Wednesday" or "breakfast in bed on Sunday" doesn't sound very exciting. For them, variety means doing things that are spontaneous and unplanned. They might hire a babysitter and go to a fancy motel and make love. They might sneak out of the house at night and go skinny-dipping. One couple likes to go to a hot tub where they can "just focus on each other in a sensuous and relaxing atmosphere," where there are no telephones and no children to disrupt them. Another couple likes to play "pickup" games in bars or any other public place. They "get a charge" from watching the response of onlookers. A gay couple creates a romantic atmosphere by wearing sensuous clothes, cooking a gourmet meal together, and then eating it by candlelight with soft music playing in the background. For this couple, variety means making love at different times of the day and in different rooms of the house. Whatever form variety takes, it always makes certain times in the lives of couples more exciting, which increases emotional arousal and rejuvenates romance in the relationship.

Appreciation. "How much appreciation and recognition do you get for things you do in the relationship?" Appreciation, it turns out, buffers against burnout.[14] Feeling appreciated and respected makes people feel good—about themselves, and about the person who made them feel that way. On the other hand, feeling unappreciated makes people feel angry and resentful at the person criticizing them and bad about themselves.

People see themselves mirrored in the eyes of the people around them. When such a mirror projects a positive image, an image of someone warm, generous, sexy, and fun to be with, that is the way they themselves come to view themselves and behave. When the mirror portrays someone stingy, nasty, obnoxious, and cold, that too becomes part of their self-image, which in turn influences their behavior.

Most of us have within ourselves the capacity to behave warmly or coldly, generously or stingily, in a sexy and playful way or in a nasty and obnoxious way. When people treat us as warm and playful, that, in and of itself, will bring out more of our warm and playful behavior than our cold, obnoxious behavior. This is the power of self-fulfilling

42

Ayala Malach Pines

prophecies (Snyder 1979). And it has a very practical implication. In a couple system, the more recognition each mate gives, the more rewards there are going to be in the system, and the more of them each mate will eventually receive.

Opportunities for Self-Actualization. The more an environment provides couples with opportunities for self-actualization and personal growth, the less likely they are to burn out.[15] Abraham Maslow believed that people have as a basic human motivation an innate drive toward actualization of their human potentialities (Maslow 1962). Self-actualization is also a major theme in the writing of Carl Rogers. "There is in every organism, including man, an underlying flow of movement toward constructive fulfillment of its inherent possibilities, a natural tendency toward growth" (Rogers 1961).

Environments that offer couples opportunities to achieve self-actualization, in which both mates are challenged to pursue spiritual growth and self-discovery, in which they can strive to fulfill their human potential, are environments that enhance the romantic spark. Lynne, a successful career woman, describes how this works:

> There is almost nothing I did when I was single that I can't do now because I am married, and so much more I dare to do and am able to do because I have my husband's support and encouragement, that I could not do when I was single.

Self-actualization involves continuous change and growth, which for some people can be anxiety provoking. It requires openness to new experiences in a positive, active, and creative way. All of which helps prevent burnout.

Other Burnout Causes and Burnout Buffers in the Environment

Overload, conflicting demands, and family commitments are, obviously, not the only burnout-enhancing stresses. Other stresses include such things as boredom, household chores, constant demands to prove oneself, crowded living conditions, noise, and pollution. Similarly, variety, appreciation, and self-actualization are not the only environmental features buffering against burnout. Other positive features include good relations with family, friends, and coworkers; unconditional support in time of trouble; feedback on performance;

autonomy; and a home that is comfortable, pleasant, and designed to meet one's needs, preferences, and personal taste. While variety and self-actualization help maintain emotional arousal, appreciation and support strengthen commitment.

Objective vs. Subjective Environments

When discussing the effects of one's environment, it is often assumed that the environment is an objective reality, when in fact this is rarely the case. We don't interact directly with the physical world around us, but rather with a psychological world that was created through the mediation of our senses. We experience a subjective, not an objective, reality. We are constantly bombarded by endless stimuli from the environment. In order to make sense of the world, we have to screen out some of these stimuli. Our senses select, organize, and interpret, and thus we end up with a personal and subjective view of the world. Our perceptions are not a passive reflection of the environment but instead the result of an active process in which we shape and create our world.

In the research cited earlier, the environmental features that were found to cause or prevent burnout were aspects of the psychological world of the people who described them. They were not based on objective measures but on subjective reports. People described overload the way they experienced it. Variety, conflicting demands, obligations, and appreciation were all subjectively defined as well. The same environment can be perceived very differently by different people. It can be seen as stressful by one person and as exciting and challenging by another. Whether couples burn out or not depends on the way they cope with their subjective environments.

According to stress psychologist Richard Lazarus, a process of "appraisal" mediates between the effects of the environment and the emotions they produce in the individual. "Appraisal can be most readily understood as the process of categorizing an encounter with respect to its significance for well-being" (Lazarus and Folkman 1984, 31–32). A situation can be viewed as either relevant or irrelevant to well-being, as harmful, potentially harmful, challenging, or potentially positive in outcome (Lazarus 1984).

The same situation will affect different people differently depending on their histories and their personalities. One person may react with anger, another with depression, another with fear or guilt.

Ayala Malach Pines

Others may feel challenged rather than threatened under comparable conditions. For example, one person may cope with marital problems by denial and another by depression. One person may handle an insult by ignoring it, another may get angry and have a fight, a third may plot revenge.

There are differences in the ways people approach life. Some are dramatically affected by the smallest stresses. These people tend to view the world as a place dominated by evil forces where one is best prepared if always ready for the worst. Each problem is exaggerated and seen as evidence that things are bad and will naturally become worse. Other people believe that when left to themselves, things will naturally turn out for the best. The most important thing is to be happy and experience life to its fullest. Such people minimize negative events.

People differ in their appraisals of stresses and their abilities to cope with them, which can influence when burnout will occur, how long it will last, and how severe its consequences will be. It is not just the objective conditions that cause misery or even happiness, but also how we interpret those conditions. An old rabbinical story makes this point very well:

> A man came to the wise rabbi in great distress begging for help. "Rabbi," he said, "I am going out of my mind. With me, my wife, and the six children all living in one little room, there is no space for breathing. The noise and the crowding are making us all crazy. I don't know what to do." "Do you have a goat?" the rabbi asked. "Yes," the man answered. "Bring the goat into the house," said the rabbi. "What do you mean, 'Bring the goat into the house'?" the man asked with great shock. "I've just told you we have no air to breathe as it is." "You want my advice, don't you?" the rabbi asked sternly. "I do, I do," the man replied meekly. So the man went home and brought the goat in. A week later the man returned to the rabbi, this time in even greater distress. "Rabbi," he said "life is not worth living. Now, in addition to everything else, we have to deal with this filthy goat. I can't take it anymore." "In that case," said the rabbi, "get the goat out." Next day the man came to the rabbi, kissed his hands, and said, "Rabbi, thank you! What a pleasure it is not to have a goat in the house. There's so much air, so much space, and no goat filth. Life is wonderful!"

People tend to perceive stresses as objective reality even when they are self-imposed. In order to reduce stresses such as overload, conflicting demands, and family commitments, every stress has to be scrutinized to clarify whether it is a real demand or a self-demand, whether it is a "have to" or a "want to." To do that, it is important to help people recognize the rewards that may be related to the stress. Being always busy, for example, may be related to feeling important. It also is an excuse to get away from other, less desirable activities.

The Effect of Expectations

Expectations about romantic love always exist as a part of people's belief system. They can be conscious or unconscious, verbalized or unverbalized, private or culturally shared. Even when a couple's expectations are achievable, after the euphoria of having a dream come true there can be disappointment with the discovery that reality is less exciting than a dream. A classic example is the couple whose romantic ideal involved being the first in their group to marry, marrying the most attractive person in high school (the homecoming queen and the quarterback), and settling down in a nice suburban ranch home with a white picket fence. Once the dream has been achieved and the enjoyment from it exhausted, the couple may feel bitterly disappointed because achieving the dream, which was supposed to give their life a sense of meaning—forever— has failed to do so.

When romantic expectations are not achieved (even if the reason can clearly be attributed to environmental stress), the feelings of disappointment tend to be directed at the mate and cause the erosion of love and commitment. The disappointment is made more painful when the mate once seemed to match a romantic image, thus promising that the ideal love could be realized and help heal childhood wounds. In time the positive emotional energy is drained out of the relationship, and gradually love burns out. The experience of burnout, in turn, weakens the couple's love and commitment toward each other. The negative downward spiral continues until love is dead.

In order to ensure the continuous growth of love in a couple relationship, expectations must be constantly redefined. This happens naturally when change is a part of the couple's romantic ideal and part of their expectations. An example is the couple for whom the ideal relationship is one in which they communicate openly about everything, in which they are committed to each other and to living life to the fullest, in which they believe that change is an opportunity, and in which they feel that the best place to grow is with each other. A relationship like this, in which the romantic ideal is achievable and growth centered, can get better with time. It can deepen and become more secure (grow "roots"). It can also allow both mates to grow as individuals and as a couple (grow "wings"). That, in turn, will strengthen the couple's love and commitment, creating a positive loop that (at least in theory) can last forever.

Roots and Wings

"Roots and wings" are the antithesis of couple burnout. The most profound characteristic of roots and wings relationships is that the partners not only maintain the romantic spark even after many years, but their relationship actually gets better with time. The roots symbolize security and mutual trust, a feeling that your mate knows you completely, with all your virtues and your faults, and loves you just the way you are. The wings symbolize excitement and personal growth, the feeling that together and alone you are getting the most out of yourself and out of life.

The first thing most roots and wings couples say when asked to describe their relationship is: "My mate is my best friend." Lynne, a renowned university professor, describes her marriage:

> We have been married for nineteen years and through
> all this time we've been talking nonstop. I can't tell you
> how many times we've missed an exit on the highway
> because we were too involved in a conversation. We are
> both very involved in our careers, but luckily our fields
> are close enough to understand what the other one is
> doing, so we can talk about it. Because we have been with
> each other all these years, we understand each other's
> way of thinking. But since we come from very different
> backgrounds we are able to provide different perspectives
> and a challenge that a person in our own field could not
> provide. But it's not just talking about work that has
> improved with time. Everything has gotten better with
> the years: our sex life, our freedom with each other, our
> feelings of security, of belonging, and even our financial
> situation. . . . Given what I see around me with our
> friends and other couples, our marriage is pretty unusual.

I worried about it a lot before I got married. This is why
I was in no hurry to get married, why I waited so long.
But when we met we both knew that this was it. And we
were right.

It is essential that there be both roots and wings to keep a relationship alive. A relationship that has overgrown roots and no wings provides a sense of security but is most often experienced as boring,
stifling, and oppressive. One woman says:

My husband is a good man and a good provider. I know he
loves me and the kids and was never interested in other
women. I have resigned myself to the fact that we are
going to remain married. But there is no spark between us.
The marriage is so boring that I find other people to do
things with us so I don't have to spend time stuck with just
my husband.

On the other hand, relationships that have overgrown wings but
no roots tend to be rather short-lived. Typically, in such relationships both partners develop their own interests, their own circles of
friends, and their own leisure-time activities, but they don't bring
these interests back to the relationship. Consequently, the bonds
that keep the couple together are loosened. A young professional
woman says:

Eventually I realized that we had nothing in common. We
weren't speaking the same language. We were awake during different times, and our lives were completely separate.
We were passing each other like two trains in the night.
Sooner or later I knew that one of us just had to bring up
the question: What's the point of staying together?

Even when a relationship has both roots and wings, they are not
always balanced. It is essential that both partners in the relationship
have both roots and wings, rather than one (usually the wife) taking
on the role of the spokesperson for roots, with the other (usually the
husband) taking on the role of spokesperson for the wings. Only in
relationships where both partners have both roots and wings is there
the foundation of commitment and security, and the growth energy
needed for keeping the romantic spark in a relationship alive.

Ayala Malach Pines

The Love and Burnout Model

The two questions I am asked most often about couple burnout are: "What causes burnout?" and "How can burnout be avoided?" The Love and Burnout Model (see page 49) addresses both of these questions.

The topics discussed in this chapter—including the three facets of falling in love, the effects of the environment, and the effect of expectations—are each parts of the model and were presented for that reason.

The model describes two paths leading either to burnout or to roots and wings. The two paths start similarly with a couple in love. How is a couple that burns out different from one with roots and wings? If we leave aside the possibility that the burned-out couple has serious emotional problems, we have to assume that the difference lies in their different environments. A stressful environment—or an environment that the couple perceives as stressful—prevents the one couple from actualizing their dream. Coping with stress drains their energy and their love. A supportive environment enables the other couple to grow and become self-actualized. The sense of significance they get from the relationship keeps their love alive.

The Love and Burnout Model has several key points:

• People who believe in romantic love expect it to give their life a sense of meaning.

• There is a direct relationship between romantic love and burnout. Falling in love is the initial stage and prerequisite for the burnout process.

• Despite the uniqueness of the experience of falling in love, the "how" and the "why" of the experience are universal.

• There is an interaction between couples and the environment. It is not the mate's disposition that causes burnout, but rather the destruction of one's romantic ideals by situational stresses that are erroneously attributed to the mate.

• The environment is not a totally objective external reality. Each one of us experiences a perceived subjective representation of the world.

• Expectations about romantic love result from learned cultural values as well as from personal experiences and always exist as part of

The Love and Burnout Model

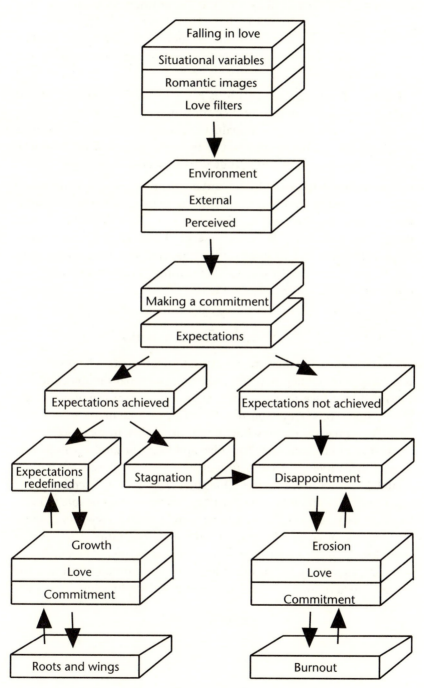

people's belief systems. Expectations are activated when people fall in love and are in full force when a commitment is made, whether the commitment is formal or not. They have a powerful effect on love relationships, even when unconscious and not openly verbalized, because they are associated with what is perceived as the essence of life.

• Frustrated romantic expectations cause bitter disappointment and with it the erosion of love and commitment. Fulfilled expectations, however, are not a guarantee against burnout. Romantic ideals can be frustrated by not being achieved or by being achieved yet failing to give life the sense of meaning they were expected to provide.

• The outcome of the ongoing interaction between a couple and their perceived environment can be positive or negative for their love relationship. In the best possible case the outcome is "roots and wings," an ideal balance between security and growth. In relationships with roots and wings, love is enhanced with time and continues to provide life with a sense of meaning. In the worst case, the outcome is burnout, the death of love.

A Note to Therapists

The conceptual framework of burnout integrates a social psychological perspective (which puts emphasis on situational variables and culturally shared love filters in mate selection and on the effect of the environment on couples' burnout) with a psychodynamic perspective (which emphasizes unconscious romantic images in mate selection). This conceptual framework (the love and burnout model) can be presented to couples in lecture format and parts of it can be demonstrated by structured exercises. One such exercise was described at the end of the section on love filters. The exercise enables people to identify their own love filters, and can be used by therapists with individuals, couples, or groups. In chapter 9 there are two more exercises that are relevant to the material presented in this chapter. One deals with romantic images and their effect on mate selection and burnout, the other (a sociodrama) provides an experiential exploration of couples' roots and wings.

3

Three Clinical Approaches to Couple Therapy and an Alternative

The play *It Was the Lark,* written by the Israeli humorist Ephraim Kishon, is set about twenty years after the events recounted in Shakespeare's *Romeo and Juliet.* Somehow the star-crossed lovers have survived their rendezvous with destiny and settled into middle age. In the beginning of the second act, an overweight, balding Romeo and a querulous, nagging Juliet wake up in their drab apartment. Soon they start arguing, with much exasperation and annoyance, over whether it was a nightingale or a lark that they heard on their first night of love. "Definitely a Nightingale!" proclaims Juliet. "A Lark!" Romeo shouts back, adding, "You were always like that! Just to provoke me, just to argue, just to tease! Black? White! Today? Tomorrow! Lark? No, definitely not . . ." "Oi, Momo, you're stubborn! . . . You're stubborn! A Nightingale!" retorts Juliet (Kishon 1974, 36). When they turn their backs toward each other, the silence of the dead stretches across time and bed.

The humor and sadness of the play derives from the contrast between our romantic images of the passionate, beautiful lovers and the drab familiarity of their middle-aged marriage. The playwright seems to tell us that the only way to make love last forever is for the lovers to die at the height of passion. Most people, however, prefer to look to places other than a crypt to preserve their love.

Even if couple burnout is a new concept, the experience it describes is clearly not new. People have fallen in and out of love before, people have gotten married and divorced before, and people have asked for help with problems before. Never before, however, have so many people asked for help from psychotherapists. As Rollo May says, we are "an age of therapy" (May 1969).

With the technological revolution has come an ever-increasing reliance on experts and specialists. In the area of human relationships, psychotherapists are the experts. Many modern couples feel that their parents can't really help them with problems, because their parents' marriages (unlike their own) are based more on commitment than on romantic love. The religious answer they get from a priest or a rabbi (that their union is sacred or at least semi-inviolate because it was blessed by God) does not quite address the problem that love has died.

Not everyone who has marital problems seeks therapy. Some people avoid therapy because they don't believe that it (or anything else for that matter) can help. A man who left his wife for another woman after fourteen years of marriage said:

> I don't believe in the notion of "working on relationships."
> You didn't have to work at falling in love, did you? When a
> relationship isn't working, it means that love is gone. It's
> better to admit it, and the sooner the better.

Other people see in seeking professional help an admission of failure. Yet others know intuitively that the therapist is going to explain their problems as some kind of pathology and they refuse to accept that perspective.

Clinical psychology, the field most involved in treating couples' problems, is defined in the *Dictionary of Behavioral Science* as "a branch of psychology devoted to the study, diagnosis, and treatment of behavior disorders." Behavior disorders, according to the same dictionary, are those behaviors defined as "disturbed, abnormal, and deranged" (Wolman 1973).

Clinical psychologists are trained to approach problems as some kind of disease or abnormality. Individual therapists tend to view couples' problems as caused by the pathology of the individual, couple therapists and family therapists see them as caused by dysfunctional patterns in the couple. One way or another some abnormality is identified. Abnormality implies uniqueness (abnormal in the sense of "not normal," "not typical"). The assumption of the uniqueness in marital unhappiness is perfectly expressed in Leo Tolstoy's epigraph to *Anna Karenina*: "All happy families are alike, but an unhappy family is unhappy after its own fashion." Indeed, the quote is a favorite among family therapists.

The disease model of clinical psychology is appropriate in the case of seriously maladjusted individuals. The unique abnormality of a particular couple, however, can hardly account for the fact that over 50 percent of all marriages end in divorce, and that the majority of the rest have had at some point problems serious enough for the partners to consider divorce.[1]

Three Clinical Approaches to Couple Therapy

Couple therapy began as a professional specialty in the United States in the 1930s, but it was only after World War II, with the dramatic increase in the number of divorces among young couples, that it started to grow rapidly. In recent years, the growing acceptance of therapy as a way to address problems, the growing numbers of troubled marriages, and the pressure to provide less expensive and shorter therapy, has led the field of couple therapy to develop at an exponential rate.

Until the development of family therapy, therapists avoided and discouraged contact with their patients' mates. Therapy was based on the premise that psychological problems arise from unhealthy relationships and can best be treated by an intense relationship with a therapist. Seeing each mate separately continued to be the most common practice of couple therapy for thirty years. It wasn't until the late 1960s that the practice of seeing couples in joint therapy was established—a practice that has become the norm today.

There are three major approaches to couple therapy: psychodynamic, behavioral, and systems.[2] When couples have a marital problem and decide to seek therapy, these are the three basic styles of therapy they are most likely to encounter. Both psychoanalysis and behavior therapy were originally developed to treat troubled individuals. Only much later were they applied to the treatment of couples, and their approach to couples isn't much different from their approach to individuals: both assume an underlying individual pathology in couples' problems. Systems therapy, on the other hand, originated in work with troubled families.

The Psychodynamic Approach

The psychodynamic approach emphasizes the role of innate drives, childhood experiences, and unconscious forces. The therapist is viewed as providing for the patient a screen on which to project unresolved and largely unconscious childhood issues that are being replayed in the patient's adult life. The patient "transfers" these past emotional attachments to the therapist. Once these unconscious childhood issues become accessible to the conscious mind, once the connection between the present and the past is comprehended by the patient, and once the transference is resolved, therapy is over. For orthodox psychoanalysts, the idea of working with a couple jointly is unacceptable because transference, the most important element in therapy, is diluted in the presence of the spouse.

Psychodynamically oriented couple therapists emphasize unresolved childhood conflicts and unconscious motivations in mate selection and in the maintenance of unhappy and destructive relationships. They see people as actively creating their life circumstances, including their marital problems. Mate selection is never viewed as random or incidental. People choose mates that are most appropriate to meet needs that were not met in their childhood. A couple's unique problems reflect parts of both partners that are conscious and unconscious, suppressed and projected.[3]

The key elements in the psychodynamic object-relations approach to couple therapy were summarized by James L. Framo (1990):

1. The human need for satisfactory object relationships is a fundamental motive of life.

2. Unable to give up their parents or change them, infants incorporate (introject) the most frustrating aspects of their relationship with them. These introjects are than maintained as enduring psychological representatives of the parents.

3. Intrapsychic conflicts arise from experiences in the original family. In an effort to resolve these conflicts, the individual shapes his or her current relationships into patterns similar to those of the original family.

4. One's mate is perceived largely in terms of one's own needs (for example, a mate may be seen as carrying one's denied, split-off traits). Mates select each other to recover lost aspects of their primary object-relations, aspects that they reexperience in the other by projective identification. A main source of marital disharmony is that spouses project disowned aspects of themselves onto their mates and then fight them in the mates.

We see that the psychodynamic explanation of couples' problems is linear. Childhood traumas are expressed in current problems. Pathogenic introjects and unconscious motivations help explain irrational behaviors (such as staying in an abusive relationship or pushing someone you love to leave you.) Mates are seen as representing denied split-off parts in each other (a woman who feels she is unlovable chooses a man who can't show love so she can blame her feelings on him.) Because mates' unconscious needs reflect pathogenic introjects that underwent splitting and repression, they tend to be complementary: a victim and an abuser, a pursuer and a distancer, a sadist and a masochist. Projections and introjects in both partners create a mutual process in which each mate projects on the other split-off and unconscious parts and responds unconsciously to the projections rather than to the mate. When the couple is undifferentiated, each mate internalizes the other's projection through a process of projective identification. Internal conflicts become conflicts between the mates. In other words, couples' conflicts are a reenactment of the same inner conflict within each mate, in which each mate expresses one side of the inner conflict.

Since a psychodynamically oriented therapist assumes that the partners chose each other based on unconscious needs and that their problems are a reenactment of intrapsychic conflicts, therapy tends to be rather long. It requires bringing these unresolved conflicts into consciousness.

With the popularization of psychoanalytic ideas in the mass media, people have absorbed much of the superficial material of psychoanalysis and started using it to explain their own and other people's behavior. A woman may accuse a man of replaying with her his unresolved hostility toward his mother. Shifting the focus from a problem within the relationship to a problem with him makes the man the subject of blame and frees the woman from responsibility for the role she plays in the relationship.

The psychodynamic approach's contributions to the field of couple therapy include its focus on the influence of childhood experiences and unconscious motivations in what would otherwise seem like irrational behavior. Another major contribution has been the emphasis on the role of unconscious motivations in mate selection and in the creation of couples' problems. Yet another is the view of people as being driven to create their life circumstances (even their relationship's problems) in order to satisfy important psychological needs.

The main objection raised by critics of the psychodynamic approach, in addition to its length and relative ineffectiveness with concrete symptoms, has been its tendency to attribute too much importance to early childhood experiences and not enough to the current environment and the behaviors of the people involved. Other criticisms have been directed at its inclination to attribute too much power to the unconscious and not enough power to the conscious mind, to spiritual needs, and to future goals; to assume excessive pathology; and to "blame" the reason for suffering on the person in pain.

The Behavioral Approach

Behaviorism focuses on observed behavior. Pathological behavior is seen as caused by learning and reinforcement. Behavior therapy specializes in methods of changing maladaptive habits. Behavioral therapists see both the causes of problems and their solutions in the current environment, and they take problems at face value. A behavioral therapist is not likely to assume, as a psychoanalyst typically does, that the patient doesn't understand his "real" problem. For example, if the problem is a morbid fear of being touched by a person of the opposite sex, a behavioral therapist will not waste time reliving the childhood trauma that created the fear, but will direct all efforts to relieving it. The person will be asked to make a list of all the activities related to being touched and rank them in order of the fear they produce, from least to most scary (from a handshake to making love). He (or she) is taught relaxation exercises. Then, while in a state of complete relaxation, he is asked to imagine the item at the bottom of the list. If he tenses, he is returned to the relaxation exercises. When able to remain relaxed while imagining the item at the bottom of the list, he is instructed to imagine the next item. This process of "progressive desensitization" continues until the person is able to imagine the most scary items on the list without panicking. Actual physical contact is the final proof that the fear is gone, and then therapy is over.

Behavioral couple therapists assume that in every social interaction people try to maximize their rewards and minimize their costs. Happy relationships are characterized by a maximum of rewards for both mates. Problems in relationships occur when mates give few rewards to each other or make the costs of the relationship excessive. Problems also crop up when there is an imbalance, when one spouse is reaping most of the rewards while the other is paying most of the costs, or else when spouses use coercion to get the rewards they want. Based on this set of assumptions, the behavioral therapist's goal is to teach couples how to provide each other with more rewards at reduced price. To do that, the therapist asks each spouse to state explicitly what he or she would like to receive from the other, and then helps the couple reach an equitable exchange of these desired behaviors or rewards (Segraves 1982).

One of the first attempts to apply behavioral principles to couples was made in 1969 by the behavioral couple therapist Richard B. Stuart. Stuart treated four couples who were in divorce court for similar reasons—basically the husband wanted more sex and the wife wanted more talking. The therapy consisted of helping each couple negotiate a contract in which the husband could earn a poker chip for every fifteen minutes of dialogue. When the husband earned eight poker chips, he could exchange them for sexual intercourse. The result: the rate of talking went up significantly, and so did the rate of sexual intercourse. After a few sessions, none of the couples wanted to continue with divorce proceedings (Stuart 1969).

More recent examples of the application of behavioral approach tend to be more sophisticated. An exchange may involve sexual activities that are pleasurable to both mates (one evening devoted to the desires of one mate, another evening devoted to satisfying the other mate) rather than exchanging sex for conversation. Yet the techniques are still aimed at helping couples learn more productive and positive means of effecting desired behavior changes in one another: negotiating fair exchange contracts and using rewards to modify each other's behavior instead of using punishment or coercion.

The contracts that therapists help couples negotiate are often written, so they can be easily renegotiated and modified. Placed in a visible location, they can serve as a constant reminder and reference. The two major forms of contracts in use are "quid pro quo" and "good faith."

In the quid pro quo (or tit-for-tat) contract, the desired changes of both mates are cross-linked so that if one person changes the behavior, the mate will also change in the requested way. For example, if Ruth wants David to spend more time talking with her and he wants her to spend more time with his colleagues, a quid pro quo contract might be written as follows: if David spends an hour talking to Ruth, Ruth will spend an hour with David's colleagues. In this contract, mates' behavior changes are contingent on one another. If you do not fulfill your part of the contract, your spouse is under no obligation to change, and vice versa. The problem with this kind of contract is that couples (especially distressed couples) can get into a "you go first" standstill.

The good-faith contract is written so that a mate who engages in the desired behavior receives positive reinforcement independent of what the other mate does. In the example above, if David talks with Ruth for half an hour, he can choose which movie they are going to watch that week. In such a contract there is no benefit in waiting for the other to change first.

The discussion of the two types of contracts demonstrates the extent to which behaviorists take people's problems at face value and their relationships as straightforward business propositions. Behavioral marital therapy (BMT) is based on principles derived from exchange theory. Couples are seen as engaging in continuous behavioral exchanges in which every behavior is both a response and a stimulus. The quality of a couple's relationship depends on the level of their mutual reinforcements. Positive reinforcements increase both satisfaction and the likelihood of reciprocation. Therapists help couples develop communication, problem-solving, and negotiation skills. Communication skills include such things as learning to listen without interrupting and to summarize what you have heard to make sure you understood it. Problem-solving skills include such general instructions as finding a special time for the discussion (not during a fight), avoiding arguments about the legitimacy of the problem, focusing on one problem at a time, and stating the problem in positive (rather than negative) and behavioral terms (O'Leary and Turkewitz 1978).

Since behaviorists deal with observable behaviors, they can measure their effectiveness, which they have indeed done. Actually, the emphasis on empirical research is one of the things differentiating BMT from other therapeutic approaches. For example, in his review of twenty years of research (his and that of others), including twenty-four outcome studies conducted in five countries, Neil Jacobson concluded that behavior exchange has an immediate but short-term (six months) effect, whereas communication combined with problem solving has less of an immediate impact but an effect that lasts longer (one year). A combination of both components has both an immediate and a longer impact (two years). However, after two years 30 percent of the successfully treated couples regress. When these are added to the 30 percent that have not gained from therapy to begin with (a similar percentage—30 percent—does not benefit from other forms of therapy), the success rate is 50 percent.

The behavioral approach's contributions to the field of couple therapy include its emphasis on empirical research, its optimism about the couple's ability to change, a focus on observable behavior in therapy, and the use of structured exercises. The main objection raised by critics has been its tendency to attribute too much importance to observable behavior and total disregard of unconscious forces. Another criticism is that the therapist is a mechanic; treatment is mechanical and impact temporary.

The Behavioral vs. the Psychodynamic Approaches

Clearly, the psychodynamic and the behavioral approaches have very different assumptions about human nature. For the psychodynamically oriented therapist, the essence of people is expressed in unconscious processes triggered by childhood experiences. Consequently, these processes are the focus of therapy. For the behavioral therapist, the essence of people is expressed in overt behavior, making overt behavior the focus of therapy. In both cases, when a couple comes for help, help is given in accordance with the therapist's theoretical perspective, which may have very little to do with the couple's own perspective. When couples give themselves over to "experts" in the hope of saving their relationships, they force themselves to fit into the therapist's perspective. More often than not, however, because they are focusing on each other in a new and positive way, because they are trying to change old patterns of behavior, and because they believe that the therapy is going to improve things, some improvement almost always takes place.

The Systems Approach

For a systems-oriented therapist, the focus is not on the two individuals comprising the couple but rather on the new system they have created jointly. A couple system is seen as having an identity that is more than the sum of its parts. A change in one part of the system (one mate) invariably causes change in the other part (the other mate), which then causes change in the first part, and so on. For example, anger in one spouse may cause a defensive withdrawal in the other, which increases the anger of the first, which increases the withdrawal of the second, which may lead to a violent outburst in the first, which may make the second close off all communication attempts.

While in psychodynamic theory causality is perceived as linear (problems in the present are seen as caused by events in the past), and in behavioral theory events are viewed as a linear series of S–R connections, in systems theory causes of events are seen as circular. Each spouse's behavior is seen at one and the same time as both a response to and the trigger for the other spouse's behavior. If the wife complains to the therapist about something obnoxious her husband has done, the therapist is likely to try to find out what preceded that event (whether there was something the wife did to provoke that behavior) and what followed it (what she did in response).[4]

The systems-oriented therapist assumes that in a couple system there is no totally passive, victimlike position. This perspective prevents attaching blame to one person because both mates are seen as contributing to every interaction. Although in certain circumstances one mate may appear like the victim and the other like the abuser, this is an illusion derived from an arbitrary designation by the couple as to who is the actor and who is the reactor. The therapist tries to change that designation. One way to do that is to suggest that the victim is getting something from the role, such as the label of victim or of "the good one." To a systems therapist, relationships over time become structured into stable social systems that tend to resist change. Consistent patterns of interaction become the rules that govern the system. When a couple is experiencing problems, the therapist assumes that their interactions consist of some dysfunctional patterns. The therapist's goal is to change those destructive patterns and to bring the couple's system to a healthy state of balance.

A common example of such a dysfunctional pattern is the situation in which the husband sees his wife as demanding and intrusive while the wife sees her husband as cold and distant. The wife complains to her husband, but rather than making him spend more time with her and express more warmth, her complaints win her the title of "nag." He withdraws to avoid her nagging. She nags even more. He withdraws even further.

When such a dysfunctional pattern is operating, no one's needs are met. Therefore, the systems therapist will try to change the pattern. The therapist assumes that the way in which a sequence of events is described and understood results from arbitrary agreements by the mates. Does he withdraw because she nags (the way the husband describes it), or does she nag because he withdraws (the way the wife describes it)? A change in the description of this sequence breaks stereotypes the couple holds and may radically alter rules of interaction and myths.

Some systems therapists use paradoxical interventions.[5] Rather than provoke the system's resistance to change, the therapist utilizes that resistance as part of the therapeutic process, by prescribing the symptom. For example, the wife may be told that it seems like the desired change in her husband is really important to her, and she should put even more effort into changing him by nagging even more. The husband may be told that he should help his wife by withdrawing even further. The assumption is that both of them will realize the absurdity of their behavior and will stop the dysfunctional cycle altogether.

Other systems therapists use more straightforward interventions. A therapist may instruct the couple that from that time on the husband is to request everything he previously received from his wife without asking (his meals, clean clothes, etc.). This is expected to change the rules governing the marriage (rules in which he gets what he needs without having to ask while she has to nag to get what she wants). Once the rules are changed, or the rules about who makes the rules are changed, the dysfunctional pattern will be broken, the couple's problems solved, and the therapy over.

The main contribution of the systems approach to the field of couple therapy is its emphasis on the third component in a couple's relationship—the couple—as an independent system. Other contributions include: the notion of circular causality and of feedback loops, in which a change in one partner always causes change in the other and where one can never not respond; the view of symptoms as part of a certain couple context and as serving a function in that system; and the close attention to communication (e.g., input vs. output, symptoms as communication).

Traditionally the systems approach has been criticized for its tendency to attribute too much to the present and not enough to the past. In recent years the approach has also been criticized by feminist writers for its disregard of gender issues.[6] Concepts such as complementarity and circularity ignore power differences between men and women and suggest that both mates are responsible for whatever happens in the relationship. In cases of violence, the woman is asked what did she do before the attack (i.e., how did she provoke it). The gender-neutral language used in discussing cases of "spousal abuse" and patterns such as that of a pursuer and a distancer does not address the fact that in almost all cases the woman is the victim in the cases of spousal abuse and the pursuer in a pursuer-distancer dynamic. In addition, there is no reference to the question of why this pattern was created to begin with (the woman is in a one-down position), and the obvious fact that the problem is gender related is ignored.

The Three Clinical Approaches and the Existential Approach

Even in this oversimplified description of the three leading clinical approaches to couple therapy, it is clear that each approach has certain advantages and disadvantages. Most couple therapists use some combination of all three approaches when working with couples. Typically, a therapist explains the underlying dynamics of the couple's issues from a psychodynamic perspective, describes negative patterns of interaction and tries to change them like a systems therapist, and teaches communication and problem-solving skills like a behaviorist.

Despite their different primary orientations, as clinical psychologists, couple therapists from these three approaches all too often explain couples' problems as a sort of disease or abnormality. This is true whether they focus on abnormalities in the individual mates or on dysfunctional patterns in the couple. The disease model denies the situational context of the couple's problems, which includes not only such stresses as illness, financial difficulties, and a demanding career, but also all the cultural trends discussed earlier—the high rates of divorce, the breakup of the extended family, and the changing roles of men and women. It also encompasses the culturally sanctioned emphasis on romantic love as the basis for marriage and the unrealistic expectations a belief in romantic love can generate.

A focus on pathology, by definition, implies a relative disregard for the healthy parts of the couple's relationship. This fact was dramatically demonstrated in a unique conference on couple therapy organized by Harvard Medical School. The most significant feature in it was a series of videotapes made during actual therapy sessions. Four of the country's best-known couple therapists (Peggy Papp, James L. Framo, Norman L. Paul, and Carlos Sluzki) were videotaped treating the same couple. The four therapists presented and demonstrated their different therapeutic styles in individual lecture sessions, during which they were able to stop the video presentation at any point, answer questions, and comment on a particular intervention.[7] The presentations were published recently in a book entitled *One Couple Four Realities* (Chasin, et al. 1990).

In a final session with two of the conference's organizers, the couple was asked to evaluate each of the four therapists and to describe what they had gained from each of their therapeutic interventions. The couple was very generous in their compliments to the four therapists and described in great length and detail the insights they gained from each one of them. In closing, the interviewer asked if there was anything that they found missing, something they wish had been discussed but was not, something missed by all the therapists. The couple answered without a moment's hesitation, "No one asked us whether or why we love each other. No one asked what was good about our relationship, what it was that kept us together for ten years."

The reason no one asked the couple about love is rather obvious. They were having problems, which is what brought them into therapy. All four of the therapists saw their goal as alleviating those problems; consequently, problems were the focus. It should be noted, however, that both the man and the woman were attractive, articulate, and professionally successful individuals. What is more important, however, is that they behaved lovingly toward each other and were committed to the relationship. These facts were never brought up in therapy.

Love is rarely the focus of couple therapy, whether the therapy is performed by a psychodynamically, behaviorally, or systems-oriented therapist. The reason is the same in each case: Since the couple presents problems, problems are the focus of therapy. When love does come up, it is addressed as a secondary issue. For couples who base their relationship on romantic love, however, love is a primary issue. Couples who are taught by the prevailing cultural values to believe in romantic love are trying to work out in their relationships an issue of major significance. They are looking for love to give their life a sense of meaning. When they fail, they are devastated. This is why they go to a "marriage expert" for help, but the therapist, who is also socialized to believe in the same romantic ideology, doesn't see the problem of the failure of love for what it is.

Helping people find meaning in life is a major goal in the existential school of psychotherapy. It is *the* major goal in one of its branches, called logotherapy (*logos* = meaning in Greek). Victor Frankl, who developed logotherapy, describes it as focused on "the meaning of human existence as well as on man's search for such a meaning" (Frankl 1966, 153–54). According to Frankl, the striving to find meaning in life is "the primary motivational force in man" (154). He quotes a public opinion poll showing that 89 percent of the thousands of people polled thought that man needs "something" to live for. Logotherapy emphasizes the power of expectations, values, choices. Frankl denies that "one's search for meaning . . . is derived from, or results in, any disease. A man's concern, even his despair, over the worthwhileness of life is a spiritual distress but by no means a mental disease" (Frankl 1966, 162–63). On the basis of his experiences as a survivor of a Nazi concentration camp, Frankl argues that there is nothing in the world that can so effectively help one to survive even the worst conditions as the knowledge that there is a meaning in one's life. Thus, logotherapy regards its "assignment as that of assisting the patient to find meaning in his life" (163).

Frankl did not apply logotherapy to couples. For one thing, he saw the search for meaning as a unique task that must be accomplished by each individual alone. In addition, he did not see romantic love as *the* solution to the existential dilemma, but as one of the experiences by which people can discover meaning in their life.[8] Similar reasons explain why other forms of existential psychotherapy were not applied to couples (Yalom, 1980).

A Focus on Love
in the Treatment of Couple Burnout

When a couple comes to therapy for the first time, they usually look grim and tense. Each mate carries a mental list of all those "terrible things" that the other one is doing, or has done, throughout their marriage. If we drew two balloons above their heads to indicate what they were thinking, each balloon would show a partner presenting the "crime list" to a shocked and dismayed therapist, who leaps to their side, where together they work to change their unreasonable (and stubborn) mate. Instead, the questions that I ask are: What attracted you to each other when you first met? What attracted you to this inconsiderate, cold, and uncaring man? What attracted you to this demanding, hysterical, and unsympathetic woman? These questions have an almost magical effect. Faces relax, and surprised smiles replace angry looks as they tell me how they fell in love with each other. Dona describes her first meeting with Andrew and what made her fall in love with him:

> Andrew lived next door to me. Once, when I was mad at my previous boyfriend, I invited him to a party. He was a very beautiful person and had many beautiful qualities, and I fell in love with him. . . . He was sort of the strong, silent type, you know. . . . He was pretty decisive about where he wanted to go. He usually went where he wanted to, and I liked that. He was a good lover, and he was nice looking. . . . He is a very elegant man and tidy. His image of himself is important, so he always looked good. He wasn't penny-pinching; he would spend money on dinner and stuff like that, which I enjoyed. I thought that chemically we had a lot in common. . . . I mean, I fell in love with him. You can't explain why you fall in love with somebody; it's not a logical thing.

When I asked Andrew why he fell in love with Dona, he said:

> We were next-door neighbors. I remember bumping into her a couple of times at the mailbox, which was next door. And then she invited me to a party. . . . She seemed professional. At least that's the overriding term one would use. . . . I thought she was attractive . . . and she was quite

friendly, not difficult to get to know. . . . And she exhibited some emotional dependency, which was also very attractive to me.

One of my favorite exercises in couple burnout workshops (the exercise is detailed in chapter 9) is to ask participants what attracted them to their mates initially and then ask what are the traits of their mate that they find most stressful at present. There is, always, a direct relationship between the original attraction and the current stresses.

It is the things that initially attract people to each other (the recognition that the other is capable of helping them overcome unresolved childhood issues) that eventually cause their burnout (when they feel that the other cannot or will not do that). For example: a man who was attracted to a woman because of her strength and energy explains his burnout in the fact that she is controlling and hysterical. A woman who was attracted to a man because he is generous with his money says when she burns out that he is a spendthrift.

We discussed in the previous chapter Marcy, who as a child adored her emotionally distant and professionally successful father; she fell in love with Marie who is a very successful and very busy business executive and very attached to her daughter. Marcy fell in love with Marie because she seemed like a superior being—beautiful, desirable, successful. She put her on a pedestal. Her greatest stress in the relationship was the fact that Marie did not seem to cherish their time together as much as she did and did not seem as needy of their relationship as Marcy.

Dona fell in love with Andrew because he was the strong, silent type. She burned out because he was controlling and didn't know how to communicate. Andrew fell in love with Dona because he saw her as a competent professional woman who showed emotional dependency. He burned out because she was too focused on her career, too manipulative, and too needy of security. Dona explained:

> We were not building something together. We were just
> always going off in separate directions. There was no cou-
> ple. There was no bond. . . . Whenever we would try to dis-
> cuss something, I would get violently angry with him
> because I couldn't get through. . . . He is always, I think,
> protecting himself from being controlled. So if I ask him to
> do something, I've got to think how can I ask him to do it.

I can't be direct. I've got to think. It's exhausting. And he began to detect that I was manipulating, which I really was, because I could never say to him I'd like you to do such-and-such, because his response would be: Oh yeah? You know, something like that. . . . And his way with money is not my way either. He has no budget. He doesn't know—he's got a business but doesn't know what anything costs him. . . . He doesn't take the trouble. It makes me feel insecure.

Andrew, describing his side of the story, said:

I have great respect for her professional qualities and always will. On the other hand, what I like in people and admire in people is to be well rounded and do more than one thing, which is why I've been willing to take a crack at this and a crack at that. Dona will never do that. Ever. There comes a point where, you know, the good news turns to bad news. . . . I think she found me unstable.

And on the issue of control Andrew commented:

She is very . . . manipulative, maybe that's a little bit too strong a word, but she was always trying to get me to do something. Most of the friction was because she wanted to do something and wanted me to go along, when I was perfectly content to sit at home, or I wanted to go do my own thing. . . . It got to the point where she realized that she couldn't control me.

Dona saw in Andrew someone strong and decisive who was generous with money and was willing to take her out for dinners. These qualities were associated in her mind with security—the security she perceived Andrew as refusing to give her. Andrew, on his part, was attracted to Dona's strength and neediness of him, but came to view them as attempts to limit his freedom.

Because of the strong connection between the things that attract couples to each other and the things that eventually cause their burnout, addressing the original attraction can serve an important diagnostic purpose. After hearing from a couple what attracted them to each other, it is quite easy to predict the things about each other that will give them the greatest difficulty.

For people who believe in romantic love, the things that attract and the things that distress are both reflections of an existential search. They are related to an internal image of an ideal love in which one's fears of isolation will be gone forever and one's uniqueness cherished. When a relationship fails to fulfill this ideal image, the pain and rage focus naturally on those aspects in the mate that cause the most acute disappointment. In other words, while the attraction represents the existential hope, the stress represents its disappointment.

When couples see how they themselves desired the things they now find so objectionable about each other, they realize their own role in shaping their relationship and their power to affect it. When a stress that has been labeled "a problem caused by my spouse" is relabeled "a frustrated hope" or "an opportunity to grow and overcome an unresolved issue," it does not seem quite as overwhelming. This is especially true when the problem caused by the spouse is seen as related to the very thing that made him or her so desirable initially. The reason for this is that while the spouse's personality is not in people's control, one's own hopes, dreams, and romantic goals are—at least to a certain degree (the degree of control increases with the increased awareness of the internal workings of our minds). Relabeling stresses as frustrated hopes and opportunities for personal growth reduces helplessness and hopelessness, which, as we know, are the hallmarks of burnout.

The search for meaning through romantic love can take very different forms for different people or during different stages of life. Yet the dreams a couple had at the beginning of their relationship can continue to play an important role in their lives for years after. I had a demonstration of that in my work with Ken and Margaret.

The couple (both in their early fifties) has been married for twenty-five years and have four grown children. They came to see me because they felt burned out in their marriage and were thinking about divorce. Margaret's main complaint was that Ken was always so involved in his work and that he was never available to her, even during her times of greatest need. "I don't see a reason to stay married," she said. "I am alone all the time anyway." Ken agreed that he may have been too involved in his work in the past, but insisted that things have changed, that he wanted to be closer to Margaret. His main complaint was that he felt rejected by Margaret, both emotionally and sexually.

When I asked Ken and Margaret what attracted them to each other originally, they told me that besides being attracted to each other's looks (they are both tall, very attractive, and rather similar looking), Ken was attracted to Margaret's warmth, and she was attracted to his strength. Since both came from very poor and unstable family backgrounds, they had a shared dream to be financially secure and have a comfortable, warm, and stable home. During their years of marriage they made that dream come true. They were very comfortable financially, had a beautiful home, a lot of "nice things," and a "wonderful" close-knit family.

But working to achieve the dream was not easy. It required a lot of hard work from both of them: Ken in his job, Margaret at home. Both felt that they had put more into the marriage than they had gotten back from it. My own sense was that Ken and Margaret were suffering from the fact that now that their dream had come true, they felt that their lives were empty, but instead of attributing their sense of disappointment and emptiness to an "existential crisis," they attributed it to each other.

I asked Ken and Margaret what would be their one wish if they met a good fairy that could fulfill any wish. Ken's response was, "I would like Margaret to love me." Margaret said, "I want to have a wild, crazy, passionate love affair with Ken." What these two people, who were on their way to the divorce court, wanted more than anything else was a romantic relationship—not with a fantasy stranger, but with each other. It would probably come as no surprise that Ken's and Margaret's wishes were related to what they experienced as most lacking about each other. Ken complained that Margaret was cold and rejecting ("She never gives me a kiss or a hug spontaneously"). Margaret complained that Ken was doing things without consulting her, and seemed much more interested in his work than he was in her ("He never asks my opinion about anything, and is always much more interested in spending time discussing a business deal than he is in spending time with me").

Predictably, their greatest stresses were related to what Ken and Margaret found most attractive about each other when they first fell in love. In those early days he loved her warmth and sociability, and she fell in love with his strength and stability. Now she was too sociable (toward others) and he was too strong and stable (too committed to his work and not enough to romance). Once they became aware of the relationship between what they found most difficult and what they found most attractive about each other, as well as between their greatest stresses and their frustrated romantic ideals, and once they became aware that they had the same romantic dream, realizing that dream became the focus of all their efforts. One time, when trying to explain how important romantic love was for her, Margaret said, "Finding a love like that (like the romantic love I have been dreaming about and hoping for with Ken) is like finding God."

The Contribution of Social Psychology: Two Kinds of Attribution

There is one more field of psychology that in my opinion has great relevance to couple therapy, even though, to the best of my knowledge, it has never been used for that purpose—social psychology.

Social psychology is the scientific field that seeks to comprehend the nature and causes of individual behavior in social situations. The situational context of problems, which is underemphasized in clinical psychology, is overemphasized in social psychology. Social psychologists are not therapists and are not concerned with treatment but rather with "understanding the situations that shape the behavior of individuals toward each other" (Wolman 1973, 300). In the case of marital problems, the question for a social psychologist is: What are the situations that cause problems for all couples? A rather different question is asked by a family therapist: What are the unique problems presented by this couple? The first question emphasizes the shared aspects in all marital problems; the second one emphasizes the individual aspects and thus fosters the misconception mentioned earlier—the "fallacy of uniqueness."

For a social psychologist, one of the most effective ways to help couples is to let them discover, with the help of other couples, the fallacy of their perceived uniqueness. When I lead couple groups, I ask group members to describe what attracted them to their mates, their expectations of their relationships, their major stresses, and the ways they cope with these stresses. During this process, couples inevitably discover how universal both their hopes *and* their stresses are. This discovery helps break their fallacy of uniqueness. This, as we know, reduces guilt and blame and frees emotional energy for more constructive coping.

We are all active participants in creating the world we live in. During our interactions with the world, we constantly form impressions and explanations for events we observe. In social-psychological terms, we "make attributions" for these events. The attributions different people make, even for the same event, can vary widely.

Seeing a man slip and fall, for example, can be attributed to all sorts of causes: to the slipperiness of the ground or of his new shoes, to his innate clumsiness or absent-mindedness, to a temporary state of physical exhaustion caused by studying late for an exam, or to intention—falling on purpose to amuse his little child. When the focus of the explanation is on the environment, the attribution is called situational (e.g., the man slipped because of the slippery ground); when the focus of the explanation is on something in the person, the attribution is called dispositional (e.g., the man slipped because he is clumsy).

People all too often explain their own and other people's behavior in dispositional terms. For example, when they have certain feelings, thoughts, and physical symptoms in response to a jealousy-triggering situation (such as their mate having an affair), they say, "The reason I am experiencing this jealous reaction is because I am a jealous person." Another person, given the exact same set of circumstances, could say, "The reason I am experiencing jealousy is that my lover is going to bed with someone else."

Interestingly, both those who define themselves as jealous and those who define themselves as nonjealous actually have a very similar response to jealousy (in terms of physical and emotional symptoms), and their jealousy is triggered in similar situations (when they perceive a threat to a valued romantic relationship).[9] The difference between dispositional and situational attributions is not semantic. It has far-reaching implications for the individual making the attribution or about whom the attribution is made. Individuals making dispositional attributions are explaining events by the fact that they are "those kind of people." That explanation puts them in what social psychologist Philip Zimbardo calls "a prison of their own mind," a mental prison from which there is no way out (Zimbardo, et al. 1973).

The person who wants to be a lawyer but does not apply to law school because he or she is shy has created a self-made prison of the mind. A person prone to jealousy who marries someone whose only redeeming quality is faithfulness, has created a self-made prison. The couple that experiences relationship problems, and is convinced that these problems are the result of each other's innate personality characteristics, is also creating a mental prison. The lists of "terrible things" mates keep about each other help keep them in these mental prisons. Because they assume that "they are the way they are, and that's all there is to it," people who are making dispositional attributions—either about themselves or about their mate—are not very motivated to change.

Individuals who make situational self-attributions, on the other hand, are explaining events by the fact that they are reacting "to the particular situation," which means that in another situation they may react very differently. For example, such people may note that they are nervous in front of large audiences, feel excluded when their mate is flirting with a good-looking stranger, or feel less romantic since the three children came along. Such people are not very likely to explain their response by the fact that they are "those kind of people" and "nothing can be done about it." They are much more likely to see their response as caused by the particular stressful situation and, consequently, to focus their efforts on changing that situation. Rather than accepting the situation as a given, such people actively seek to improve their lives and their relationships by changing the situation.

In my work with burned-out couples, a very important goal is to help both mates make the transition from dispositional to situational attributions. Typically, couples define their marital problems dispositionally: "He is a cold, uncaring, emotionally closed person. He is incapable of communicating his feelings." "She is insatiable in her demands; nothing I ever do is enough for her." In response, I typically ask whether there has ever been a situation in which he communicated his feelings or she appreciated something he did. As luck may have it, there is always at least one case in which both mates agree that was indeed the case.

Even if there was only one instance of this atypical ("abnormal") behavior, it still means that he is not a closed person, but rather a person who opens up more easily in certain situations; and she is not an insatiable person, but rather a person who is more easily satisfied in certain situations. The challenge for the couple is to try to identify what it was about that particular situation (often it is the same situation that brought out the unusual behavior in both of them) that enabled him to open up and her to be satisfied. As difficult as that task may seem, it is much easier than trying to make a cold person warm or an insatiable person satisfied.

A similar shift from a dispositional to a situational attribution can be made in the case of a problem such as jealousy. When a person comes for therapy because of jealousy, most often the dispositional attribution of "a jealous person" has already been agreed on by both mates. In order to challenge it, I usually ask, "Have you been that jealous in all your intimate relationships?" or, "Have you always been that jealous in this relationship?" The answer to either one of these questions is most often no. My next question is: "What is it about this relationship or this particular period of time that triggers your jealousy?" or, "What was it about the relationship or the period in which you were least jealous that made you feel different?" These questions are rather different from: "Why am I a jealous person?" and "How can I change myself to stop being jealous?" Instead of attributing the jealousy to a dispositional pathology it is attributed to a jealousy-producing situation.

Couples often make dispositional attributions about their relationship. The words that serve as a clue are "always" and "never." These attributions can be challenged by an alternative—situational—attribution. When a couple says, "We never communicate," they can be asked, "Was there ever a time or a situation in which you did communicate?" "What was it about that situation that made it easy for you to talk to each other?" When a couple says, "We never do fun things together," they are begging to be asked: "What did you do together (no matter how long ago) that both of you thought was fun?" "What is it about that activity, or the circumstance in which it happened, that enabled both of you to have fun?"

Although social psychology has not been applied directly to couple therapy, the above examples show that it can provide couple therapists with an important addition to the clinical approaches. Couples can be helped to shift from dispositional to situational attributions both in and out of the therapy room. The examples presented above demonstrate how it is done in reference to outside issues the couple brings into therapy. In the therapy room it is done by noting every time the couple does something that contradicts a dispositional attribution they make about themselves or about each other. For example, when a wife complains that her husband is uncaring, the therapist will note every time the husband does something which shows care. The shift from dispositional to situational attributions is similar to Michael White's concept of "unique outcomes" and to Franz Alexander's "corrective emotional experience."[10]

Of course, real life is a mixture of attributions, some situational and some dispositional. We fall in love because of endearing traits of our beloved, and certain dispositional attributes about ourselves give us a consistent and secure sense of self. Social psychology, while emphasizing the interaction between the person and the environment, does not deny the importance of individual traits and dispositions. Rather, it suggests that human experiences such as shyness, jealousy, and couple burnout have an important situational component that is more amenable to change than are people's personalities.

Couples' vs. Observers' Attributions of Couple Burnout

Environmental pressures such as money problems and work stresses can erode love relationships, while environmental support and growth opportunities help feed the romantic spark. Nevertheless, even couples who carry a heavy burden of stresses are often far less likely to see them as the major reason for the deterioration in their relationships than are objective observers. They tend instead to attribute their marital difficulties to each other's character deficiencies or else to some inherent incompatibility in their personalities. Similarly, couples benefiting from environmental support tend to attribute its positive effects to themselves more than would outside observers. For obvious reasons, this misattribution is far less costly psychologically to the couple than is the tendency to attribute to themselves the blame for the negative effect of environmental stresses.

How easily people can see the effect of environmental influences on other couples' relationships! In two studies on couple burnout (one done in the United States the other in Israel), 300 subjects were presented with eight short scenarios and asked in each case to guess the couple's level of burnout.

The box on page 75 presents the eight scenarios, the instructions given to the studies' participants, and the scale used to evaluate the level of burnout they projected on each couple.

Some of the scenarios emphasize personality compatibility, like Mark and Mary, who have very similar personalities and enjoy similar activities. Some of the scenarios emphasize personality incompatibility, like the scientist David and the social worker Dalia whose personalities and preferred activities are very different. Some emphasize environmental stresses, like Tom and Tina, who have four young children, or Joe and Judith, who have been married for five years but can never afford to take a vacation. And some describe positive home

> **Try to imagine the following couples and, despite the limited information provided, guess their levels of marriage burnout using the following scale:**
>
> 1   2   3   4   5   6   7
> not at all   somewhat   totally
> burned out   burned out   burned out
>
> - John and Jacky have been married thirty-five years. They have three children and four grandchildren. __
> - Mark and Mary are very similar in their personalities. Both love reading, hiking, and listening to classical music. __
> - Joe and Judith have been married for five years. Joe works very hard. He comes home very late and continues working into the small hours of the night. Because of his work, they can never afford to take a vacation. __
> - Gary and Gina got married three months ago and this week have entered their new home. __
> - David and Dalia have very different personalities. David is a scientist who enjoys most of all spending time with his science books. Dalia is a social worker who enjoys most the company of people. __
> - Tom and Tina have four young children. The oldest child is six years old; the youngest one is still a baby, Tina does not get help with the care of the house or the children. __
> - Benjamin and Beth have been married five years. They have an eight-month-old baby and a nice suburban home. __
> - Eli and Iris love doing things together, but each one of them also has a very full and rich life as an individual. __

environments, like Gary and Gina, who just got married and entered their new home.

Results comparing the average burnout scores attributed to the eight scenarios showed that in both studies the rank orders for the burnout levels were identical.[11] The highest levels of marriage burnout were attributed to the couple experiencing the most stress: the hard-working Joe and his wife, Judith. Tina and her husband, Tom, with their four young children, came in a close second. The newly-weds Gary and Gina, entering their new home, received the very lowest burnout scores. In other words, the situation explained both the highest and the lowest scores: a stressful environment explained the two highest burnout scores, and a positive environment explained the lowest score. Compatibility or lack of compatibility also had an effect on the burnout ratings. The compatible Mark and Mary were seen as less burned out than the incompatible David and Dalia. Yet the difference due to compatibility was much smaller than the difference due to environment.

These findings suggest that, when presented with brief descriptions of couples, "observers" attribute burnout more to environmental stresses than to personality incompatibility. It is interesting that those same "objective observers" were all subjects in a study on marriage burnout. When asked about their own marriages, they tended to attribute the causes of their own burnouts to personality incompatibility! A woman who, like Tina, had four young children and not enough money to afford help with the house or the kids gave Tina's marriage the highest burnout score. Yet she explained her own marital difficulties by the "fact" that her husband is "a cold and uncommunicative person who does not have the same needs for intimacy and sharing" that she has. The fact that most evenings she was so wiped out that the only thing she could do before falling asleep was to watch television somehow did not seem as important in her evaluation of her marriage as was her husband's supposed coldness and inability to communicate.

Now, it may very well be that her complaint about her husband is a legitimate one, but she fell in love with him "as is," and there is a much smaller chance that his personality will change than that the environment will change.

Finally, in any discussion of the effect of environmental stresses on couples, gay couples deserve a special mention. Most gay couples deal with many more stresses from their families, their work, and society at large, than do straight couples. These stresses can, but do not have to erode their love.

In summary, I have presented in this chapter five approaches that, in my view, have the greatest relevance to couple burnout. Among these five are the three major clinical approaches—the psychodynamic approach (which views couple problems as a result of unresolved childhood issues that are reenacted in the couples' conflicts), the behavioral approach (which sees couples' problems as caused by lack of communication and problem-solving skills that can be taught), and the systems approach (which views a couple as an independent system and couples' problems as the result of dysfunctional circular patterns of interaction). The clinical approaches have the advantages of well-developed theories and techniques for working with couples, but their disadvantages are an overemphasis on pathology and a relative disregard for the existential and situational context of couples' problems. The existential and social-psychological approaches are important for drawing attention to the existential and situational contexts of people's problems. Their big disadvantage is their not having been applied specifically to the treatment of couples.

In my own thinking about couple burnout, and in my work with couples, I incorporate the contributions of all five of these approaches. I find this integration to be the most complete and useful approach for dealing with couples' issues, whatever they are (Pines 1987a).

While in certain sessions I may lean more on one approach than another, the tenets of all five approaches and the possibility of using them are always present in my mind. This integrated approach serves as the theoretical foundation for this book.

The next three chapters are devoted to an exploration of couple burnout in three of the most important facets of people's lives: work, home, and sex. Work involves the couple in their interaction with the outside world; home involves the couple in their interaction with the inner circle of their family; sex involves the couple in their most intimate interaction with each other.

4

Couple Burnout
and Career Burnout

The ability to love and the capacity for work are the hallmarks of
full maturity.

—Sigmund Freud

"What is more important: your work or your relationship?" I presented this question to thousands of people in lectures and workshops. The almost unanimous response: "My relationship, of course!"
Then there is the question: "What is your favorite day of the week?"
My data suggest that for most people the favorite day is Saturday
("The weekend is here!"). The next most favorite day is Friday ("The
whole weekend is still ahead"). The third is Sunday ("It's good to
have a day off, but it's getting too close to the work week"). Most people prefer weekends—time spent with their family—to workdays.[1]

Yet when I asked how much of their prime time—time they are not
totally exhausted or preoccupied with something else—they spend at
work and how much of their prime time they spend at home, most
often work came out ahead.

Most people give the best of themselves to the "strangers" they
come in contact with through their work. To those strangers they are
polite and attentive. By the time they come home to the person who

is supposedly most important in their life, they have neither the energy nor the patience to be polite and attentive. So they dispense with tact and other niceties, and tell themselves: "At least at home I can be myself." Why is it, though, that being oneself almost never implies being one's best?

All too often, once people feel assured of their mate's love and commitment, they start taking this love for granted. They make demands they would not think of making during the early stages of the relationship, demands they would never make of other people. The mate becomes the one person in their lives who is "supposed to" understand their work stress. "Who can I ask to be understanding and supportive if not my mate?" they ask self-righteously. Leah, who has been too often on the receiving end of this attitude, says:

> When my husband Dan was a student, he told me he was
> under terrible stress because he had to study. I was sup-
> posed to understand. When he was a junior faculty mem-
> ber, he said he was under terrible stress being junior faculty.
> I was supposed to understand. When he became a senior
> faculty member, he was under terrible stress being senior
> faculty. And I was supposed to understand. It seems that
> every period in our fifteen years together has been "the
> most difficult period" in his life. And I was expected to be
> sympathetic, understanding, and never make demands.
> When I realized that this was the way things were going to
> be forever, I knew I had to get out of the marriage.

By the time Dan realized his job was destroying their marriage, it was too late. A romantic relationship can withstand only so much chronic stress. This is not to say that a relationship can't survive, or even benefit from, a short dose of crisis-at-the-factory. In short doses a mate can provide loving support. But when crisis becomes a daily event, it imposes stress on relationships that erodes love. Dealing with continuous stress at work in effect makes work a higher priority than the relationship. No romantic relationship—gay or straight—can withstand that kind of continuous assault indefinitely.

Comparing Couple and Career Burnout

In a "good" relationship, the career doesn't come first, and such a good relationship can prevent career burnout. That is what I discovered in three studies in which 1,187 participants described their work, marriage, and levels of burnout. People who were stressed at work but felt supported by their mates were able to cope with work situations that were otherwise intolerable.[2] A young lawyer who was working on a lengthy and complicated divorce trial describes it:

> I am almost at the end of my rope. The pressures of a court trial are immense, and this one has been dragging on for weeks with no end in sight. I feel very responsible to our client, and I think that the senior lawyer working with me on the case is totally incompetent and irresponsible. Not only that, but the other side is one of the biggest law firms in town. Our team is no match for them under the best of circumstances, and these are definitely not the best of circumstances. . . . It is very important for me to know that I can come home at night and be with someone I love who loves and appreciates me. It keeps intolerable things in perspective.

If, on the other hand, people are in a bad relationship, the stress involved can have a very negative effect on their work. A computer consultant whose marriage of fifteen years was ending says:

> I sit in front of the computer and I see blank. Since I am a freelance consultant, and consequently am never sure about my next project until the contract is actually signed, the pressures of supporting a family have always been very difficult for me to bear. Now that my marriage is on the rocks, the tension is draining all my creative energy. And being creative is essential to my work. It is the essence of what I do, of what I sell my clients. For weeks now, since the serious problems between us began, I haven't been able to work. I know what needs to be done, but I can't concentrate enough to be able to do it. I am so drained I feel like throwing everything away.

Findings of the three studies comparing job and marriage burnout show that overall burnout was more related to marital problems than to work stress.[3] Apparently, the overall quality of people's life is more affected by the quality of their marriage than by the quality of their work. This is an important finding considering that most people concentrate their best energies on their jobs—perhaps in the belief that they have to work at their jobs while their relationships will somehow take care of themselves. The greater importance of marriage was also documented in national surveys showing that only a small percentage of people rank work as the central factor in their lives. Family life is consistently described as more important than work for most people.[4]

Participants in the three studies described their marriages not only as more important to them but also as more satisfying emotionally and as less pressured than their work. They had better personal relations at home, they got more emotional rewards, more support, more sharing, more opportunities for self-actualization, and a greater sense of meaning. Work, on the other hand, was a source of bureaucratic and administrative hassles; there was pressure to make decisions without enough time or information, few opportunities for influencing decisions, and the physical environment tended to be more uncomfortable and impersonal. What saves some people from going crazy at work is their family life. David, a fifty-year-old training expert at a government agency, is married and the father of six children. He describes how his family protected him during a crisis:

> After thirteen years in the same department, I was told I
> was going to be transferred to another department the next
> day. I felt devastated; I felt a total lack of self-worth. I did
> not trust the person I was transferred to and I resented the
> unfair and inconsiderate way the transfer was done. But I
> had no choice. I know this is not at all uncommon, but it's
> devastating when it happens to you. I found it very hard to
> take. I felt that the company was playing games with my
> life. I felt angry, humiliated, and used; they were going to
> pick my brains and then dump me. The stress was eroding
> away my soul. I felt like I didn't exist. I was doing my job
> like a machine, like a warm mannequin, not a person. . . . I
> felt trapped. That was the worst thing. . . . I wanted to
> escape at any cost, but there was no way out. The obliga-
> tions of a large family didn't give me the latitude to simply
> walk out. And there was the pressure of having put all those
> years into a retirement system that I knew I was far enough
> into so that I couldn't go somewhere else. I knew that if I
> left I was throwing a lot of my future away. . . . The most

devastating thing was the feeling of worthlessness. And I
couldn't get out of it. I was so miserable, I couldn't see any
of my friends. I was in no shape to be a loving husband and
father. At times I thought I was at the point of murder. The
pressure builds up and builds up until something has to
give and you've got to cash in all your stamps. And then
you just do it. You simply have to escape. We are a good,
warm, and loving family, and this is the thing that got me
through all this. . . . That's the thing that has held me
together. The love and support of my wife and my children
prevented me from committing an act of violence, either
on someone else or on myself, which I contemplated seriously. The pleasure of the day wasn't worth the pain.

I am often asked which is more prevalent: burnout on the job or in
relationships. While estimates of burnout in the population are as yet
unavailable, I was able to compare the levels of burnout on the job
and in marriage in the samples I studied. In a combined sample of 960
men and women, the average score of relationship burnout was 3.3
(for details about the calculation of the score see Appendix 1). This
score was identical to the average score of job burnout obtained in a
combined sample of 3,916 men and women. Similarly, the average
couple burnout score in a study of 200 Israelis—2.8—was identical to
the job burnout score in a combined sample of 393 Israelis (Pines and
Aronson 1981).

The similarity between levels of burnout in relationships and jobs
in such very different samples is less surprising when one considers
the fact that they are both measured using very similar self-report
measures (see the Burnout Measure in Appendix 1 and in Pines and
Aronson 1981). Since both tests ask how frequently the individual
has had a series of negative experiences, a certain similarity in
response can be expected. The similarity between job and relationship burnout is also less surprising when one considers the fact that
these two spheres cover most of an individual's life in our society,
and are also the two primary paths for finding a sense of significance
in life. Because both work and marriage so often fail as answers to the
existential dilemma, job burnout was described as the social epi-
demic of the eighties and the modern institution of marriage as being
in a state of calamity.

Judging by the similarity in people's levels of burnout on the job and in couple relationships, we can assume that there is a parallel not only in the intensity but also in the subjective experience of both. Indeed, just as in couple burnout, people experience job burnout as a state of physical, emotional, and mental exhaustion caused by long involvement in emotionally demanding situations. People burn out in their jobs for the same reason they burn out in marriage: their experience doesn't match their "romantic" ideal. Just as lovers fall out of love because married life isn't what they imagined, workers burn out because they can't achieve what they expected in their work.

Not surprisingly, the process leading to career burnout is very similar to the process leading to couple burnout.[5] Consequently, the couple burnout model discussed in chapter 2 is very similar to the career burnout model presented next.

The Career Burnout Model

Like the couple burnout model, the career burnout model addresses two key questions: What causes burnout? and, How can burnout be avoided?

Just as couple burnout can happen only to couples who started their relationship in love, career burnout can happen only to idealistic and highly motivated individuals. Highly motivated people don't work hard because of money (even though it's always nice to get paid well), and they don't work hard because of the threat of discipline or censure. Idealistic people work hard because they expect their work to make their lives matter in the larger scheme of things and give meaning to their existence. They don't need either a "carrot" or a "stick" to motivate them (Pines 1993). They are motivated enough as it is because they identify with their work.

Work motivation includes three types of expectation: universal expectations, those shared by everyone who works (the most important of which is to do something significant); profession-specific expectations (for people in the human services, for example, this includes helping people and making the world a better place); and personal expectations based on an internal "romantic" image of the work, inspired by a significant person or event. Combined, these three types of expectations form the motivation that the work will make one's life matter in the larger scheme of things.

The Career Burnout Model

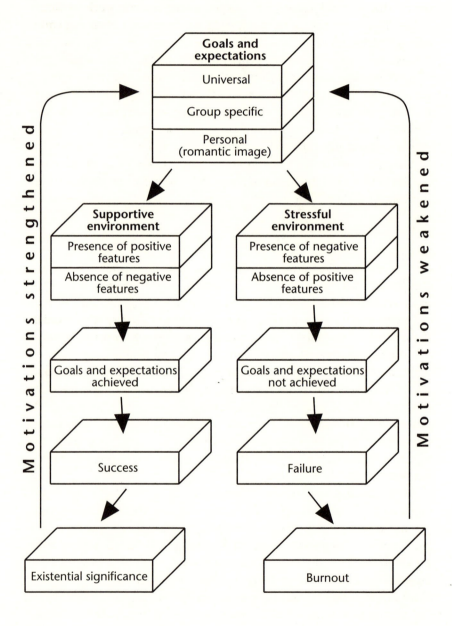

When people who have high expectations of their work enter a career, they can either reach peak performance or burn out, depending on the interplay between the expectations and the work environment. The outcome, in either case, is the result of a dynamic interaction between the people and their perceived environment.

In a supportive environment (where workers have the autonomy, resources, and support needed to accomplish their goals without the frustration of bureaucratic hassles and red tape), highly motivated workers can reach peak performance. Reaching peak performance increases their sense of significance and success, which, in turn, increases their original motivation.

When the same highly motivated workers are thrown into a stressful environment (where they are overloaded with work; where their ambition is stifled by bureaucratic interference, poor communication, and endless paperwork; where they can't get the support and resources they need to get the job done well; where they feel unappreciated and stuck below their level of competence; where they don't get a sense of meaning from their work), burnout is almost inevitable. This can be clearly seen in situations where failure is built in. A typical example is a job in which there is no way to have the quantity of work demanded done to the level of quality it demands. For motivated people whose egos are tied to their performance, failure is a most powerful cause of burnout.

Job and relationship burnouts not only parallel each other, they also affect each other. It is very difficult to isolate the experience of burnout, either at work or in the marriage. When people start burning out on their jobs, typically they pull back from coworkers and begin to feel isolated. They think they are not getting enough appreciation for their work or that the work is not challenging enough. Consequently, they start putting increasing demands on their mates for professional appreciation and challenge. Such demands are both unfair and unrealistic, since the mate is probably not well enough informed or qualified to fulfill them. Yet the atmosphere of disappointment and regret becomes associated with the marriage. Noticing the close connection between burnout on the job and in relationships made me, after ten years of studying career burnout, shift my focus to the study of couple burnout.

Burnout can work the other way as well, spilling over from home into work. Most often this involves people who escape marital problems by totally investing themselves in their work. People like that usually come to work very early, leave very late, and take work home with them so as to avoid the danger of having to talk to their mates. As long as work gives them a sense of significance, of making a difference, of success, of belonging, they are able to avoid burnout. But if a problem comes up at work, if they experience a crisis, a major disappointment, or a big failure, they have nothing to fall back on at home. Consequently they start feeling burned out in their career as well as marriage.

Overinvolvement in work is not always motivated by a need to get away from a burned-out marriage. There are those who are "workaholics," a term coined by Wayne E. Oates, a religion psychologist and a priest, in his book *Confessions of a Workaholic* (Oates 1971). Typically, workaholics are people who are "addicted" to work—for whom work has become an all-involving preoccupation. It is the only thing in life that seems to matter, the only thing that makes them feel alive. They invest all their time and energy in their work, so there is little or nothing left for other people or activities.

Since they get their sense of "cosmic significance" from work, most workaholics, like most devoutly religious people, don't need to get it from love. Consequently, many of them never marry, limiting themselves to dating people who won't interfere with their work. When they are forced for some reason (such as pressure from their company or their family) to marry, the demands the mate makes to spend more time together (sooner or later) eventually start the pattern of escape into work described earlier—unless the mate is also a workaholic.

When both mates are workaholics, their involvement with each other is more like dating than marriage. Such couples are often childless (and if they have children, they hire full-time care for them). At times they keep separate apartments and even live in separate cities. Often they keep different hours and know different sets of friends. Their limited involvement in the marriage leaves them plenty of time for their careers. Needless to say, burnout at work for a workaholic is a traumatic and devastating event, far worse than the breakdown of a marriage that has been firmly kept in second place.

This leads to the worst case of all, when people who get their sense of significance from both work and love, burn out simultaneously in their work and in the relationship. The physical, emotional, and mental exhaustion of burnout becomes so all-encompassing that in some cases the individual is completely immobilized. Things are as bad as they can be, the failure is total, and there is no hope for anything to improve. Nothing seems to matter, and there is nothing worth living for. A probation officer, burned out in his job and recently separated from his wife, says:

> I sat all through the night with a gun pointed at my head. I couldn't see a reason to live. My wife left me, and I couldn't blame her. I was really impossible to live with. She needed to get away to save her own sanity. And I felt like a total failure at my job. It all of a sudden dawned on me that I was trying to do an impossible thing. I couldn't really change anything in the lives of the kids I was responsible for. And besides, I no longer felt they deserved help. I couldn't believe I had sacrificed my marriage for them. What a stupid fool I'd been. I felt all alone in the world, trapped in a corrupt and inefficient system . . . my whole life had been wasted. What reason was there for me to go on living?

After this lengthy discussion of the similarity and direct correlation between burnout on the job and in marriage, it may be worth noting that neither the similarity nor the correlation is obvious to the people who experience both of them. At times people blame burnout at work for problems in the relationship, and other times people blame the relationship for problems at work. Many a time, after an intensive burnout workshop, a participant will confide in me, saying: "If I knew then what I know now, I would still be married." What they mean is that with the insight they gained during the workshop they realize that they were too quick to blame their spouse for their problems at work, and too quick to give up on the relationship—when the real problems lay elsewhere.

People don't see the obvious, not because they are dense or lacking in sensitivity and insight, but because they have simply focused on the closest thing at hand. When they burn out, instead of focusing on the situational stresses that caused their burnout, they focus on their own failings and on the presumed failings of the person closest to them—their mate.

Men and Work

Balancing work and an intimate relationship is equally important for men and women, yet traditionally men have been expected to get their sense of existential significance from work, while women get theirs from relationships. As a result, in traditional marriages the balance between work and marriage occurs more between husband and wife than within the individual man or woman.

In her book *Intimate Strangers,* Lillian Rubin describes what happened when she asked hundreds of people of all ages and walks of life, "Who are you?" Almost invariably, she reports, a man responds by saying what kind of work he does: "I am a salesman," "I am a physician," "I am a police officer." Having identified himself by his career. He then, sometimes as an afterthought, may mention something about being a husband or a father. A woman, on the other hand, is far more likely to start by saying "I am a mother and a wife" and only then mention something about her career (Rubin 1983, 162).

Despite the recent changes in sex-role definitions, the majority of men and women still define themselves in terms of traditional sex-role stereotypes.[6] Men are socialized in our culture to identify with their work to the extent that both professional success and professional failure are seen as personal success and failure. Women, on the other hand, have been socialized, until very recently, to define personal success and failure more in terms of their roles as wives and mothers. For men (as well as for modern career women) who believe in romantic love, finding an answer to the existential dilemma in work conflicts with the alternative—romantic—solution.

The inherent contradiction between the idealized image of romantic love and that of a successful professional career does not become apparent until one tries to actualize both of them simultaneously. For example, there was Dan, the professor whose wife, Leah, left him because she couldn't identify with the role of a faculty wife. For Dan, becoming a successful scientist was supposed to be not just his dream, but their joint dream. He expected his wife to identify with his professional ambitions and to take personal pride in his successes. He expected her to enjoy his international reputation and all the benefits it offered them in travel and in leading a rich and exciting life. All he wanted in return was her trust and support while he worked to make that dream come true. The problem that eventually destroyed the marriage was the fact that Leah did not share his dream.

Leah's sense of meaning in life was tied much more to the quality of their daily communication than to the idea of being married to a successful scientist. She did not identify with his success and was acutely aware of the personal price she was paying for that success. Leah remained in the marriage as long as she believed that the turn of her own dream of closeness and intimacy would come some day. When it became clear to her that the sacrifices demanded of her and of the marriage for the sake of her husband's success were not temporary, that there was a basic discrepancy between her husband and herself in what they both wanted from life, she saw no choice but to leave the marriage.

Obviously, the situation is different when both husband and wife identify with the husband's achievements. Sarah and her husband are an example. Sarah grew up in a very poor family, trained as a nurse, and married a successful doctor. Her life as the wife of a well-to-do man fulfilled all her fantasies. She was happy to quit her job as a nurse and to take on the job of supporting her husband's career. Her greatest joy at the beginning of their marriage was decorating their big beautiful house. Sarah spends hours every day taking care of the house and the big garden surrounding it. She takes great care of her own appearance, and always looks slim, tan, and elegant. She is proud to entertain her husband's colleagues, and sees her life as a fairy tale come true.

What is the difference between Sarah and Leah? Both their husbands had achieved top positions in their fields. Both their husbands made a good living, although, granted, the doctor made more money than the professor. Sarah, however, identified with her husband's career and was thrilled to stand in his reflected glory, while Leah did not and was not. Sarah and Leah show that the impact on a relationship of a very stressful career depends to a large extent on the subjective costs and rewards the career provides for both members of the couple.

The same cost/benefit analysis happens when a man is a failure at work. Whit, a mechanical engineer in his thirties, is an example.

Whit chose engineering because he liked to build things with his hands and was good at it. For twelve years his work at a large oil company gave him ample opportunity for success. The work involved creating new instruments and improving old ones. Whit loved the excitement of each new challenge. He even enjoyed the stress involved. Sometimes he worked twenty hours straight to meet a deadline. He was often so absorbed in his projects that he ignored his wife and children, but he believed that his wife understood that he was working for both of them. Whit made a lot of money, which enabled him and his wife to buy of expensive "toys" they both enjoyed. He felt respected and successful in his work. Whit was happy with his life and felt it gave him everything he wanted.

Things started to go wrong when Whit was promoted to a managerial position. It was the natural career step for him, but he had never been trained in management. It wasn't something he wanted to do, except for one thing—it was an important promotion, and his colleagues noted that "if you don't get promoted, you're actually getting demoted." The first months on his new job were stressful for Whit because he didn't know exactly what he was doing. But there was something exciting about managing a team to get a project done, and he enjoyed the new challenge. After this brief period of getting acquainted with the new job, he got a project that was beyond his budding skills as a manager: he needed to guide 60 people through a $5 million project in just nine months. Whit started working twenty hours a day, the way he had when, as a hands-on engineer, he needed to get something done. But he found that his subordinates didn't care as much about the project as he did. In addition, they resented his authoritative style of management. Their dissatisfaction grew until they rebelled openly by going over his head and demanding his removal from the project. To his great shock, top management sided with them. Three months before the project was to be finished he was transferred.

Whit was devastated. He had failed in his work, the thing that meant most to him, and he had failed royally. Everyone in the whole company heard what had happened. Every day he ran into people who had once been on his team, people who knew about his failure. The embarrassment and humiliation were almost too much to bear. When he first got the news about his dismissal from the project he contemplated quitting the company, but his wife urged him not to, at least not until he had another job to replace it. (His professional position was very important for her own sense of significance and security.) But Whit did not start looking for another job. His ego was so crushed by his failure as a manager that he couldn't summon the emotional energy needed to go job hunting. He felt depressed and emotionally depleted, couldn't concentrate, and had problems sleeping. Life lost its meaning. Eventually his wife, who tried for as long as she could to be strong and supportive, said she couldn't take it anymore.

Within the same company, Whit reached peak performance and then burned out. Reaching peak performance increased his sense of significance and success, which in turn increased his work motivation. He remained in this positive loop for twelve years and probably would have remained in it indefinitely if he hadn't been promoted. When he was given a job in which he was bound to fail, he burned out in less than a year. Because his relationship with his wife and children were secondary to his career, they couldn't give his life the sense of meaning that work had given it.

Although Whit's involuntary removal as head of the project, like David's involuntary transfer to another department (which was described earlier in the chapter), is not uncommon in large bureaucratic organizations, they are extreme events. For most people, burnout is caused by a slow and gradual erosion.

Rona and Ben provide an example of burnout caused by the daily tedium of work. When they first met and fell in love, Ben had a good union-protected job that provided a secure and comfortable income. Unfortunately, the secure job was also very boring, and after fifteen years in it Ben decided to quit. He wanted a business of his own, and chose to open a restaurant. He wanted Rona to help, at least in the beginning, until they could afford outside help. Reluctantly, Rona agreed. After five years of hard work, which was neither exciting nor financially rewarding, both felt burned out in the job and the marriage, but there was no easy way out.

Sometimes a man's burnout (either in work or marriage) is triggered by a midlife crisis. Like burnout, the midlife crisis tends to happen to people who are highly motivated, with great ideals and enthusiasm. It happens particularly to people who have made their career choices at an early age—say, when they were in their twenties. They start out convinced that being a lawyer, a doctor, an architect, a teacher, a police officer, means making a major contribution to society. By the time they reach midlife they either realize that their contribution may be far smaller than they had hoped or else they begin to think that society doesn't deserve the sacrifice they are making. They start feeling empty and disillusioned, painfully aware of their mortality and the passage of time—both the time remaining and the time spent. Someone once said we should look at our lives as days of the week, with each day representing a decade. Well, one day, these people look up from their work and discover it's Wednesday, or Thursday, or even Friday morning, and they say, greatly distressed, "Wait a minute. This isn't what I want." William Bridges describes it:

> When the dream has been gained, the vice-presidency, the book, the three kids and the handsome home—there is the moment of realization: "O.K., I've got it, now what?" And even: "Is this it? Is this the destination that I've sacrificed everything for?" The discrepancy between public image and private awareness can be excruciating at this point in life. And what of the person who didn't make it? The denied dream is the other gateway to reality. There, one is faced with the nevers. "I guess I have to face the fact that I'm never going to be the head of the company . . . never going to be the parent of four happy, well-adjusted children." And with that acknowledgment comes the strange sense that one has been chasing a carrot on a stick, that the sunset into which one was riding was painted on the other end of the train car. (Bridges 1977)

Burnout is less likely to happen, and if it does happen is less likely to be devastating, if work is balanced by an intimate relationship. This balance is a difficult one to achieve and a difficult one to maintain. One of the ways to identify the balance—or imbalance—between them is to list, side by side, demands at work and demands at home. Doing that can help one ascertain to what extent these demands are current, legitimate, and reasonable, and prioritize the responses to them. This exercise can be done in the context of a burnout workshop, or as part of therapy.

Gerald, for example, is thirty years old, has two young children, and works as an attorney at a large law firm. Gerry's lists looked like this:

Work

1. Be a brilliant lawyer.
2. Not make any mistakes.
3. Protect my clients.
4. Keep up with new laws/court decisions.
5. Bring in new clients.

6. Pal around with my colleagues without making it seem like I am malingering.
7. Get along with my bosses without making it seem like I am toadying.
8. Be a good boss to my secretary and the back-office support staff.
9. Dress appropriately.
10. Be entertaining, charming, someone other lawyers like and respect.
11. Be a team player and represent the firm well.

Home

1. Be a good husband and father.
2. Support my family financially and, of course, emotionally.
3. Take care of the yard.
4. Be a role model for the kids and a good disciplinarian.
5. Share chores.

Gerry not only has many more items in his work column, but the work column is more specific and well thought out. Gerry feels that all the things he does at work are important and that he must meet these demands if he is going to make partner at his law firm, which is his paramount concern. Compared with this, the demands imposed by his family are extremely light. I would wager that if we had asked him about any of the items on his work list—say, "What does it mean to be a 'good boss'?" Gerry could tell us exactly what that meant, from being clear in his instructions to his secretary to taking her out to lunch on National Secretary Week. But if we were to ask him what it meant to be "a good role model" for his kids, it might have taken him quite some time to come up with an answer.

Interestingly enough, as is often the case, Gerry seemed to resent far more the relatively small demands made by his family than he did the huge list of demands made by his job. Moreover, Gerry considered his family much more important to him than his job. What Gerry learned from making the lists was that he was shortchanging his family. In addition, by scrutinizing his lists in a careful and honest manner, he came to realize that some of the demands he listed as imposed by his career were actually self-imposed.

In other words, under close inspection, Gerry gained insight into the fact that he was making demands on himself as a lawyer, boss, and colleague far in excess of what his law firm expected of him. He also had to admit to himself that the people he loved most—his wife and children—received far less of what he had to offer than did his work.

Gerry's experience is not unique. It tends to characterize high achievers: top-level executives, politicians, lawyers, doctors, psychologists, scientists, and all other professionals who get involved from a very young age in a demanding and ego-involving career. Unfortunately, many of them don't stop to evaluate their self-imposed demands and priorities until it is too late. Typically, they start their careers very early. In elementary school they work very hard to be accepted into the best high schools. In high school they work very hard to be accepted into the best colleges. In college and in graduate school they work very hard to get the best possible position at the best company, political office, law firm, hospital, clinic, university. Once they get that desired position, they work very hard to be promoted and stay on top of the field.

During those years they typically also fall in love, marry, and have several children, but since the job has the highest priority, they rarely have time for family. It usually takes a dramatic event to shake up this single-minded involvement with work. The dramatic event can be positive, such as a major achievement, or it can be negative, such as a major failure, a life-threatening illness, an accident, or a divorce. In all such cases, the precipitating event makes what seemed to be a substantial world look fragile and unreal. When the dramatic event happens between the ages of forty and fifty, the result can be a serious questioning of the value of one's entire life.

Women and Work

If professional identities are more important to men, and if domestic identities as wives and mothers are more important to women, and if people burn out because they are disappointed in their expectation that the role with which they identify most will give meaning to their lives, then it follows that more men will burn out at work than women. (Following the same reasoning, we can make the equally obvious prediction that women will be more burned out in their marriages than men. We will return to the second prediction in chapter 5.)

Despite the "obviousness" of this prediction, studies of gender differences in career burnout indicate that women report higher levels of job burnout than men. For example, in one study involving ninety-six professional men and ninety-five professional women,

women reported extreme levels of burnout four times as often as the men (Pines and Kafry 1981b); similar results were reported in many other studies conducted by myself and my colleagues.[7] These studies involved, separately, groups of 205 professional men and women; 220 professionals; 118 human-service professionals; 89 schoolteachers; and 66 managers.[8] In every study we attempted to find occupations in which the percentages of men and women were similar. In business, that meant looking at middle management, in medicine at family medicine and pediatrics, in education at the high grades of elementary school or at high school.

Why do women report more job burnout than men? While it is possible to explain it by the "fact" that women are innately weaker, less able, more vulnerable to stress, use inadequate styles of coping, or are more willing than men to acknowledge weakness, it is also possible to explain the gender difference in burnout by different expectations and different stresses the two sexes have in their work. Many of these differences can be traced back to the greater difficulty women have in achieving a balance between their work and their home responsibilities.

Study results suggest that one reason for women's higher levels of burnout is the relative absence of rewards in their work (such as worse pay and work conditions) and the increased number of stresses when compared with men. Women have less freedom, less autonomy, less influence, less variety, less challenge, and a more negative work environment. They have fewer opportunities for self-expression and actualization and, on the whole, fewer rewards for their work. Studies also show that women suffer from discrimination and harassment, especially in male-dominated professions.[9] No wonder they report higher levels of job burnout.

For many women, the most stressful aspect of work is people's demands—both at home and work—that make them feel harassed and overextended. Women's attempts to respond to these demands leave them feeling overloaded, torn, and conflicted.

In addition to the dissimilar stresses they encounter, men and women often bring with them into work distinct sets of expectations. Studies of gender differences in work attitudes suggest that women are more emotionally involved in their work than are men and are likely to see their careers as a source of personal growth and emotional fulfillment (Hennig and Jardim 1976). When these high expectations are not met, women burn out.

The Helping Professions

The high emotional involvement in work can be seen as a result of women's sex-role socialization. While this socialization has the greatest impact on women's roles as wives and mothers, it does also influence their work. Such an involvement is most clearly evident in the helping professions (nursing, counseling, teaching), where women are disproportionally represented. Working in the helping professions puts women in a high risk group for both career burnout and couple burnout because of three basic traits shared by many of these professions, traits that are also characteristic of intimate relationships:

• They are emotionally taxing; the demands of the work are often similar to the demands involved in parenthood or marriage.

• Certain personality traits shared by those who choose these professions also lead them to see marriage as the most important relationship.

• These professions share a "client-centered" orientation that is modeled after the parent-child relationship.

Each of these traits is a major cause of burnout. When combined, they multiply each other's effects.

Emotionally Taxing Work

Work with people always involves a certain degree of stress. The specific degree and kind of stress depend on the particular demands of the job and the resources available to the professional. It means dealing with people's idiosyncrasies, remaining professionally skilled and personally concerned. Marriage requires similar skills. For some people, the emotional demands of work and marriage are so similar that the stress multiplies exponentially. A therapist described the difficulty:

> After eight hours of listening to people in my office, I simply don't have the patience to listen to my husband when I come home. I love him. He is the most important person in the world to me. I know he has more right to my time than all my patients. But at the end of the day I am so emotionally depleted, that I simply can't be available to him. It's very sad.

Self-selection

If work with people is emotionally taxing for everyone, it is particularly so for people who choose such work because they like people, have great empathy for their plight, and value themselves most as being empathic and helpful. Whenever I ask such professionals to list their reasons for choosing to work with people, whatever their occupation, the reasons always include some variation of "I like people," "I am a people's kind of a person." Many of these professionals see being people-directed as the essence of themselves. It is an essence they express not only at work but even more so in their intimate relationships. This positive self-perception is shaken when such a person burns out in either sphere. A counselor in a mental health clinic, who specialized in work with couples and who burned out in her thirteen-year-old marriage, described the devastating effect it had on her self perception:

> Even when I knew that I didn't love him anymore, that I
> couldn't stand his touch, that I had to get out of the mar
> riage, I continued fighting that knowledge. I simply
> couldn't face the fact that I, of all people, was failing in the
> relationship that was the most important one to me. How
> could I continue counseling other couples if I couldn't
> counsel myself? How could I help others when I couldn't
> help myself?

Client-centered Orientation

Most human relationships are expected to be symmetrical, with both partners contributing their fair share. Two major exceptions are parenthood and client-centered occupations. In client-centered work, the professional provides a service of some kind, and the client receives it. The professional's work is justified only so long as there is a client to be helped. All training focuses on the client's needs and the best ways to serve them. Very little attention is paid to the needs of the professional or the stress of serving clients who are particularly difficult or demanding. Parental love, which is the model for many helping professions, is supposed to be unconditional—not depend on reciprocation. Parents whose love is conditional (on the child's performance, for example) are criticized, as are professionals who satisfy their own emotional needs through their clients.

An asymmetry in relationships can be very stressful. The stress is increased when combined with the emotional demands of work with people, particularly for idealistic people who choose to work with people because they love people. Of course, all of this is equally true for men and women. The difference is that more women go into the helping professions, and women, more than men, are socialized to identify with the giver role. Even career women who are not in the helping professions often experience difficulty combining career and family. A successful businesswoman describes it:

> The work of a professional woman who is also a wife and mother is never complete. There is always more that can be done and should be done. I carry all these "shoulds" in my head all the time and that means that I can never come home from work, flop down in a chair, and just unwind.

In a study done by Dalia Etzion, twenty-nine women and twenty-nine men middle managers were compared regarding their job burnout, life and work satisfaction, and various life and work features. The men and the women were matched in age, seniority, and managerial level. As in all previous studies, results indicated that the women were more burned out than the men. It was also found that with the same level of education, a man was likely to climb to a higher managerial position. For women, burnout increased with education; for men it decreased. It seems that the higher expectations associated with a higher education were more easily achieved by men, and at a lower price (Etzion 1984).

Women also paid a higher personal price for their careers in terms of family life; 31 percent of the women in this group remained unmarried, yet not one of the men was single. In addition, the more successful a woman manager was in her career, the less successful she felt about her home life. For men, success at work was not correlated with either success or failure at home. In interviews I conducted with other women managers, they talked with great pain about the personal sacrifices they had to make for the sake of their careers; many times they doubted whether it was all worth it. A public relations director in a government agency said:

> Now that I am getting close to my fiftieth birthday, I spend a lot of time thinking about my life, evaluating things,

wondering. If a young woman came to me today and asked if I recommend this life to her I would have to say no. The price you pay is just too high. Look at me. I am the head of the department, but I am home alone at night. My marriage couldn't sustain the pressure of my career. And it wasn't that the household chores weren't taken care of. I always made sure that the house was clean and food was on the table on time. What got to my husband was that I was more successful than he was. At parties people knew who I was and knew him only as my husband. He just couldn't take it. My marriage was literally the price I paid for my professional success. Now I am no longer sure it was worth it.

Despite all the recent advances in the status of women and the changes in sex roles for both men and women, the reality is still that most women who combine a home and a career are carrying the double burden of two full-time careers: the regular duties of a job, as well as most of the duties of child care and housework. The career woman/housewife/mother is frantically trying to respond to all her competing demands. Typically, she is the first one up in the morning, preparing breakfast for her family. During lunch and on her days "off" she takes care of family errands. She shops for groceries on her way home, and while her husband and children relax, she prepares dinner. Afterward, she cleans up and then helps the children with their homework. On evenings and weekends she does the laundry and drives the children to their various activities.

Women's daily routines have many domestic interruptions. It is usually the mother who takes the children to the pediatrician for their physicals and shots and to the dentist to get their teeth cleaned. It is the mother who stays home with them when they are sick. It is the mother who goes to parent/teacher conferences and is called when there is a problem. Thus, it should come as no surprise that one of the most consistent sex differences in my research on burnout has been the greater conflict between work and home experienced by women. In Etzion's study, the conflict between work and home was correlated with burnout—but only for women, not for men (Etzion 1984). The best interpretation of this finding is that the conflict between the demands of work and the demands of home life is more intense for women and thus more stressful. This interpretation was supported by the findings of a study in which the conflicting demands women had both at work and at home were more frequent and more stressful than those men had (Pines and Kafry 1981b).

In addition to the job stresses that working women share with men, and the heavier burden of housework and child care that they tend to take on themselves, women are burdened by other stresses that originate in external or internalized social norms and mores that put women in a double bind in which they are doomed if they do and damned if they don't. Rose's life is an example of such a double bind.

Rose was twenty-nine, attractive, warm, sensitive, and exceptionally bright when I met her. She graduated Phi Beta Kappa from an Ivy League college and met her husband while working on her Ph.D. in science, which she received with the highest honors. Throughout her education she was supported by the most prestigious grants, fellowships, and scholarships. Rose played competitive tennis and appeared with a local amateur orchestra playing the violin. When her husband took a position with a law firm on the East Coast they moved. Soon after they settled in their beautiful new home Rose discovered, to their great delight, that she was pregnant. Several months after the baby was born, Rose, who was preparing her dissertation for publication, was offered a position at a prestigious university located sixty miles away. It was a great professional compliment and the ideal job for her. But now she had a baby with whom she wanted to spend all her time. Rose was torn. When she stayed home with the baby she felt she was disappointing her mentors who recommended her for the job. When she worked at the library she felt guilty about leaving her baby with a sitter. The more Rose thought about her two choices, the more torn she felt.

Since Rose seemed unable to resolve the conflict, I suggested that she get some perspective on it with the help of a group of strangers. In order to do this, Rose agreed to be videotaped showing the two sides of her role conflict. Both tapes started with Rose talking about her background, education, and interests—-but the endings of the two tapes were different. In one tape she presented only her career plans, saying she wanted to accept the university position, teach, do research, and publish scientific articles. In the second tape she only talked about her family plans, saying she wanted to stay home with her baby for a few years and fix up their new home.

Male and female college students were shown the two tapes. After viewing the career tape, they described Rose as success-oriented, ambitious, aggressive, dominant, independent—adjectives traditionally applied to career-oriented males. By contrast, after viewing the family tape, they described her as less competent overall and less able to withstand pressure. In spite of, or because of, her reduced competence, women liked Rose less while men liked her more in the family tape. Men found her more feminine, open-minded, sincere, intelligent, well adjusted, kind, sensitive, warm—and wanted more to spend time with her (Pines 1979).

It is possible that men are threatened by career women, especially a woman as brilliant as Rose. It is also possible that a woman who stays home with her baby follows a sex-role stereotype and is, consequently, more understandable and more likable. Whatever the explanation, it seems clear that even among students—who are more liberal in their attitudes toward career women than most other groups—a career woman is in a double bind. If she chooses a career she will be seen by men as less feminine and less desirable. If she chooses a family, both men and women will see her as less competent professionally.

Such conflicting cultural messages can affect a woman only if she internalizes them. An exceptionally bright woman, Rose internalized both messages. That was why she was conflicted. She believed she could have both a career and a family. She expected both roles to give her life meaning, although, of course, not of the same kind and not at the same time. The two idealized images did not conflict until she had to make a choice between them. What did she do? Did she take the job, because superb child care can always be found and it was her big chance to make a splash in academia? Or did she stay home, because her baby was going to be young only once? Rose did not take the job. She had another baby and started teaching part-time at a local four-year college.

Many women feel disappointed when they hear about her decision. Why? Because women want to believe that a woman can, in the catch phrase, "have it all." Although Rose might tell us she does have it all—she has a loving husband, two children, and a teaching job she loves—it is also clear that she did not try to become a "super woman," to "go for the brass ring."

Every choice means giving up an alternative, and disappointment causes burnout. This is equally true for men and for women. The difference is that women are presented with more of these conflicts and therefore tend to burn out more.

People who successfully combine a career and a family find a way to achieve balance between them, and that balance protects them from overinvolvement with either role. When they feel they have failed at one, the other gives meaning to their lives. A science professor who is married to a man who is also a science professor in the same department, and with whom she has two young children, says:

> When I feel like a failure as a wife and mother, I say to myself, "Well, at least I am a decent scientist." When I feel like a failure as a scientist, I say to myself, "At least my husband and children think I am wonderful."

Indeed, several studies report a positive association between the number of roles a person (woman or man) occupies and psychological well being (Barnett 1993). The balance can be achieved by the individual—man or woman—and it can be achieved by the couple. While all couples, gay and straight, have to deal with issues related to the home/work conflict, those couples where both mates have a career about which they care deeply represent a special category termed by social scientists "dual-career couples."

Dual-Career Couples

The term "dual-career families" was coined by Rhona and Robert Rapoport to designate a type of family in which both heads of the household—the husband and the wife—pursue active careers and family lives. "Career" designates those types of job sequences that require a high degree of commitment and have a continuous developmental character (Rapoport and Rapoport 1969).

Studies show that dual-career couples have a number of advantages over traditional couples (in which the husband works and the wife stays home).[10] The most obvious advantage is a considerable financial edge gained by having two incomes. Dual-career couples also have stronger marital relationships; marital satisfaction is increased and self-esteem rises when both partners have careers. In several studies, women who work reported greater self-esteem, efficacy, well-being, and marital satisfaction than did housewives. Furthermore, a challenging job was found to protect women from the stress involved in their role as mothers (Barnett 1993). Similarly, husbands of women who work full-time reported being happier in their marriages, had fewer infectious diseases, and were less susceptible to psychiatric impairment than husbands married to housewives.

While the gains reported by the wives are more in terms of self-actualization, the gains felt by the husbands are more in terms of the egalitarian relationship. Several of the husbands whose wives started working after being housewives for many years discovered, sometimes to their own surprise, that not only were they—the husbands—skilled and competent in their new domestic responsibilities, but they actually enjoyed the extra time they were spending with the kids.

As for the careers of dual-career couples, several studies find that couples who share the same career, or the same field, benefit. In a study of eighty-six sociologist couples who were at the same academic departments, it was found that sociologist wives were more successful than women sociologists in general. They obtained higher degrees and more promotions and continued with their careers longer (Martin, et al. 1975). In another study of 200 psychologist couples, it was found that when compared with a group of men and women who were not married to colleagues, the psychologist pairs produced more publications than their same-sex counterparts (Bryson, et al. 1976). Similar findings were obtained in a study of dual-career lawyer couples (Epstein 1971). The husbands of professional women were more likely to respect professional competence and achievement not only in their wives but in women in general.

Children (especially daughters) also benefit when both parents work. It was found, for example, that daughters of working mothers were more likely than daughters whose mothers stayed home to choose their mothers as role models and as the people they most admired. Adolescent daughters of working mothers were active and autonomous and admired their mothers but were not unusually tied to them. For daughters of all ages, having a working mother was associated with seeing the world as a less restrictive place (Nye and Hoffman 1963).

While dual-career couples have advantages over traditional couples, they also have a higher divorce rate. It appears they are pressured to make adaptations that are not required within more conventional marriages. Psychiatrists Carol and Theodore Nadelson believe that dual-career couples often face difficult choices:

> The husband who is transferred to a new location may
> have to consider not only his wife's social adjustment and

interests, his children's schooling and relationships with peers, but, to a greater extent, his wife's career possibilities. She may not be able to obtain a position equal to her present one, or her career advancement may, in fact, be jeopardized by a change in location. Wives share a complementary dilemma. The wife may be offered a potentially gratifying career opportunity, only to recognize that this shift might put added pressure on her family, especially if a location change may be required. She may decide to decline the offer, or she may seek another apparent solution: that one partner commute. This latter pattern has become frequent in recent years. The costs of these changes may be significant enough to cause a rupture in the marital relationships. (Nadelson and Nadelson, 1980, 95)

The Nadelsons also say that dual-career couples may be forced to reconsider their family roles and may have to adapt emotionally to new roles and expectations. Among the areas of conflict they mention competition, envy, and unmet expectations.

In my own work with couples, the main complaint of dual-career couples—both gay and straight—is lack of time. This is especially true when both mates have careers they value that demand a lot of their time. Anthony explains:

I find the inability to resolve the conflict between money and time to be the most stressful. Making the kind of money I want to have obliterates the emotional connection that I want to have. But I don't want to give up the income of a good job. Yet, I am working too much for it to really make sense if I'm going to balance my life the way I believe I want to—and the way I believed it would be when we fell in love. While there is no question in my mind about what I would choose if I had to make the choice between my work and my relationship with Ellen, luckily (or maybe unfortunately) I don't have to make a choice. So I end up giving the best part of my days to my work.

Ellen's response reflects a similar sentiment:

I love my work. It has always been a very important part of my life and of my definition of myself. Tony has not

always been as happy in his work, so I am delighted that
he enjoys and is successful in it now. And yet, the time
commitment both jobs require is the greatest strain on the
relationship. It takes so much out of us that when we are
together, in the evening or on weekends, we are totally
wiped out. Even though I have complete confidence in our
love for each other, I know from personal experience the
accumulative effect such continuous stress can have on a
relationship. I know that if we want the romance to remain
in our relationship we have to be on guard and make sure
it doesn't get lost.

Certain conflicts around issues of time management are inevitable
when both partners are constantly negotiating the demands of a
career and an intimate relationship, each of which they are deeply
invested in. Time is one resource that cannot be recouped or
expanded. No matter how energetic, clever, and skillful a couple is,
they can never have more than twenty-four hours in a day. One practical way to address issues, such as time, is for both mates to list their
work and home demands side by side (with a rank of importance
from 1 to 10 next to each demand) and for both of them together to
examine each other's lists (adding their own rankings). Even when
couples have been together for many years and claim to know each
other intimately, this process can produce some surprises.

A wife may discover that the demand to have dinner on the table
by a certain time and the guilty feelings associated with going out
for dinner are values and judgments she carries in her head that
were imprinted in her childhood. She may discover that for her husband, going out for dinner has far more positive and exciting associ-
ations and that he would love to do it more often. A husband may
discover that being a good provider, which he considered the most
important responsibility of a husband, is not so important to his
wife. For his wife, the time spent together as a family may be more
important than the raise her husband might get if he spent extra
time working after hours.

Even when a certain demand is recognized as being real by both
mates, after close scrutiny they may decide that, given their current
preferences and priorities, the demand is no longer essential. In other
cases they may decide that even if a demand was legitimate and reasonable in the past, it no longer is. Listing the home and work
demands, examining those demands together, being willing to recog-

nize self-imposed demands, and being open to negotiating all demands are important first steps in achieving a marriage/work balance. A balance between work and marriage enables people to get a sense of meaning from both. This solution to the existential dilemma has (at least in theory) twice the chance of succeeding as does relying on either work or marriage alone.

Work can be very ego gratifying. It enables people to be "heroes" in a culture-prescribed "hero system" (to use Becker's terminology). For such people, work can have a transcendent value. A politician who manages to get to the top of a political structure can get his sense of "cosmic significance" from his political power; a businessman who manages to get to the top of a financial empire can get it from his monetary power; an artist can get it from her art and the recognition it gives her. For such recognized "heroes" of society, having power, money, and recognition can provide enough meaning to life so that the romantic solution can be skipped. But these are rare cases, in which people are totally self-actualized in their work so they can forswear love.

Unfortunately—or maybe fortunately—our culture's hero system works only on rare occasions. In addition, there are very few places at the top (not to mention the sad fact that some of the people who make it to the top still feel empty). For the majority of people, the most intense, most moving experiences are those related to love. Even for people who are successful in their careers, work is often not enough to give life meaning unless there is love too.

A Note to Therapists

A subject of great importance that has not been addressed throughout the chapter is the unconscious issues involved in the choice of a career—issues that tend to be rather similar to those involved in the choice of a mate. In both cases we can assume that the choice is influenced by an internal "romantic image" that developed during childhood. As a therapist, helping people identify this romantic image and noting its effect on burnout is a very valuable exercise.

In chapter 9 I describe a multiple-step workshop exercise aimed at helping couples note the connection between the things that attracted them to each other and the things that have become the most serious problems in the relationship. It is possible, similarly, to show people the connection between their hopes and expectations when their entered their career and the major stresses in their work.[11]

Here the group is divided into foursomes, but this time the task for each foursome is first to discover what hopes and expectations they all had in common (e.g., to be successful, to do something significant); second, the stresses they now have in common (e.g., can't do the work the way it should be done); and third, the connection between the hopes and expectations on the one hand and the stresses on the other (both lists were put on the board as each foursome was presenting their lists).

In a workshop on "burnout in work and marriage," both of these exercises can be done back to back (only three steps in each) and thus demonstrate the impact of people's romantic images in both. These romantic images are invariably tied to people's notions of the kind of work and the kind of relationship that is most likely to give their life a sense of meaning. Needless to say, both these exercises can also be done in the context of individual therapy.

A note about gay couples: all the issues discussed throughout this chapter are as relevant for gay couples who are trying to negotiate the demands of an important career and the demands of an important relationship as they are for heterosexual couples. In both cases, the person who is more involved in the career tends to be the distancer and the person more invested in the relationship the pursuer.

5

Gender Differences in Couple Burnout

> In marriage, a man "enlarges into a husband," while a woman "by degrees dwindles into a wife."
> —William Congreve, *The Way of the World*

Who is more burned out in marriage, men or women? When asked, most men claim that they are the ones who suffer more in marriage. In popular literature and movies, many plots describe how men desperately want to escape the trap of marriage set for them by women. Indeed, men in traditional marriages have the lion's share of the burden of financially supporting a family. In addition, as Warren Farrell complains in his book *Why Men Are the Way They Are* (1986), marriage defeats men's basic drive in life—to have sex with a large number of young female partners.[1] Male comics have for centuries complained about the general incomprehensibility of women.

On the other hand, if we ask women which sex is more likely to burn out in marriage, their answer is invariably "Women!" Rosemary, a thirty-year-old woman living in a small northwestern town, explains: "Women carry more of the burden at home, they expect more from their marriages, and their marriages are more important to them than they are to men." The vast majority of the women with whom I shared this observation agreed. Since men and women have such different perceptions of who is more burned out in intimate relationships, it is interesting to examine the results of objective research on the topic.

Research suggests that marriage benefits men more than women, both physically and emotionally. Rates of mental disturbance, for example, indicate that while married women have higher rates of mental illness than married men, single men are more likely to be mentally disturbed than single women (Gove 1972). When marriages break up, divorce tends to have a more adverse effect on the health of divorced men than it does on the health of divorced women. In addition, recent research suggests that the psychological well being of men is more dependent on their family roles than on their work roles (Barnett 1993).

The eminent sociologist Jessie Bernard presented some of these and other data in her book *The Future of Marriage* (1983). The data show that married men are happier and healthier, both physically and mentally, and live longer than single men. Married men are less likely to commit suicide, have fewer mental and physical health impairments, and have fewer symptoms of psychological distress than do their single counterparts. They are more likely to earn good money and less likely to be involved in crime. (It can be posited, of course, that women choose to marry the kind of men who earn more money and don't commit crimes, rather than that being married makes men earn more money and commit fewer crimes.)

Despite their protestations, men seem to be well aware of the benefits of marriage and their dependency on women. Even if their marriages end in divorce, men usually try marriage again right away, or as soon as an appropriate marriage partner is available. Bernard argues that "whether they know it or not, men need marriage more than women do." Yet men resent marriage because they are so dependent on it (Bernard 1983, 16–27).

For women, marriage is not nearly as positive. Actually, for many women who view marriage as their ultimate goal in life, marriage ends up being a health hazard (Basow 1992). Bernard cites studies indicating that wives lose self-esteem and a sense of personal identity because they conform to their husbands' needs and expectations. Married women are significantly more likely than married men to experience psychological distress, including depression, anxiety, phobias, passivity, and nervous breakdowns. Since single men show more distress in these same areas when compared with single women, the conclusion seems justified that marriage is harder on women than it is on men. Further, more wives than husbands report feeling frustrated and dissatisfied with their marriages, while fewer wives report enjoying positive feelings of companionship; more wives than husbands seek marriage counseling and therapy; more wives regret their marriages; more wives consider separation and divorce; and more wives actually initiate divorce proceedings. Following a divorce, women are far less eager than men to get married again (Bernard 1983, 28–58).

As noted during the discussion of changing sex roles and their effects on couple burnout, couple therapists report that most couples coming into therapy do so because of the wife's dissatisfaction (Prochaska and Prochaska 1978). In addition, the results of a large survey including several thousand men and women indicate that when a woman's expectations for her marriage are not met, and it is possible for her to leave the marriage, she will do so (Blumstein and Schwartz 1983).

But it is not always possible for women to leave a marriage, because most women are financially dependent on their husband's income or on their joint incomes. Barbara Ehrenreich, in *The Hearts of Men,* mentions Jessie Bernard's work, but she argues that while Bernard may be right about men's dependence on women's care, her analysis of marriage has missed a far more important factor: women's financial dependency on men. Why is a financial dependency more important than an emotional one? Because, says Ehrenreich, a financial dependency is likely to last longer (Ehrenreich 1983, 10–11). Ehrenreich argues that women's financial dependence traps men in marriage and burdens them with the struggle to support a wife and a family. Indeed, there are data from a number of studies that document the health hazards of the men's breadwinner role: an increase in peptic ulcers, heart attacks, and strokes among unemployed middle-aged men (Liem and Rayman 1982). One study, for example, found that one hundred men whose jobs were going to be terminated had significant increases in blood pressure and levels of cholesterol and norepinephrine—changes that are known to have an adverse effect on the cardiovascular system (Kasl and Cobb 1970). According to Ehrenreich, since the 1950s medical opinion noting the lower life expectancy of men has explained it by the fact that "there was something wrong with the way men lived, and the diagnosis of what was wrong came increasingly to resemble the popular (among men) belief that men 'died in the harness,' destroyed by their responsibility (Ehrenreich 1983, 70–71).

So who is right—Bernard or Ehrenreich? Are men more burned out in marriage because they feel trapped by financial responsibilities and because they suffer the health hazards associated with the breadwinner role? Or are women more burned out in marriage because they carry a heavier burden of child care and household responsibilities, experience more emotional and psychological stress, and find their needs for intimacy less satisfied?

To answer this question, I did four studies involving 458 men and women (Pines 1989). The gender differences in couple burnout in all four of these studies was the same. Interviews and clinical work with burned-out couples showed the same gender difference: Women report higher levels of burnout than do men.

The first study involved one hundred men and women from the San Francisco Bay Area who had been together for an average of eight years. The relationships varied from very traditional to very non-traditional, but across the styles women were more burned out than men. They reported feeling "depressed about the relationship," "emotionally exhausted," and "wiped out" more often than did men, and felt more often that they had "nothing left to give." Men reported only two burnout symptoms more often than women: feeling trapped and being anxious.[2]

Bear in mind that in my clinical work with couples, I discovered that when marriages broke up, men often seemed to be in the dark about what had happened. In interviews, these men frequently said things like, "I don't know what happened to her. We were very happy, or at least I thought we were happy. Then one day, out of the clear blue sky, she said she wanted a divorce. I still don't understand what went wrong."

The women, on the other hand, were aware for some time that there were problems in the marriage, but they were unable to make their husbands understand: "I tried to explain it to him for years. He just wouldn't listen. I could never talk to him and make him understand. Finally, I just gave up trying and asked for a divorce."

The question that remained after the San Francisco study was whether these findings were unique to that particular group of people. Were the findings influenced, for example, by the liberal attitudes the San Francisco Bay Area is notorious for? (One might argue that because of these liberal attitudes women had higher expecta-

Ayala Malach Pines

tions that were frustrating.) So I repeated the study in the conservative Israeli port town of Haifa (a sister city of San Francisco). One hundred couples, married an average of sixteen years, completed the Burnout Measure (see Appendix 1). Again, Israeli women reported significantly higher levels of burnout than did Israeli men. Out of the twenty-one symptoms included in the Burnout Measure, the wives reported experiencing nineteen more frequently than did the husbands, including feeling "depressed," "emotionally and physically exhausted," "weak," and "anxious."[3] The sex differences in the Israeli sample were identical to those in the American sample, with the exception of anxiety, which Israeli women reported feeling more often than did Israeli men. American women reported feeling anxious less often than did American men.[4] This can possibly be explained by the "tough soldier" image of Israeli men.

Women also reported higher levels of burnout in two other studies on marriage burnout. One study involved one hundred Israeli adult college students, the second, fifty-eight American adults who participated in a marriage-burnout workshop in the southwestern United States.

In spite of the consistency of these findings, an important question still remained: Are women indeed more burned out in their intimate relationships, or do they only report higher levels of burnout? Is it possible that women, in actual fact, suffer the same level of burnout as men, or even less than men? When data are based on questionnaires in which people are asked directly to describe how they are feeling, as was done in the couple burnout studies, the researcher is always left with the problem of interpretation. In our culture, gender stereotypes make it more appropriate for women than for men to be weak and vulnerable. Does that mean that it's easier for women to admit that they are burned out?

In *Men and Women: How Different Are They?* John Nicholson reported that if you ask people how they feel in an emotional situation, women typically say they are more deeply affected. Yet, when hooked up to machines that measure blood pressure and heart rate, men actually show greater response. On the other hand, when erotic films are shown, men typically report higher sexual arousal, but women's bodies react just as strongly (Nicholson 1984). In other words, men and women respond verbally the way they think they are supposed to respond.

Sometimes people aren't aware of how burned out they really are. They may know how physically, emotionally, and mentally exhausted they feel, but they attribute it to something other than the real cause. (Think, for example, of the man who believes that his long commute to and from work leaves him exhausted when he gets home, but who in fact dreads facing his wife and uses his "exhaustion" as an excuse for retreat.) This psychological deception happens most commonly in situations where admitting burnout will require actions people don't want to take, like getting out of the marriage. Perhaps men have better reasons to suppress their burnout and find it easier to do so. Perhaps women are more in touch with their feelings and, therefore, quicker to attribute them to burnout.

Should we trust what people say? Should we trust their physiological responses? Should we listen to the insights of a psychotherapist who interprets their unconscious motivations? Every choice has advantages and disadvantages. The advantage of self-report data, in the case of couple burnout, is that it provides information about people's subjective experiences. This is very valuable information in and of itself, whether it is the "whole" or the "true" interpretation. For even if physiological responses to stress are the same, the fact that men and women interpret these responses differently is likely to influence their likelihood of burning out.

In my research, I made it easy for people to admit to being burned out by telling them that only those who were once on fire can burn out. Consequently, I felt I could trust the honesty of their responses. Furthermore, the questionnaire data regarding gender differences in burnout was confirmed by my experience as a therapist. I saw many burned-out individuals and couples both in the context of couple workshops and in the context of therapy. In the majority of cases, the wives were more burned out. One last point: If a woman says she is burned out, there is a greater likelihood that she will seek a divorce because of it. Self-report can be an indication of future action.

If we accept that women are, in fact, more burned out in their intimate relationships than men, we are still left with the question of why. Jessie Bernard would say it is because women carry the heavier burden of stresses in marriage. Barbara Ehrenreich might point out that comparing husbands' and wives' levels of burnout is an unfair test of gender differences in marriage burnout because men who burn out leave the marriage, because, unlike their wives, they can afford to. A selection process leaves in marriages the husbands who are not-burned out and the wives who are. Another proposition made by Ehrenreich is the notion that some men who can't face breaking up the marriage themselves therefore make their wives' lives so miserable that they end up walking out of the marriage. Looking only at the self-report data, we may find that these wives have higher levels of burnout, since the deterioration of the marriage was something they did not wish or cause. My own assumption is that there are two other reasons why women burn out in marriage: First, women enter marriage with higher expectations that marriage will give their life a sense of meaning. Second, the hassles and stresses married women have to deal with in their roles as wives and mothers are significantly higher than are those married men have in their roles as husbands and fathers. Some of the data generated by my research that had a bearing on these two issues are presented next.[5]

Men, Women, and Romance

Women do not necessarily have higher expectations of romantic love than do men. Women do, however, seem to attach their expectations of romantic love to marriage more than do men. For most women—because of the way they were socialized—finding true love in marriage means security, companionship, and happiness ever after. My research findings reveal that many women describe their relationships as a more significant part of their lives and as more important than their careers. Women also report expressing themselves more in their marriages than men do. Many men, on the other hand—because of the way they were socialized—view marriage as a trap—one of the few negative emotional experiences men report more frequently than women.[6] When women make marriage so important, it is easy for them to burn out. Men, who view their wives and families as important but not central to their lives, are less disappointed.

The sex differences in expectations of marriage are also evident in data on romantic ideals. When asked how important different aspects of romantic love are to them (see box on next page), women's ratings were higher on nine of the ten items, including trust, understanding, friendship, security, emotional and intellectual attraction, life sharing, romance, and money. Of the ten items, only one—physical attraction—was rated higher by men than by women.[7]

This questionnaire can be used in the contexts of both couple therapy and a couple workshop. In both cases couples are asked to compare their responses and note such things as: Are the responses similar? Is the rank order of the ten items similar? What are the differ-

---

How important, to you personally, is each of the following aspects of romantic love? Please use the following scale:

1	2	3	4	5	6	7
not at all important			somewhat important			extremely important

Physical attraction ___
Emotional attraction ___
Friendship ___
Long acquaintance/life sharing ___
Intellectual attraction___
Trust ___
Understanding ___
Romance ___
Security ___
Money ___
Some other aspect (please explain) _____

---

ences? Why do they think they see things differently? And what effect might these differences have on their relationship.

Why do women expect marriage to give meaning to life more so than men? A historical explanation is offered by sociologist Robert Bellah and his colleagues who suggest that since the early nineteenth century, "while men's work was turning into a career or a job, women's work had the old meaning of a calling, an occupation defined essentially in terms of its contribution to the common good" (Bellah, et al. 1985, 88). While the roles of men emphasized "self-aggrandizing individualism," the roles of women emphasized "un-selfishness and concern for others" (88). Men were identified with the head and women with the heart. The contrast between men and women was not "wholly disparaging of women, since the romantic movement exalted feeling above reason as the wellspring of genuine humanity" (89). This was especially true in the area of love and marriage, an area that required the participation of both sexes. Love, which was a matter of the heart and not the head and an essential basis for marriage, was woman's sphere. Women accepted much of this ideology (Bellah, et al. 1985, 88–89).

Ayala Malach Pines

Modern psychoanalytic theory provides an alternative—personal history—explanation for the greater existential significance that relationships have for women. The psychoanalytic explanation for the development of gender differences in the centrality of relations has been discussed in the works of such feminist writers as Nancy Chodorow (1978), Dorothy Dinnerstein (1976), Carol Gilligan (1982), Harriet Goldhor Lerner (1988), Jean Baker Miller (1976), and Lillian Rubin (1983).

According to this psychoanalytic feminist perspective, there are some deep-seated psychological differences between men and women who grow up in our society, differences that are not born in nature but result from the fact that a woman is almost always the primary caregiver during a baby's infancy. As Lillian Rubin notes in *Intimate Strangers,* since it is a woman who "feeds us, shelters us, comforts us, and holds us in her arms to allay our fears," it is with a woman that we form our first and most important emotional attachment (Rubin 1983, 50). In growing up, there are two tasks of paramount importance: developing an independent and coherent sense of self and developing a clear gender identity as a man or a woman. These tasks are accomplished differently by each sex.

For a boy, developing a clear masculine gender identity requires renouncing the emotional attachment to Mother and seeking instead an identification with Father. Accomplishing this difficult separation enables boys to establish strong ego boundaries. Therefore, boys have a stronger sense of being unique and separate. For a girl, developing a feminine gender identity is much easier because it requires identifying with mother, with whom she already has the primary emotional attachment. But because of the strong identification daughters have with their mothers, it is more difficult for girls to separate and develop an independent sense of self. These developmental differences have a profound effect on the psychological makeup of men and women and on the relationship between the sexes, making them in effect "intimate strangers" (Rubin 1983).

Because boys have to repress their feelings toward their mothers at an early age—before their ability to express complex feelings has fully developed—as adults men have difficulty connecting words with feelings. For most men, therefore, words are not a major aspect of intimacy. Since women never have to renounce and repress their emotional attachment to Mother, they are more in touch with their feelings and more comfortable talking about them. This, says Rubin, is why talking about emotions is easier and more important for women than it is for men. Sharing their inner life is at the center of most women's definition of intimacy. These early-childhood experiences can explain why women attach more significance to all aspects of communication than men do. Indeed, as the romantic ideology data showed, trust, understanding, friendship, and emotional attraction were more important to women. Other data indicated, similarly, that self-expression in marriage is more important to the women than it is to the men.

When women fall in love and get married, they expect their intimacy needs to be satisfied by intimate conversation in the context of marriage. Unfortunately for those needs, women marry men who often don't have the same needs for intimate talk (Tanne, 1990). Dara describes her frustration:

> Ben just doesn't seem to have the same need to talk that I
> have. He reads the newspaper every day but never wants to
> talk about anything he has read. I, on the other hand,
> want to talk about things that I read, things that I feel,
> things that I think. And I can't do it with him. And it's ter-
> ribly frustrating. I find it so easy to talk to my friends. We
> can talk for hours and hours. Why can't I talk in this way
> to my husband, who should be the closest person to me?

Ben doesn't understand what Dara wants:

> She tells me she wants to talk about a problem. I listen,
> and then I tell her how she can solve the problem. I don't
> know what else you can do with a problem but try to solve
> it. But instead of being grateful, she gets furious with me.[8]

Men and women also feel differently about sex, argues Rubin. For women, there is no satisfactory sex without emotional connection. For men, the two are more easily separable. The reason, again, has to do with those early stages of development when a boy represses his emotions toward Mother but does not have to repress the erotic aspect of his attachment. A girl, on the other hand, has to repress her erotic attraction to her mother but can maintain her emotional attachment and identification. As a result, "for men, the erotic aspect of any relationship remains forever the most compelling, while, for

women, the emotional component will always be the more salient"
(Rubin 1983, 103).

From the perspective of couple burnout, these differences in childhood experiences make their mark on men's and women's romantic
images. A more salient component in women's romantic images is
emotional attachment, while in men's it's the erotic aspect. As a
result, men and women enter relationships with different romantic
images and different sets of expectations, which influence their likelihood of burnout.

I found in my research that a poor sex life, the lack of physical
attraction, and boredom were more highly correlated with burnout
for men than they were for women.[9] Physical attraction was the only
aspect of romantic love rated higher by men than by women.[10] In
addition, men described themselves as more desirable sexual partners
and rated sex better than women did. Kathy describes the difference
between her and her husband in their approach to sex:

> We may have a terrible fight and not talk to each other for
> a week, but when we get to bed he wants to make love.
> How in the world he can even be thinking about sex with
> so much tension between us is beyond me. When we fight
> I get all tight inside. I need to feel close and loving before I
> can relax enough to open myself up for lovemaking.

Murray, her husband, sees things differently, of course:

> To me sex is a way of getting close. After we have a fight, I
> think that making love is the easiest way to make up.
> Unfortunately, Kathy doesn't see it that way. She would
> rather continue sulking.[11]

If women, more so than men, expect marriage to give meaning to
their lives, if the major component in women's romantic image
involves emotional attachment and communication, and if the
major component in men's romantic image involves sex, then it is
rather hard for both men and women to have their romantic images
actualized in the same relationship, and women's expectations are
more likely to be frustrated. In other words, gender differences in
marriage burnout are obvious and burnout is almost inevitable. I

devote chapter 7 to a discussion of this pessimistic conclusion. But for now, let me leave it and move from a discussion of expectations to a discussion of stresses.

Marital Stresses—Men's and Women's

What are the most stressful, burnout-causing aspects of marriage for women? Are they the same as the most stressful aspects of marriage for men? According to my research findings, the answer to the second question is a very clear "no."[12]

As for the first question, "conflicting demands" ranked first on women's list (it had the highest correlation with burnout) but only seventh on the men's list. "Unselfish concern for others" is a more important part of women's role definition and romantic ideal than it is for men. In addition, women are socialized far more than men are to actualize their romantic ideal in marriage. The feeling that they are failing is very painful. Susan describes the stress of conflicting demands:

> The hardest thing for me is feeling that I am disappointing people who depend on me and trust me. They include my family, my friends, and people in my work. It's not that their demands on me are unreasonable or unfair. It's that there's only one of me. I only have twenty-four hours in each day and I feel like I'm being torn apart.

Feeling pressured by family commitments, which was the second highest burnout-causing stress for women, was fifteenth on the men's list. Susan gives an example:

> Weeks before Thanksgiving I am beginning to worry about whom to invite for dinner. My brother can't stand Steve's sister and her husband, but Steve's mother would never come if his sister didn't come. And while I find his sister a bore, I think that the family should be together for the holidays. So I talk to everybody for hours, trying to make them accept each other, in addition to shopping, cooking the meal, cleaning the house, and all the rest. Steve couldn't care less who comes for dinner, and since the hol-

idays are the busiest time of the year at his work, he
doesn't help much with the preparation of the meal either.

Conflicting demands and family commitments have something
important in common. As we know, they both can reflect a failure to
perform according to some standard or expectation. The perceived
failure generates feelings of guilt and anxiety over not doing things
the way they "should" be done, a very powerful cause of burnout for
women that ranked a mere 14 for men.[13]

When discussing the stress of conflicting demands, family commitments, and guilt, parenthood deserves a special mention. Books,
songs, television commercials, and sitcoms all celebrate the cotton-
candy world of parenthood. The archetypal images are of cherubic
little children, wearing soft nighties, all washed and combed, with
rosy cheeks and cheerful smiles, coming to give Mom and Dad a
goodnight kiss. But, as every parent knows, parenthood is far from
being a state of constant bliss. You have to feed children, wash them,
dress them, shop for them, keep them healthy, keep them happy, and
take care of them when they are not. When they grow up you have to
negotiate their moods, fights, and heartaches. You have to give all of
yourself, all of the time, without expecting anything back.

In other words, you ideally have to love with no strings attached.
Furthermore, there is no training for your role as a parent, a role that
for many people (especially women) is the most ego involving. Not
only that, you can't get out of being a parent the way you can get out
of a bad marriage or a bad job. You don't get weekends off. You can't
postpone a child's need the way you can put off unpleasant paperwork. You can't quit parenthood, you can't take a sabbatical, and you
can't trade in one difficult child for an easygoing one.

Under the weight of these stresses some parents burn out, most
likely those who had unrealistic expectations of parenthood, who
expected their child, even as a baby, to love them unconditionally and
give meaning to their lives. It tends to happen more to those who are
isolated, ignorant about the tasks involved, and lacking in resources
and support. It also happens most often during difficult periods in the
child's or the parent's life. In one study that included seventy-three
mothers, for example, a significant correlation was found between
their burnout as mothers and the impulsiveness of their school-age
children.[14] Even normal, yet undisciplined or frustratingly active children can be very taxing for mothers.

In interviews with professionals and volunteers working on parental stress hot lines, I learned that, most tragically, burnout is one of the main causes of child abuse. Parents calling on those hot lines often say that they have reached their limits: "I can't take it anymore," "I am totally wiped out," "My child is driving me crazy," "I am falling apart," "I can't cope." The triggers of abuse, like the triggers of burnout, are rarely dramatic events. They are most often mundane daily problems of childrearing, especially with children between birth and five years of age. During these years parents are most likely to feel trapped in the house and bound by all that is required in the care of a young child. Socially isolated, unable to separate themselves from the child, and ignorant of what can be expected of their child, they feel a deep sense of failure and guilt.

In a study that included in-depth interviews with twelve abusive parents, we found that the burnout level of these parents was the highest of any group we have ever investigated.[15] Virtually all the abusive parents in the small sample suffered from financial hardship, poor family relations, and lack of support from spouse or friends. They expressed an inability to cope with their emotional and economic problems and resorted to violence because they had few skills to help them face the demands of parenthood. In light of the stresses that parenthood can entail, it is interesting that the number of children a couple had and the number of children still living at home were not correlated with marriage burnout.[16] This suggests that while in some marriages children are a stress, in other marriages they are a joy and part of the glue holding the couple together. Which part the children play depends on the couple's expectations, stresses, and available resources.

The stresses of parenthood do not discriminate between the sexes. Single fathers are as stressed as single mothers. But since, in our society, women still carry the lion's share of the parental role in most families, they also end up shouldering most of the physical and emotional burdens that come with that role.[17] Since societal norms define motherhood as the most important role in a woman's life, feeling that she is not performing to the high standards of the role can cause a worse feeling of personal failure in a woman than a similar less-than-perfect performance can cause in a man. Actually contrary to folk wisdom, recent studies reveal that while men's psychological well being is more dependent on their family roles than on their work roles, women's work roles buffer them from the stress of family roles (Barnett 1993).

From everything said so far it seems that women's stresses in relationships are related to their higher expectations both of their relationships and of themselves. They are more stressed by conflicting demands because they accept the various demands as legitimate. They are stressed by family commitments because they accept them as their responsibility. The feeling that they are not performing up to the high standards they impose on themselves causes them tremendous guilt—the severe internal judge that decrees they have failed. For many women an ideal life often includes a perfect relationship that encompasses a shared inner life, shared goals, mutual recognition, mutual appreciation, and self-actualization. Their emotional involvement in the marriage (which in most marriages is bigger than the men's) makes them take on the job of "the keepers of the spark." They work hard to do what is "right." When they feel they have failed and their relationship is not all it is "supposed" to be, they burn out. Women, it seems, burn out because they care too much.[18]

This is not to say that couple burnout is exclusively a woman's experience. Some men report higher levels of burnout than women; in some marriages the husband is more invested in the marriage, and in some more burned out than the wife. As is often the case, statistical averages don't apply to all individuals. The reason for men's burnout is the same as the reason for women's burnout—the relationship failed to meet their expectation and give their life a sense of meaning. Two couples I worked with are an example of role reversal in couple burnout.

One couple was in their 30s, the other in their 50s. The husband in the younger couple was an engineer; the husband in the older couple was a high-school teacher. Both men had enjoyed their work at one time but were, by the time I saw them, disillusioned and bored with their careers. Both men described their relationships with their wives as the most important thing in their lives. In both cases, the wives had started careers late in life. The younger woman had gone back to college after working to put her husband through. She had been extremely successful in her studies and obtained a good academic position. The older woman started working for a local politician after the three children left home. With intelligence, maturity, hard work, and enthusiasm, she became the politician's campaign manager. Both women loved their work, were excited about their successes and were delighted for the chance to prove themselves, to reach their full potential.

Their marriages were important to the two women, but not more important than their work. They derived their sense of meaning in life from their work as much as from their marriages, but they were married to men who now put the relationship first. This situation caused great tension in each couple. The tension was aggravated by the couples' realizations that they were reversing traditional sex roles. The men were afraid they were caring "too much" about the marriage; the women worried they were caring "too much" about their work. These couples demonstrate the stress of different priorities in life, no matter whether it is the husband or the wife whose interest is focused on work rather than on the relationship.

For men who are in more traditional marriages, the most stressful and burnout-causing aspect of marriage is overload, which ranked third on the women's list.[19] Steve describes the stress that overload imposes on his marriage:

> When I come home at night, after a long and very stressful day in the office, I am exhausted. I have neither the emotional nor the physical energy Susan expects me to deliver as a husband and a father. I need a few minutes of peace and quiet before I unwind enough to be able to listen to her or the children. When I'm not available emotionally or I'm not supportive enough, she gets resentful. I wish she could come to work with me some day and see what it is like. That might help her understand the stress I deal with and maybe make her slightly more supportive of me.

For other men, whose professional identity is the most important part of their definition of themselves, the romantic ideal is different. After spending a whole day in "the jungle out there," these men expect home to be a refuge and a haven. Similarly, men who are socialized by what Barbara Ehrenreich called "the breadwinner ethic" (Ehrenreich 1983) expect in return for the economic support they provide their families to receive the nurturing and care wives are "supposed" to provide. When their marriages don't turn out the way they expected, they burn out.

Sexual variety is another aspect of the romantic image that seems more significant for men. This gender difference was documented recently in meta-analytic studies of attitudes toward sex.[20] My findings also show that the second most stressful aspect of marriage for men is boredom, which ranked only sixteenth on the women's list.[21] A businessman, married twelve years, observes the effect of boredom on sex in his marriage:

> I am a very sexual person. I just love the sexual energy
> between a man and a woman, even if it doesn't involve
> sexual intercourse. I have many sexually charged (yet
> unconsummated) relationships with women I come in
> contact with. But not with my wife. With her there is no
> sexual energy left at all, just boredom.

All these findings suggest that often men and women enter relationships with different romantic ideals and experience, very different stresses. This conclusion was reached by other scholars as well, most notably Jessie Bernard, who went so far as to distinguish between "His marriage" and "Her marriage" (Bernard 1983, 5).

Given their divergent ideals and stresses, it is not surprising that men and women describe marriage differently. In all my studies on marriage burnout, men have recounted their marriages more positively than have women. In the San Francisco study, for example, men described their communication with their partners as better than women did. Men were more likely to say that their mate was their best friend and the one person in their lives they could completely open themselves up to. (Women were far more likely to have a female friend with whom they talked about "everything," including problems with their mate.) Men described themselves as sharing more of the household chores than women gave them credit for. (Women described themselves as carrying more than their share of chores.) Men described sex as better and themselves as more desirable sexual partners than women did. All in all the men seemed, indeed, happier in their marriages than the women.[22]

One day I was a guest on a radio talk show. After I spoke for a while on couple burnout, the host invited listeners to call in. One of the callers, who sounded extremely upset, told us that he had been married for over fifty years. He said that until very recently he and his wife had had "a wonderful marriage." They were both "very happy" together, their "communication was very good," and "sex was wonderful." He was perfectly content in the marriage until "two weeks ago," when he discovered, to his great shock, that his wife "was a whore." When I asked what he meant, he said that he found out she had been seeing other men all through their marriage and was sleeping around even before they got married. He described himself as "terribly upset and burned out." "Wouldn't you be?" he demanded. I did not have a chance to talk to the man's wife, but my experience leads me to believe that if I did, I would hear a markedly different description of their fifty years of "marital bliss." If she indeed had been involved with other men throughout the marriage (which might or might not have been true), she most probably would have described the quality of their marriage, their communication, and their sex life as far less wonderful.

Because of the different perceptions that some husbands and wives have of their relationships, one of the first things I do in working with couples is to establish that in my office there is almost never an absolute truth, but rather two versions for everything.

For a couple therapist, establishing "dual empathy" is one of the most important aspects of the therapeutic work. From their first meeting with the therapist, both mates have to feel understood, validated, and empathized with. Only in this way can the therapist convey to the couple the message that both their perspectives can be legitimate—at one and the same time.

The observation that women have higher expectations from intimate relationships and carry a heavier burden at home have been confirmed by a number of findings in my studies.[23] These expectations are also evident in prevailing cultural stereotypes and in the findings of other investigators, who show that a wife's general life happiness and overall well-being are more dependent on marital happiness than are her husband's. Consequently, when problems occur, women tend to be more distressed.[24]

For a long time women's responses to stress were attributed to their dispositions rather than to their situations. For example, the higher frequency of depression among women was said to be caused by women's psychological vulnerability and weakness of character. Only recently did scholars begin to attribute women's complaints to the reality of their lives. It has been noted, for example, that depression is greatest among low-income women with young children—a group and a period of life characterized by the greatest stress.[25] Contrary to the myth of legions of depressed "empty nesters," women whose children have left home are relatively unlikely to suffer from depression—much of the stress in their lives has flown the coop along with their children. Only "supermothers" who define themselves in terms of their maternal role suffer from depression when their children leave home (Scarf 1979). Single women and married men, who are burdened by the least amount of stress, are least likely to suffer from depression.

How Women and Men Cope with Burnout

If too-high expectations and the daily accumulation of stresses cause burnout, the obvious cure for women's higher levels of burnout is to lower their high expectations and to reduce the perceived stress in their lives.

For most women—and most couples—the idea of lowering their expectations of a love relationship is unacceptable. When two people fall in love, they don't want to hear that the chances of their love enduring will improve if they limit their expectations to those that are realistic and statistically likely to be achieved. During infatuation, when expectations are formed, couples want the best and the most for themselves and for each other. Someone has to be designated the keeper of the spark, even at the risk of higher vulnerability to the dangers of burnout. Women tend to take on the job because of their sex-role socialization. But keeping the spark alive is not exclusively a women's domain and can be defined as a man's responsibility as well—or instead. The best possible solution seems to be a "joint custody" of the romantic spark, in which the couple jointly defines expectations for the relationship, and jointly sees to it that the relationship does not depart too much from that shared ideal. In relationships where this is the case—whether the task is done simultaneously or is alternated—the romantic spark is more likely to stay alive.[26]

Perceived stress in couple relationships can be reduced in two ways: by reducing the stress itself and by improving buffers against it. Some couples are able to discuss their perceived stresses and negotiate contracts for sharing of tasks. The sharing can include earning money, paying bills, taking care of the children, and keeping house. The success of this solution is evident in dual-career couples who have a companionship marriage. It is also possible in traditional marriages where husbands have avoided domestic responsibility because they grew up in a family that defined it as "women's work" (and because they earn all the money so they won't do "her" job). Research indicates that when these men have to share child care with their wives, they often discover that it can be extremely rewarding. (They also understand better what their wives are complaining about.) Marriages in which there is a sharing of household and child-care responsibilities were described as happier by both mates (Pepitone-Rockwell 1980). It may also be worth noting (again) that for both men and women the more roles one occupies the better the physical as well as psychological health (Barnett 1993). It is not the number of roles, but the stress involved in them that causes burnout.

The second solution—improving the buffers against burnout—is best accomplished by an effective social-support network. Women, it turns out, value and use social support more than men do. In a study involving eighty men and women in which six functions of social support were examined, five of the functions were rated as important by more women than men: someone who listens, someone who acknowledges work well done, someone who accepts and supports unconditionally, someone who confronts on emotional issues, and someone who shares one's view of reality. The only function valued more by men was "professional challenge," which many women tended to see as criticism (Pines 1982a).

In another study involving 220 professional men and women, in which coping with career burnout was investigated, we found that talking to a supportive friend was a much more frequent and effective method for dealing with burnout for women than it was for men. Men preferred to confront stress directly, and when they could do nothing about the stress, men preferred to ignore it.[27] I discovered similar gender differences in coping in my studies of couple burnout —for example, talking to a supportive friend was more often used to deal with stresses by women than by men. Men tended more to ignore the source of stress and to avoid it.[28]

There was an interesting reversal in the way the sexes coped with career stress as opposed to couple burnout. On the job, women were more reluctant than men to confront the source of their stress directly ("Confront the boss? Me? Oh, no!"). Yet in their relationships women were likely to use confrontation more frequently than men. They were the ones who most often demanded that a problem be acknowledged and discussed; they were the ones most likely to complain about not enough quality time together.[29] Similar findings were reported by the psychologist John Guttman, who discovered that wives were more likely to complain about problems in the relationship, and that in good marriages when such problems were raised, wives managed the negative emotions so they did not escalate (Gottman 1994).

The largest dissimilarity between men and women in their coping styles, however, had to do with the way they used friends. Women used a network of friends—both at work and at home—more frequently and more effectively than did men. Women found it easier to talk to a good friend about problems and conflicts, and found talking more helpful. Bear in mind, however, that while talking to a supportive friend can be very comforting to one's ego, it is not the best way to confront problems with one's mate. A woman who talks to her best friend about her husband's beastly behavior is likely to receive all the needed support for her contention that the behavior in question is indeed beastly, but she is not likely to gain much insight into the husband's reasons for that behavior. This is why, research findings show, the more one talks to a supportive friend the more burned out one is likely to be in the relationship. This finding was true for both sexes, but more so for women.[30] It can even be argued that women's tendency to talk with their friends (or their therapist) instead of with their husbands is in part responsible for their higher burnout rate. This finding should be of great concern for therapists who work on couple issues with only one member of the couple.

Even if it is tempting for people to use the easy way of getting support for their own perspective, it is much better, in the long run, to take the harder approach and talk directly to their mate. In the context of therapy, this means seeing a couple therapist rather than an individual therapist. In couple therapy, self-focus helps avoid a blame frame. ("Why is this behavior so upsetting to me?" "What have I done to provoke, condone, or encourage this behavior?"). In cases where one partner would not go to couple therapy—one way to bring him (or her) is to say that you (the therapist) need their perspective in order to understand what is going on in the relationship.

Besides direct talk about problems and couple therapy, another recommendation for couples is to develop a social-support network of other couples who share their particular kinds of stresses and role conflicts, who view the world the way they do, and who can provide feedback, emotional sustenance, and assistance in times of need. Such a support group can help the couple break their fallacy of uniqueness and generate new and creative coping strategies.

While women report higher levels of burnout, thus creating a temptation to offer solutions that apply more directly to women, burnout is a couple's problem and can be solved only within the context of the couple. If burnout is indeed a couple's problem, and the recommendations for dealing with it are the same for both husbands and wives, why devote a whole chapter to sex differences in burnout? I had two main reasons for doing that: First, the question, "Who is more burned out in marriage, men or women?" is one I am asked very frequently and therefore seems to be of interest to many people. (As a matter of fact, this whole book is organized around the most frequent questions I am asked about couple burnout.) Second, awareness of gender differences in burnout can help men and women appreciate the universality of both their perspectives.

When a woman expresses frustration with the fact that her husband does not care about the marriage as much as she does, that he is involved in his work to the exclusion of everything else while she is left to carry the full burden of their home and family responsibilities, the knowledge that they are not the only ones who have this problem is helpful in reducing blame and guilt. It also enables couples to hear each other more clearly and to understand each other's perspective.

For the therapist who works with couples, using couples' groups or couples' workshops can be a way of demonstrating the universality of the gender issues that manifest themselves in couples' problems. Even when the therapist works with one member of the couple, it is important to remember that couple burnout is a relationship issue and should be treated as such.

Homosexual Couples

Research shows that homosexual relationships have more equality and less role playing than heterosexual relationships. Actually, they more closely resemble relationships between best friends with a sexual/romantic component than they do heterosexual marriages (Basow 1992, 226–28). Yet, as a result of gender roles and stereotypes, men in same-gender and cross-gender relationships are more similar to each other than they are to women. Blumstein and Schwartz found that gay men's relationships were the most sexually active and least monogamous when compared to both heterosexual and lesbian relationships. On the other hand, they characterized lesbian relationships as most compatible, supportive, emotionally expressive, and sexually monogamous, but with the least sexual activity when compared to gay men and heterosexual relationships (Blumstein and Schwartz 1983, 1990).

The stresses on homosexual couples are greater than those on heterosexual couples. The social stigma connected with homosexuality means that many homosexual couples cannot be public about their relationships (e.g., they go alone to couple functions, such as office parties). Homosexual couples also get less social support for their relationship from family members (Kurdek 1989).

Nevertheless, the variables that determine relationship satisfaction are similar for heterosexual and homosexual couples (Eldridge and Gilbert 1990). They include strong attachment to and perceived attractiveness of the partner, a constructive attitude towards disagreements, and shared decision making.

Conclusion

In conclusion, work and marriage address what most people's lives are really like, how most people try to find meaning in their lives using our culture's prescribed solutions. The actual process of living is what beats people down, whether they are successful in what they do or not. This is why established relationships are not as exciting as the first stages of falling in love. Yet it is the day-to-day existence that makes romantic relationships stable; it is what gives them their "roots." As we will see in chapter 6, sex is what gives intimate relationships their "wings."

6

Burnout in Sex:
The Slow and Steady Fire

> Just because you don't see shooting stars,
> Doesn't mean it isn't perfect . . .
> It's the stuff that dreams are made of,
> It's the slow and steady fire.
> —Carly Simon, "The Stuff That Dreams Are Made Of"
>
> The best aphrodisiac is a passionate partner.
> —Anonymous

During the break in a couple burnout workshop I led, a woman in her late forties came over and said:

> After listening to you I no longer think I am burned out in
> my marriage. I still love my husband, and I know he loves
> me. Our communication is good, and we both consider
> each other our very best friend. The problem is that sex has
> become so boring and listless that it's almost not worth the
> effort. Mind you, it's not because we don't know what to do
> in bed. We know each other's bodies so well that we can
> always make each other come. But why bother? We both
> would rather read a good book or watch TV than make love.
> Our sex is efficient but soulless . . . like peeling potatoes.

What this woman wanted to know can be summed up by one of the most common questions couple and sex therapists hear: "Can sex be good and exciting even after many years of marriage?"

Some people, who believe the only honest response to this question is "no" and yet who want the security of marriage, look for sexual excitement in illicit affairs. (At times, the split they make between love and sexuality is a reflection of a split in their internal romantic image, a subject I will return to later.) For most people, however, living with one person and looking forward to sex with another is not a desirable solution.

People who consider sex the most important thing in an intimate relationship do not accept the solution of splitting love and sex, and may choose instead "serial monogamy." They remain in a relationship only as long as the sex is exciting. When sex becomes less exciting, they become restless and, sooner or later, leave. Such people, at times, end up with a long series of brief love affairs with little or no emotional bonding.

Other people bring sexual excitement into their long-term relationships by opening them up to sexual involvement with other people. Examples of such "safe" sex outside the marriage are triangles, mate swapping, and open relationships.

In triangles, a couple invites a third person to join them in bed. In mate swapping, a couple engages in sex with other couples as a recreational activity. In open relationships, sex outside the marriage is permitted within certain agreed-upon rules, which may differ widely depending on the couple. For some couples the rule is "only when out of town." For some there is a condition such as: "Never spend the whole night together with someone else." Since the advance of AIDS, there is an additional rule: "Always practice 'safe' sex." For one couple the rule is "every Tuesday and Thursday night." On those nights the wife brings her lover home, while the husband goes over to his lover. Such agreements are aimed at limiting the emotional involvement outside the primary relationship and protecting its priority. However, keeping feelings in check is not easy; more often than not, couples eventually choose to "close" an open relationship because "it was just too much hard work."

A San Francisco–based commune, which called itself Kerista Village, developed an unusual method for keeping sex exciting in their intimate relationships. The Keristans, who numbered nineteen adults, were together for over twenty years. They maintained a rotating sleep cycle in which every night another man slept with another woman according to a prescribed schedule. This arrangement, the Keristans argued, assures a high level of sexual variety without the otherwise inevitable loss of trust, security, emotional depth, and commitment. (And yes, they did have children; two children, now teenagers, were raised by "joint parenting.")[1]

Other cultures have found different ways of keeping sex exciting. Orthodox Jews, for example, must practice partial abstinence. Because of the purity laws, which prohibit intercourse during and a week following the woman's menstruation. Sex is permitted for only about two weeks a month. The forced abstinence, I was told by Orthodox couples, ensures that sexual intercourse will not become a boring routine.

An extreme form of this "abstinence makes for passion" is the eleventh-century courtly love. Developed and idealized by troubadours and poets in the courts of the aristocracy, courtly love required that the exalted passion between a man and a woman remain unconsummated. Only desire that remained unfulfilled and unsatisfied was believed capable of fueling passion and bringing it to its ultimate heights. In their tales, consummated affairs—like those between Lancelot and Guinevere or between Tristan and Isolde—always ended in great tragedy.

Open marriages, sexually liberated communes, Orthodox Judaism, and the troubadours' ways no doubt seem like pretty remote prescriptions for normal married life. Most couples (and most couple therapists) would probably prefer to have a passionate sexual relationship with the person they love, the person they plan to spend their life with, and would rather not resort to forced abstinence, an open relationship, or illicit affairs.

In modern western culture, sexual attraction is a very important component of romantic love. The media, which reflect our cultural values and act as a powerful socializing force, offer an image of romantic love that has a very strong erotic component. Most people today find it difficult to imagine falling in love with someone to whom they are not sexually attracted and most women as well as men find that sex is most exciting when done with someone they are in love with.

This connection between sex and love, which to us seems so natural and necessary, is very recent. There have been many cultures and social systems in which sex was important but in which romantic love played no part at all. In those cultures people had sex, most likely enjoyed it, and saw it as normal and natural—without the overlay of love. In other cultures, love played an important part but was completely divorced from sex. For the Greek scholars and artists, for example, true love was possible only between men, because only such love could be spiritual. Sex with a woman was procreative and thus could not be connected with true love.

In our culture, birth control has taken sex out of the realm of procreation and romantic love has made sex spiritual. Most women, as well as many men, feel they are missing something important when sex is without love. They don't want sex to be just a biological function; they want it to be an expression of love and to have a spiritual meaning. Ernest Becker, in *The Denial of Death,* argues that sex is part of man's "animal nature." Man has always struggled to overcome his animal nature because it is part of his mortal body. "Sex is of the body," writes Becker, "and the body is of death" (Becker 1973, 162).

In Greek mythology too, Eros and Thanatos are inseparable; death is the natural twin brother of sex. People who exclude sex from their definition of romantic love are people who deny the reality of the human body and its animal nature. The reason they do it—and why that kind of an approach has appeal—is because it helps deny the body's ultimate mortality.

A case in point is Scott Peck's best-selling book *The Road Less Traveled.* In it he argues that sexual attraction is not a component of true love, that falling in love is nature's way to trick people (men?) into getting married, and that romantic love is a great lie. Peck defines "true love" as a very different experience from romantic love. It is a conscious "act of will," a "discipline." Thus he succeeds in totally removing "true love" from the realm of the body and moving it into the realm of the spirit (Peck 1978).

Peck's distaste for sex is understandable. Sex is a lower function and spiritual love a higher function. People in love, however, do not make such distinctions. In their infatuation (a bad word in Peck's dictionary), they raise sex with their beloved from a biological function to a spiritual act of bonding, from "intercourse" to "making love."

The Role of Emotional Arousal

When people fall in love they are sexually as well as emotionally aroused. The connection between emotional and sexual attachment is not surprising. The two are combined in babies and are split only in later stages of development. In addition, we are socialized to equate love with intense sexual arousal. Sexual arousal has a definite physiological basis, and can affect and be affected by any other arousal, physical or emotional. Lillian, an attractive woman in her mid-thirties, married ten years, describes it:

> As must be typical, the symptoms of the problem come up most glaringly in the bedroom. I no longer feel sexually attracted to or excited by Dave. Dave says he is still attracted to me—and that the lack of enthusiasm comes from me rather than him—but the predictability and low-key style of his lovemaking cause me to think that perhaps our lack of enthusiasm is shared. I have absolutely no complaints about his willingness, frequency, sweetness, or consideration and givingness during the lovemaking. It is the lack of creativity, genuine excitement, and passion that I refer to. And I do nothing to introduce these elements myself, since I no longer feel any passion or strong attraction. I do not find myself motivated to exhibit feelings I am not having—although some pretense on my part might get the ball rolling, perhaps. It's just not something I want to force myself to do. Passion can exist only in a circuit between two people . . . truly, I don't think either of us feels it . . . though we both want to. Is it too much to expect sexual passion after over a decade of living together? And if so . . . does that mean that you give up having it so as to preserve the marriage?

I will describe Dave and Lillian's case in great detail throughout this chapter, but even at this point we can assume that they are probably matched in terms of background, attitude, and personality. We can also assume that they fit each other's romantic images. They still love each other, and are committed to the marriage, and desperately want to recreate the exciting sex of their early years together. They do not want to break up, even though the idea kept returning. "When I contemplate life without Dave and his love," said Lillian, "I can almost feel myself shriveling up."

What seems to be missing in the marriage that was there during infatuation was the emotional arousal that comes from the newness of a relationship, from the uncertainty of the other person's love, from the excitement of finding someone who so perfectly meets one's needs and dreams.

After ten years the relationship isn't new, and since the commitment to the relationship has been made, the uncertainty and insecurity are gone. Most important is probably the fact (well known to the courtly lovers) that once our needs are fulfilled, they lose their intensity and motivating power. And when certain needs are satisfied, other needs may emerge. Lillian describes the process:

> Maybe I am no longer the same person who fell in love
> over ten years ago. I have blossomed and grown confident
> under the steady sunshine of Dave's love. Certainly I have
> very different needs today than I did when I met him. A
> decade ago I needed his nurturing and love so much that I
> was not aware of having any other needs. He was the
> answer to all my prayers.

Lillian was saying, in effect, that she expected Dave's love to give her life a sense of meaning, which it did, but only for a time. As suggested by the love and burnout model (see page 49), once expectations are achieved, if they are not redefined, they can lead to stagnation, disappointment, the erosion of love, and eventually burnout. Once satisfied, Lillian's need for nurturing and security was replaced by the need for passionate sex:

> As a thirty-five-year-old woman, no children, successful
> career, I find that passionate sex, or the lack of it, is far
> more important to me than ever before. I am no longer
> working to build a career. I enjoy my work and I feel suc-
> cessful. I think this is the age when a woman is supposed
> to reach her sexual peak . . . perhaps that is why I crave
> passionate sex in a way that I did not use to do.

Her dissatisfaction and boredom with the sex precipitated Lillian's involvement in a passionate illicit affair:

> About six months ago I became involved with another
> man who elicited passion in me that I did not know I was
> capable of feeling. For years I had just figured that I was
> not a very sexually oriented person. Though my husband
> and I had had much more exciting sex before we were mar-
> ried and during the early years, we had not had passionate

sex for at least three years prior to my affair with this other man. Although my affair was with a strange and crazy man whom I no longer have any interest in or desire to see, it elicited some very powerful feelings at the time . . . so much so that it was impossible for me to hide the fact that I was having an affair. Indiscretions on my part aroused Dave's suspicions and I ended up telling him in stages the full extent of my extramarital involvement.

Dave was wounded to the core, his infinite trust in me dissolved. He said he lost the capacity to trust completely. It would do him no good to divorce me and try to find another woman he could trust, since he lost the capacity for complete trust in another person. If I—whom he loved and trusted so completely—could betray him that way, then anyone could at any time.

When I was so close to losing Dave, my emotions swung back powerfully toward him. I no longer cared about the other man or the affair, but cared only about repairing the damage I had done to the man I love—my husband. I felt that I would kiss his feet for the next ten years if that was necessary to win back his love and trust . . . to restore the bond and comfort that I had ruptured.

The drama surrounding the affair and Dave's discovery of the betrayal not only served to remind Lillian of the sense of meaning her marriage gave her, but also was, in and of itself, emotionally arousing:

It was mostly my intense desire to right the wrong and stay on the good-wife path in the future (as well as his love and need for me and perception of my love for him) that convinced Dave to give me another chance. And the passionate desire I felt in wanting so much to heal Dave's pain and repair the damage I had done . . . and not lose the man I had loved all these years and still loved so much. . . . All those feelings created at least a semblance of sexual desire and passion, so I thought it might all be restored.

During the aftermath of the affair Lillian and Dave talked, for the first time, about the stagnation in their sex life:

At that point—while I was caught up in the passionate desire to repair the damage I had done and restore his trust—we talked about the sexual stagnation that had driven me to an affair. Dave said that I should have told him about my boredom with sex, and we would have found a way to make it exciting between us again. He said it just takes some time and attention and communication. He said he had noticed that I did not seem very interested in sex anymore. Even though that bothered him, he loved me so much that he was willing to sacrifice passionate sex in order to continue our marriage. He figured that passionate sex was small in relation to all that we did have between us. Neither of us realized that the lack of passionate sex caused a growing hunger in me that left me open for this devastating affair. Now that we knew, we both set about "working" at having better sex between us. So we took these steps:

- We got a layer of foam to soften our too-hard bed.

- I got an IUD so that the inconvenience and unpleasantness of my diaphragm would not continue to get in the way of spontaneous sex.

- I told him that sometimes his breath bothered me and turned me off sexually and personally, and we identified the food items that caused this problem and eliminated it with 90 percent success.

Dealing with the "bad breath" issue pointed to a problem in the communication between Lillian and Dave, a problem that, as they later discovered, was evident in other areas of their life:

Dave was angry that I had not told him this for fear of hurting his feelings, when in fact his feelings were not upset. He took it like any other problem—where you identify the cause and come up with the solution. I myself would have been devastated if he complained about my breath, which is why I did not say anything for the past few years. . . . We took some other steps as well:

We tried to make love at times other than late at night when we would be too tired for passion . . . we tried to do it more during the day, or early.

We went to a sex store in search of some interesting sex toys but did not find anything new!

We did much less genital sex (a pattern we had gotten into) and much more face-to-face sex, to have a greater feeling of intimacy. By more attention to forceful movements and proper placement of pillows, we found that I could have reliable orgasms even without direct oral or digital stimulation.

Unfortunately, as is most often the case, the technical improvements were effective only in the context of the renewed emotional arousal. Once the emotional arousal temporarily generated by Lillian's affair was diminished, the improvements in sexual technique couldn't maintain the sexual spark:

All of these steps seemed relatively successful in the beginning. They made important (though mechanical) improvements in our sex life. And when combined with the passionate desire I felt to repair the damage I had done, I thought that the steps we were taking might work. But I find that sex between us has again become boring for me. I am not sure what Dave is feeling. He gives lip service to interest, but his sexual actions demonstrate affection and technique rather than passion for me.

The Emotional Arousal of Resolving Conflicts

How can emotional arousal be generated and maintained in a long-term relationship? One interesting answer, suggested by Jordan and Margaret Paul, is by resolving conflicts, as they emerge, in an open and nondefensive way aimed at learning (Paul and Paul 1983). Conflicts are, of course, inevitable because people are, by definition, different and see—even the same reality—differently. These differences cause conflicts, whether or note they are acknowledged. According to the Pauls, and most couple therapists, it is rarely the conflict itself that creates difficulties in the relationship, but rather the way couples handle that conflict. Couple therapist Dan Wile goes even further in suggesting that a couple can build their entire relationship around a problem (Wile 1981, 1995).

The Pauls believe that all responses to conflict can be reduced to two intents: to protect or to learn. When people try to protect themselves, they do it in one of three ways: compliance (giving up to avoid the conflict), control (trying to change the other's mind or behavior), and indifference (ignoring the conflict). When both partners protect, they create what the Pauls call "protective circles." These circles (e.g., one mate always controls and the other mate always complies, or both mates ignore the conflict, or both try to control each other at the same time) are the cause of such things as communication problems, emotional isolation, angry arguments, and—most relevant to our topic—infrequent and listless sex.

The intent to learn requires a willingness on the part of both partners to be open and nondefensive. (Not an easy order, by any means.) It can facilitate an exciting process of mutual exploration and discovery. The process of exploration can use whatever conflict emerges, and in it both mates have to face questions like: What reason did my mate have for doing that? What part did I play in creating the problem? How did my mate's behavior make me feel? Why is that so? What childhood fears, internalized values, or unconscious expectations were triggered for me? How is my behavior affecting my mate? Why is that so? What are the consequences for the relationship? The process of exploration can produce pain and fear, especially when the issues discussed are very sensitive, but ultimately, the Pauls believe, the feelings it generates are those of passion and love:

> As we share pain, the weight of our protections is lifted and we feel lighter and clearer. We see our mate with a heart so full of love it wants to burst. We want to be as close as possible, to be one with, to be inside of. Our entire being comes alive with the intensity of our passion. (Paul and Paul 1983, 119)

I would argue that mutual exploration into sensitive areas of conflict has such a positive effect because it is emotionally arousing. The emotional arousal generated can intensify and rejuvenate sex. As the Pauls note:

> In a long-term relationship intense sexuality will endure only if partners continue to share and explore. When each person begins to pull back to protect, loving feelings and passion fade. The physical aspect of sex alone cannot keep it exciting, no matter how practiced the techniques, how

beautiful the partner, or how perfect the bodies. Without emotional intimacy, sex eventually becomes boring and infrequent (or nonexistent). (Paul and Paul 1983, 122–23)

When Lillian and Dave began "exploring," Dave discovered that for several years Lillian had been angry at him but had great difficulty expressing that anger directly. She was afraid that if she would express the full extent of her disappointment and anger and (if she let her emotional monster out of the closet) something terrible would happen (Dave would be so upset that he would leave her, and then her whole world would collapse). Dave felt that something was wrong but also preferred not to confront the issue. In the Pauls' terminology, Lillian and Dave created a "protective circle" in which each of them ignored the conflict.

When Dave and Lillian first met, Lillian was living an unstable ("flaky") lifestyle and was extremely insecure. She was attracted to Dave's strength, stability, and self-confidence. Dave, for his part, was attracted to Lillian's high energy and emotional intensity. Their marriage fulfilled both of their romantic ideals. During the first years of their marriage, Dave was a good provider and a stable breadwinner, which enabled Lillian to go back to school and get a degree. After about six years, however, Dave decided he needed a change, so he left his secure and lucrative job to become a stockbroker, a career Lillian deemed "gambling and not a real job." Shortly after Dave became a stockbroker, the stock market slid, and the two of them found themselves dependent on Lillian's salary. During all this time Lillian told Dave it was "all right" in order not to hurt his feelings, but deep down she did not think it was all right at all.

> Dave's career has not been successful. For the past four years I have been the steady breadwinner while Dave has tried to break into the field of high finance. Although he did have one fairly good year, he brought in a total of about $40,000 during a four-year period. Even when he made some money, neither of us felt it could be freely spent because there was no way to know when or if he would make another commission. Being a broker, especially during these hard times for the stock market, can be very stressful work. Dave has put out a lot of effort, undergone a lot of stress, and gotten very little back for it.

Lillian understood that what she perceived as Dave's "failure" was "due to a series of bad-luck conditions, rather than a symptom of inherent failure tendencies or inadequacies in Dave." Still she felt "emotionally impacted by a sense of his 'failure.'" It triggered childhood fears and insecurities that were, at least in part, related to the fact that her own father was "a total and complete failure in the business world." Her feelings of security in Dave and in the marriage were shaken and with them the sense of meaning the marriage gave her life. The experience had a noticeable effect on her sexual feelings:

> The sexist woman in me expects a man to be stronger and steadier and more financially successful than I am. Someone inside me wants to be a delicate, charming little girl with a big powerful successful man to take care of her and overwhelm her with his forcefulness, his sureness, his surefooted successfulness. I think I expect a husband to be successful just as Dave expects a wife to be faithful. We have both disappointed one another. Although I don't consciously make his career success a condition of my love, I am sure that on an emotional level I am experiencing deep disappointment in him. I wonder if this disappointment is behind my lack of sexual attraction. . . . Dave's financial dependency is the crux of my anger and disappointment. . . . The whole failure issue—men should succeed; my father was a failure—has a lot of emotional energy around it and generates its own dynamic.

Clearly, Dave's perceived career failure disappointed Lillian's romantic image. The disappointment had a very concrete manifestation in Lillian's sexual feelings:

> And then there is the size issue. Dave is relatively short for a man (about 5 foot 5 inches; I am 5 foot). He is also very slender. I am fairly slender but more solid than he is. I never used to think about it at all, but lately I have been craving largeness in a man. Dave is wonderfully endowed sexually—and fills me up as no other man has ever done quite so well. But in terms of body size and weight I have lately found him lacking. I crave bigness and power on top of me when we make love these days. I feel cheated

because my arms wrap so easily around his slender body. I feel like a protecting mother/companion/comfort-giver, when I want to feel like a nymphet overwhelmed by a large, powerful, and passionate man who is driven to frenzy by my loveliness.

Her disappointment in Dave has had an effect on Lillian's romantic image:

I wonder why, after over a decade of marriage, I am all of a sudden disappointed and turned off by Dave's slenderness and shortness. I used to love the way he seemed on my level. I liked the fact that he was not overwhelming. I was trying to express myself and achieve confidence and power in the world in my own right. I was sick of being overwhelmed by egocentric men. Dave was, and is, the most caring, loving, giving, wonderful man I have ever met. And I used to love his body. It hasn't changed a pound or an inch. Where have I changed, and why?

Is this body-disappointment based on failure-disappointment that I feel emotionally? Have I got his smallness of body mixed up with his smallness of income? Will this body-disappointment go away when Dave gets a new career underway and has success? And will sexual excitement ignite between us then?

Lillian started examining some other questions having to do with the meaning of her life in the larger scheme of things:

Or am I just going through some midlife crisis, wanting to recreate the fun, the dating, and the exciting sexual encounters I never had before I was married, because I was insecure and miserable? Or am I experiencing the downside of deciding not to have children . . . the emptiness—the "so, what's next?" feeling. . . . The lack of forward movement in life. . . . The lack of a major shared project to bring Dave and me together around something meaningful to both of us. Or are we experiencing the downside of not sharing some basic interests? Dave is more of an outdoors person; I am more of an abstract armchair philosopher type. . . . Perhaps we have each deadened ourselves by not pursuing independently the basic interests that we do not share. Desperately clinging to one another, perhaps we are losing ourselves as well as each other.

The "emptiness," the "lack of forward movement in life," the lack of a "meaningful major shared project" were all manifestations of Lillian's "existential" disappointment in her marriage. But the over-grown roots, the strong commitment to each other, compensated for the undergrown wings, the absence of excitement, growth, and sense of significance in the marriage:

> Will we continue to cling to one another—though rigid
> and frigid—too scared of losing each other to voice the
> feelings and fears and disappointments that prevent us
> from the passionate experience of one another? Or—
> through painful-yet-loving communication—can we break
> down the walls now stifling our love and need of growth?

Having focused so much on Dave's supposed career failure, I need to emphasize that Dave did not share Lillian's negative assessment of his career as a stockbroker. Dave, who is a very likable, bright, ener-getic, and emotionally solid person, mainly spoke of how much money he *did* make and described his continued prospects in rather rosy colors.

As I noted earlier, despite the intensity of her rage and disappoint-ment, Lillian still valued very much the security her marriage pro-vided and could not imagine life without Dave. She was afraid of what Dave might do if she expressed her negative feelings openly, so she repressed them. But it is impossible to block emotions selectively: once an emotional shield is put on, it inhibits all emotions. Conse-quently, with her repressed anger Lillian repressed her feelings of love and passion toward Dave. Dave, at the same time, while not admitting his failure as a stockbroker, was still worried about his financial future. He wanted to protect Lillian from his fears and feel-ings of insecurity and inadequacy, which he perceived as caused by his "unmasculine" dependency on Lillian's earnings. Dave couldn't admit those feelings even to himself, so he blocked them out, block-ing with them his love and passion.

When Dave and Lillian started talking about all those strongly felt yet unexpressed emotions, they focused first on the most obvious issue of conflict between them—Lillian's affair—and discovered some interesting things:

> My affair needed to be looked at as a communication to
> Dave, rather than as an inability to restrain my impulses. I
> needed to look at what I was feeling toward Dave and try-
> ing to communicate to him by having an affair—and by
> being so obvious about it. Clearly the affair had more to do
> with what I was feeling toward Dave than what I was feel-
> ing toward the other man, especially given that the other
> man is of absolutely no interest to me anymore. Now that I
> am not acting out affair-type behavior, feelings about Dave
> are surfacing that I was not allowing myself to experience
> before. Perhaps the affair was a way of doing something to
> prevent myself from knowing what I was feeling toward
> Dave, since these are very threatening feelings. I experi-
> enced anger, resentment, disappointment, concern,
> fear. . . . I am beginning to see the affair as a way of not
> having to experience these feelings.

When in a teary and highly emotional session Lillian and Dave were able to open up and discuss all of their feelings, they both experienced a tremendous relief. Lillian discovered that in spite of her "terrible feelings," Dave still loved her and actually was delighted to find out what had been troubling her all along. Dave discovered that Lillian's feelings toward him were not altered because of his "unmasculine" feelings. With the emotional relief they felt came the excitement of finding, once again, how important their marriage was and how much meaning it had in their lives. With this realization came a powerful surge of the old passion. As they both reported to me later, "sex has never been better."

Dave and Lillian were able to confront the sensitive issue of money and come up with a solution that was comfortable for both of them: they rented out a room in their house, which provided an added monthly income and allowed Lillian to cut down on her work. This was something she wanted very much to do but felt unable to do earlier because of her financial obligations. Even after the money issue

Ayala Malach Pines

was resolved, Dave and Lillian made a conscious effort to continue handling their conflicts in the same open, nondefensive way. Working through sensitive issues maintained a high level of emotional arousal in the marriage, which in turn kept the sexual spark alive.

The Emotional Arousal of Jealousy

In addition to demonstrating the power of an open and honest discussion of conflict issues, Lillian and Dave's case demonstrates the power of jealousy to arouse emotions. Jealousy is a protective reaction to a perceived threat to a valued relationship (see Pines [1992]; and Pines and Aronson [1983]). If your mate is having an affair, but you don't perceive it as a threat either to your ego or to your relationship, you are not going to be jealous. If you have stopped loving your mate, and you no longer value the relationship, you are also not going to be very jealous. However, if you value the relationship and your ego is invested in it, you are likely to find your partner's involvement with someone else threatening and to respond with jealousy.

Jealousy can drive people to do things they would never do otherwise. One man started spying on his lover in a fit of jealousy. One night he hid in bushes under her window for hours in the freezing cold. He sounded incredulous when he told me about it. "I am a stable, well-adjusted person," he said. "I don't know what is happening to me. I have never done anything as crazy as this my entire life." A woman told me that on seeing her ex-lover with a "gorgeous Los Angeles type blond," she lost all control. She snatched the hat off the fellow's head—a hat she had given him—and kicked him in the groin. Then she ran to his car and locked herself in it. "As I sat in the car panting," she said, "I asked myself who that wild woman was. I wondered if I had gone completely nuts."

Romantic jealousy can be extremely painful. A woman in one of my jealousy workshops said that jealousy was the most painful emotion she has ever felt. "I've tried everything to get some control over it," she said, "but nothing has worked. The only thing left for me is lobotomy." People in the midst of a jealousy crisis often feel as if they are going out of their minds. At times they also do extreme—even violent—things as a result of these feelings.

Most people have great compassion for those in the grips of intense jealousy. Nowhere is this better demonstrated than in the response to those who commit violent crimes as a result of jealousy.

In my work with prisoners who committed "crimes of passion," I discovered that people (as well as juries) tend to be rather lenient toward these criminals.[2] Their hot-blooded murders seem somehow more human (and more excusable) than the same murders committed in cold blood, say, for money. My guess is that people empathize more with passionate criminals because they can identify with the powerful force that motivated them.

Jealousy appears to be universal. It is experienced even in cultures that condemn it and was experienced at some point even by people who report that they are "not jealous" (Pines 1992). Evolutionary theorists explain the universality of jealousy in the role it plays in assuring a certain man's genes are passed on. Psychoanalysts explain it in developmental processes that all children experience.

Because of the great pain associated with jealousy, it is interesting to note the positive effect it has at times on the quality of sex. Jim and Stacy's story is a case in point. I met them during one of my intensive five-day "Emotions of Intimacy" workshops. Jim was fifteen years older than Stacy. They had met as boss and employee, and Stacy still looked up to Jim as her mentor. Jim had been divorced for over five years when they became romantically involved and during those five years had had many affairs. While Stacy had several boyfriends, she was still a virgin when she met Jim. The difference between them in age and sexual experience created, at least for Jim, a problem. Sex, he said, had become boring. While he loved Stacy and was flattered by the fact that such a young and beautiful woman was in love with him, and while he still felt committed to the relationship, he said that Stacy's lack of sexual experience made their love life unexciting. Because of that, he wanted to be able to see some of his former girlfriends. He encouraged Stacy to get sexually involved with other men, an experience he said would be good for her and good for the relationship. "It would help her become more experienced and sophisticated sexually," he argued with great enthusiasm, as he was pursuing different women in the workshop. Stacy, for her part, was very jealous of Jim's former girlfriends and felt inferior to them. While she was extremely attractive and had ample opportunities to date other men, she was not interested in anyone else. She said she would have been happiest in a monogamous relationship with Jim. Knowing that Jim didn't consider having sex with her exciting enough was very painful.

During the first days of the workshop the group's attention focused several times on Stacy's "jealousy" and "insecurity." On these occasions Jim was extremely understanding of "Stacy's problem." Then, one sunny afternoon, something happened that changed things considerably. Following a particularly intense session, Stacy was comforted by an attractive man in the group. This man had indicated several times that he was attracted to Stacy, but she had not responded. His nonsexual comforting hugs gradually changed to more sexual caresses. They went off to his room to "talk" and eventually made love. Since the sexual encounter was spontaneous they did not use contraceptives. Jim was furious. He could see Stacy and the other man getting physical with each other, and he felt disregarded and betrayed. "How could you do that to me?" he demanded. Interestingly, the focus of his anger was not the fact that Stacy had had sex with another man (which is what he claimed all along he wanted her to do), but rather her carelessness about contraception. "You hurt me more than any other woman has ever done," he said, "and I trusted you to protect my feelings."

While processing the experience, I asked Jim and Stacy whether there was anything positive about the experience. I was not at all surprised to hear Jim say, with great amazement, "When we made love it was the most passionate sex we had ever had. It was unbelievably intense and exciting. . . . I can't figure it out." Stacy, with tears rolling down her cheeks, nodded in agreement. The reason sex was so exciting, of course, is that it happened in the context of intense emotional arousal. For both Jim and Stacy (as was the case for Dave and Lillian), the safety of the committed relationship was shaken. All of a sudden the certainty of their world and their security in the relationship were called into question. The feelings associated with jealousy—fear of loss and abandonment, envy, rivalry, feeling excluded, and feeling betrayed—were intensified. And emotional arousal is a prerequisite for passion.

Jim and Stacy's story is not unusual. I have seen many similar cases in which one partner pushes to open a relationship because sex became boring, and then is shocked and hurt when the other partner starts enjoying sex outside marriage. That shock and hurt, "for some reason," help to revive the sexual passion in the relationship. The reason, as Dave and Lillian's case also demonstrated, is that passionate sex, even more so than love, depends on emotional arousal. Love gives the biological function of sex a higher, existential significance. A jealousy crisis reaffirms this higher significance, which is probably why I have never heard anyone complain about boring sex when in the midst of one.

Noting the emotionally arousing effect of jealousy is not meant as a recommendation to use jealousy to keep the sexual spark alive in long-term relationships. Rather, it is aimed at demonstrating the powerful effect of emotional arousal—even negative arousal—on the intensity of sex.

I asked twenty-four men and thirty-four women who took part in a couple burnout workshop: "How often do you experience intense jealousy in your relationship?" Analysis of the data revealed that the more frequent intense jealousy, the higher the level of burnout.[3] It is possible, of course, to interpret this finding as indicating that people who are open about their feelings and who are not afraid to admit things that might present them in a negative light are more likely to admit to both jealousy and burnout than people who are not open or who are invested in presenting a positive image. Discussions with the workshop participants, as well as clinical experience with people who had jealousy as a presenting problem, make me believe that even if such response biases exist, they account for a very small part of the finding.[4]

If jealousy has such a powerful effect in rejuvenating sex, how can it also cause burnout? The answer has to do with the difference between short-term and long-term arousal. While people vary tremendously in their tolerance for arousal, most like it when it is short. Almost everyone enjoys, for example, hearing a moving story, participating in an exciting adventure, or even being scared by a film or a fast-moving roller coaster, not to mention being passionately in love. Long-term arousal, on the other hand, is most often experienced as unpleasant and stressful. When the arousal is extreme, over a long span of time with no relief in sight, it can cause physical, emotional, and mental exhaustion. In small measure, jalapeno peppers can give food an exciting taste; but the same peppers can burn the mouth when excessive.

In a relationship with a strong foundation of trust and security, jealousy can serve both as a reminder to mates of how important they are to each other and as a trigger for growth. In a relationship controlled by the routines of daily living, in which the mates take each other for granted, jealousy can put the relationship as the number-one priority. It can remind the couple of the significance and security the relationship has given their lives. On the other hand, when jealousy is an ongoing problem, it threatens the fabric of security and trust that is the foundation of a relationship. The constant need to cope with jealousy can be both physically and emotionally exhausting and thus lead to burnout.

It bears mentioning here that positive emotions can also be arousing. According to Stanley Kelleman, who studied the body and its connection to psychology, emotional arousal has similar physiological consequences whether positive or negative (Kelleman 1985). This suggests that positive emotional experiences can have the same energizing effect on sex as negative experiences. Positive emotions can be generated by outside events (making love during the ecstasy of a big professional success) or by events inside the relationship. A woman, married eight years, describes it:

> At times, when we are in the middle of a particularly good conversation, when all of a sudden we understand something we've been struggling with for a long time, I am overcome with a flood of warm gushy feelings. I always dreamed about having this kind of intimacy in my relationship, and I actually have it. The feelings of love have a very strong sexual connotation for me.

Expectations

When they talk about the quality of sex deteriorating with time, couples often use the first stage of falling in love as a yardstick. When they talk about rekindling the sexual spark in a relationship that has lost its passion, this is what couples want back. Even Ellen and Anthony, whose marriage is still vital and exciting, look back with nostalgia on this stage. Ellen recalls:

> We made love five times a night and as many times during the day as our schedules permitted. We didn't want or seem to need sleep; we felt so energized by our passion. When we took a week off and went to a fancy beach resort, all we did most of the time was make love. We would go and get something to eat and then come back and make love, go for a swim, then come back and make love, get some sleep, then make love again. Nothing else mattered, not really. . . . We lived for the time we could be together. We didn't know how long the magic would last, so we wanted to take advantage of every possible minute.
>
> Now things are different. Both of us are back to being the great sleepers we have always been. Sex is still great, but it is

a far cry from those early days. Sometimes we are both tired
and several days will go by without making love. When we
do, we remember the great joy our bodies can give us. And
we keep wondering why are we letting the trivia of life
deprive us of this joy. But no sooner do we make a resolution to give sex the high priority it deserves than some
emergency comes up and again sex is pushed back in its
order of importance. This could never have happened during our early days together.

Not for all couples is sex such a wonderful experience during courtship. Looking back at the early stages, some couples don't remember
the thrill of passion but rather the awkwardness, insecurity, and nervousness. For those couples, the quality of sex does not diminish
with time but actually improves. Mimi married her husband relatively late in life, after getting out of a very passionate and very
unsatisfying relationship. She married less because of passionate love
and more because she saw her husband as a man she could share her
life with and be happy. Talking about sex she said:

I don't really understand what people are talking about
when they complain that sex gets boring. For me personally, after eighteen years of marriage, sex is much better
than it ever was. Now I feel relaxed and comfortable during
lovemaking. I don't need to pretend or impress. I feel secure
enough to try out anything I want to. . . . We both know
our own bodies better, and we know each other's bodies
better. We know better how to give and receive pleasure.

For Bill, a systems analyst, who has been married over twenty years
to a woman who is thirteen years younger than he is, sex has also
improved with time:

Before I got married I had been a bachelor for many years.
During that time I had many wild affairs with exciting and
unusual women. But I never considered marrying any of
them. When I first met my wife I knew there was something different about her. I knew she was someone I could
share my life with. And the years have proved I was right.
During those years sex has become much better than it was

> in the beginning of our relationship. It is more than just a
> sexual act, because it happens in the context of our whole
> relationship. It's like a rich, complex, many-layered fabric.
> I feel none of the pressures to perform sexually that I used
> to feel. Since I feel secure, I can relax and enjoy the bene-
> fits of a truly intimate relationship.

In addition to the effects of growing intimacy and security on the quality of sex, the expectations mates have also play an important role. When the norms created at the start of a relationship are very high (as was the case for Ellen and Anthony), sex is likely to fall short of them. Conversely, when the norms are low (as they were for Bill and Mimi), sex is likely to surpass them. In spite of the obviousness of this observation, it is rarely taken into account by couples.

The initial stage of a relationship, while important, is only one of the factors shaping couples' expectations of sex in a romantic rela- tionship. Childhood experiences (were the parents free with their sexuality and expressive physically toward each other and toward the children), past relationships (was sex exciting and mutually reward- ing, or was it anxiety provoking), as well as cultural myths also have a profound effect. In our culture, the expectations of sex in a love rela- tionship are very high indeed. Simply stated, the expectation is that sex will remain forever exciting, just as exciting as it was during infat- uation. Couples who internalize these unrealistic expectations uncritically respond to the inevitable decrease in the intensity of their lovemaking with disappointment, guilt for their part, and blame for their partner's. Some couple and sex therapists may take issue with my choice of the word inevitable to describe the decreased intensity of sex in long-term intimate relationships and would cite Mimi as a case in point. I would argue in response, that Mimi did not describe an increased intensity and passion in her sex life with time, but rather an increase in comfort, security, and ease that for her were translated into increased sexual enjoyment.

The effect of myths on the quality of sex was confirmed by some of my research findings. In the study of romantic truisms (see chapter 1), I found that the more couples believed that "love is like a good wine, it improves with time," the worse was their sex life. (If the expectation is that things will get better with time, then finding out that not only don't they get better, but they actually get worse, must be quite devastating.) On the other hand, the more couples believed in myths like "a match made in heaven," the better was their sex life. (Feeling that one chose a unique and special mate gives sex its emotional significance.)[5]

What Affects the Quality of Sex in a Long-Term Relationship?

How would you describe the quality of sex in your intimate relationship? When I analyzed the responses that one hundred married couples gave to this question, I found that the quality of sex tended to deteriorate with time.[6] This was true even of couples who described themselves as very loving of each other.

One possible reason for this finding is that sex is more of a physiological drive than love. Infrequent sex, like hunger or thirst, is unpleasant. When one is not involved in an exciting love relationship, on the other hand, one may wish one were, but the wish is not likely to cause the same degree of physical discomfort. And as with food, the same dish all the time—even if that dish includes desired food items such as caviar and champagne—eventually gets boring.

Another possible explanation has to do with the natural process of aging rather than with processes indigenous to long-term relationships. For males, the peak intensity of the sex drive (even if not the highest point in the enjoyment of sex or ability as lovers) occurs around the age of eighteen; for women it occurs later, at around the age of thirty. For the majority of people, following the peak, the intensity of the sexual drive tends to gradually decrease. While the data reveal, indeed, that the younger the couple, the better the quality of their sex life, it may also be argued that such things as small kids and mortgage payments are more to blame than age.[7]

Whatever the explanation, if the conclusion it forces us to reach is that the quality of sex inevitably deteriorates with time, then the outlook for love relationships in which sex is an important component is very grim indeed. The variations on the sexual act are, after all, limited, and the act is repeated at least once a week for most married couples. After being in a relationship for ten years—and having approximately five hundred sexual encounters with the same person—isn't it quite inevitable that boredom will set in?

Not necessarily. Since sex is not merely a physiological drive, boredom is not inevitable. In my research I found that the quality of a couple's sex life had almost as much to do with their emotional and intellectual attraction to each other as it had to do with their physical attraction, which originates in our internalized romantic image, and is, of course, a major ingredient of good sex.[8] But physical attraction cannot, in and of itself, sustain a long-term relationship. In casual sexual encounters with no emotional or mental bond, once passion is over it is often replaced by boredom or even disgust. Mark, who is thirty-eight, described his life as a swinging single:

> I would find myself, after sex, wondering what in the hell I was doing there. I would try to find the best excuse I could to get out of there as soon as possible. Sometimes I was so desperate to get away I wouldn't even look for an excuse. I would just say "I have to go" and I would leave.

Those sexual encounters in which the physical attraction is combined with an emotional and intellectual attraction, are the encounters that transform sex into the magic of making love. Joel Block writes:

> Without the intimate exchange of thoughts, feelings, and desires even the most fiery of sexual relationships will soon dry up. Sexual satisfaction often corresponds to the degree of nonsexual satisfaction within the relationship. (Block 1982, 86)

In my research, partners who described each other as "the biggest love of my life" reported better sex than those who did not. Similarly, those couples who described each other as "my best friend" had better sex than those couples for whom that was not the case.[9] Sadly, it seems that such friendships are the exception. Joel Block, in a large-scale study on friendship that involved over 2,000 people, reported that scarcely more than one-third of the married respondents regarded their mates as friends. Couples living together fared no better (Block 1980).

Good sex affects and is affected by the emotional bond between lovers. It also affects and is affected by the general quality of a relationship—good sex helps make a relationship good, and a good relationship helps make sex good.[10] In rare cases a couple may say that they have no emotional connection to speak of, and yet describe sex as good. ("We have nothing left to talk about, and yet I must say that sex is still good. It is definitely not as fantastic as it used to be . . . but it still is better than with anyone else.") In bad relationships, sex is seen most often (especially by women) as an unwelcome invasion or as a cold exercise of marital privilege. Based on all these findings there can be two approaches to improving the quality of sex in long-term intimate relationships: one is to improve the sex, the other is to improve the relationship.

Traditional sex therapists believe that improved knowledge and technical skills of lovers can improve the quality of their sex life and therefore of the whole relationship. The problem is (as Dave and Lillian showed us) that in the absence of emotional arousal the effects of improved technique are likely to be temporary.[11] Indeed, in the 1990s, sex therapists tend to be more holistic in their approach.[12] They tend to view sexual problems as relationship issues rather than as performance issues.

The approach, preferred by most couple therapists, is to improve the relationship, assuming that once the relationship is good, sex is bound to be good as well. Ruth provides an example of what anger can do to sexual feelings:

> I get so mad at him sometimes that I see red. Every time I run out of gas because he used the car the night before and "forgot" to fill it, every time a check bounces because he "forgot" to mention to me a check he wrote, every time I have no milk for the children in the morning because he developed all of a sudden an irresistible thirst for milk in the middle of the night, I feel like screaming. I can no longer look at each incident in isolation. There have been far too many incidents like that during our million years together. Every annoying thing he does provides a further demonstration of his narcissism, inconsideration, and total self-centeredness. But I can never express any of those feelings directly, because he goes wild at the slightest criticism. . . . I get so furious that even if I had some sexual feelings—simply because it has been such a long time since we had sex—my anger and resentment cure me real quick. I once considered myself a sexual person; by now I have learned the easiest road to celibacy—a bad marriage.

If Ruth and her husband were to go to a sex therapist, her husband would most likely complain that Ruth is not sexual. He has a "normal, healthy, sexual appetite" and is frustrated by Ruth's disinterest in sex. Ruth, on her part, is unable to express the extent of her anger and resentment ("How can I tell him that I'm so angry that even seeing his body in the mirror is enough to make me sick?"). So what is the solution?

The answer is open, nondefensive, and direct *communication.* Sounds like an old and tired cliché, doesn't it? Nevertheless, when communication is good, the data show that sex and the relationship are also good. Conversely (as both Lillian and Ruth demonstrate), when communication is bad, sex is bad.[13]

If a couple can talk openly and freely about sex, there is a much better chance they will get what they want in bed than if one or both of them is too embarrassed to talk about it. But communication is not limited to sex. It includes the permission to express anger, frustration, and irritation openly—something many couples have a great deal of difficulty doing. When couples talk like best friends, there is little chance that small resentments will accumulate to the point of interfering with sex.

Such openness also enables couples to be inappropriate sometimes and contradict whatever image they have of themselves or try to project. Even a "sexy person" at times does not feel sexy; and even a "terrific lover" sometimes doesn't feel like making the effort. Breaking such images and old patterns of behavior can be exciting and arousing. Research shows that androgynous people (those who combine in their personalities both masculine and feminine traits—and therefore tend to be more free and flexible in their behavior) have better sex than people who are sex-role stereotyped (and more limited in their behavioral scripts) (Safir, et al. 1982).

Open communication, as Dave and Lillian demonstrated, helps sustain the emotional and sexual intensity of a relationship, because it enables couples to discuss emotionally loaded taboo subjects. The emotional intensity enhances the general level of arousal, which heightens sexual arousal, which makes sex more exciting.

There are other things, however, that enhance the general level of arousal and thus can increase sexual arousal. One such thing, which was mentioned before, is *variety.* Variety is indeed the spice of sexual life. The more variety there is in a couple's relationship, the more positively the couple describes their sex life. On the flip side, the more boredom, the poorer the quality of sex.[14]

Is it possible to have sexual variety in a long-term relationship with one person? The answer, it turns out, depends on one's definition of sex. If it is defined as genital sex—i.e., intercourse—the answer is no. The number of possible permutations in genital sex is, as we know, finite, and the number of those sex positions practiced by most couples is even more limited than that.

If sex is defined as a total body experience, however, then the answer is yes. The number of possible permutations in touching, kissing, stroking, petting, necking, masturbation, massage, dirty talk—to mention just a few of the possible activities—is virtually infinite. In addition, sex that involves the whole body can be fast or slow, intense or relaxed, and most important, it can, but does not have to, end in orgasm.

People for whom sex is mostly genital tend to burn out fast in long-term relationships. Typically, an attractive new person is the most arousing sexual stimulus for them. The nervousness and mystery before the first sexual encounter are the most exciting aspects of the experience; everything else pales by comparison. The excitement makes them feel alive and makes life worth living—which is why they seek it so desperately. After such a person becomes familiar with the other person's body and sexual response, the novelty wears off and with it the sexual arousal. Boredom sets in, and the search for a new partner begins. These people rarely develop close intimate relations with their sexual partners. Their "best friend" is usually someone with whom they have not been sexually involved. The separation between sexuality and intimacy is deep-seated and reflects a split romantic image. Even when such people are aware of its emotional cost, they find it difficult to change.

For other people, the intimacy in a relationship is its most rewarding aspect, while getting involved with a new person generates emotional arousal of the wrong kind—feelings such as insecurity, embarrassment, and anxiety. Because of their emphasis on intimacy, their need for variety in the sexual act itself tends to be limited. Nora Ephron describes it in her book *Heartburn*:

> I have never been big on invention in [the sex] department.
> Why kid around? Every so often I browse through books full
> of tasteful line drawings of supplementary positions—how
> to do it standing, and in the swimming pool and on the

> floor! Why would anyone want to do it on the floor when a
> bed was available? I'll tell you the truth: even sex on the
> beach seems to me to be going too far. (Ephron 1983)

When we talk about "people for whom sex is mostly genital" or "people for whom intimacy is the most important part of a relationship," we are making a dispositional attribution about these people ("That's the way they are"). Such dispositions can, nonetheless, change under the appropriate circumstances. An example may help clarify this point. Earlier I quoted Mark, a thirty-eight-year-old man who talked about his frequent urge to get away after sex. It may be worth noting that in addition to being a very successful attorney, Mark is also good-looking, sure of himself, extremely flirtatious, and very successful with women. Mark described himself as someone who could maintain an interest in a sexual relationship for a maximum of four months, after which he would get bored and start pursuing other women. A less charitable acquaintance described him as "a vagina tourist." Mark specialized in short affairs, often with several women at once.

Then, one evening, Mark met the woman of his dreams at a party. He had never felt as strong an attraction and pursued her with passionate determination. He wanted to marry her. He wanted her to have his children. He wanted to spend the rest of his life with her. Sex was no longer a physical need that he sought to satisfy with the least possible hassle. With her it became a magical expression of love and intimacy. He had no interest in other women and didn't want her to see other men. His excitement about her did not diminish after four months or four years of marriage.

People who had known Mark for years and had only seen him wild and reckless, chasing women and disposing of them shortly thereafter, were amazed at the transformation. Several of them who had a chance to meet Mark's parents noted the incredible similarity between Mark's mother and the beautiful woman he finally managed to convince to marry him (but only after months of persistent pursuing). "It is almost as if his wife were a younger version of his mother," one said. Both women had a classic face, with petite and well-proportioned bodies, short dark hair, green eyes, and strong, vivacious personalities. The similarity went even beyond appearance and personality to a seeming replay of a childhood trauma. Mark's mother was an alcoholic. When sober, she was very loving and nurturing. When drunk she was unavailable and rejecting. The woman Mark fell in love with was very attached to her South American family. When she was with Mark she was warm and loving. When she was away she was unavailable and Mark felt abandoned and rejected by her. In short, Mark's love fitted his romantic image in every possible way.

The circumstances were also ripe for Mark to fall in love. He had just finished a law apprenticeship and was leaving town to join a prestigious law firm on the East Coast. The emotional arousal generated by this big change in his life made it more likely that he would interpret as love meeting someone who fit his romantic image. The love gave sex a significance it never had before for him.

So, variety in sex, like in other things, is in the eyes of the beholder. Variety in sexual partners may be the prerequisite for sexual arousal for one person and may be totally unnecessary to another. Similarly, variety in sexual positions may be wildly exciting to one person and may seem utterly ridiculous to another. The difference between couples who have good sex and those who don't does not lie in the particular expression of variety, but rather in the acknowledgment of its importance.

The techniques for introducing variety into a sexual relationship are as different as people are. One couple with five teenage children posted on their bedroom door a sign saying "NO!" and proceeded to spend a whole afternoon giving each other a sensuous massage. Another couple likes to make a date for sex so they can look forward to it, make the practical arrangements, and begin getting in the mood well in advance. For a busy dual-career couple, a luxurious breakfast-in-bed ceremony as the backdrop for slow and lingering lovemaking provides welcome relief from the quick and hurried sex they usually engage in during the week. A couple with four young children hires a live-in babysitter one weekend a month so they can get away to some nice hotel in the city where they can have "wild sex." A gay man orchestrates major theatrical happenings (of bondage, etc.) that make sex exciting. Creating a special time for sex requires planning ahead and scheduling. Such planning may take away from the spontaneity of the sexual experience but, according to the couples, it does not reduce its intensity.

Some couples, in order to increase the level of arousal in their sex life, watch erotic movies or read pornographic books and magazines together. Other more daring couples go to sex clubs or swingers' parties (nowadays these practices are more rare because of the danger of sexually transmitted diseases, especially AIDS). Some couples smoke marijuana, wear erotic clothes, or use sex "toys." In all cases the techniques are aimed at making certain sexual encounters special and different. A gay man in a five-year-long relationship says:

> We have a routine form of sex that we have regularly, that is, without the special kind of intimacy and the production number. A production number would be a more full, complete, intimate expression. It takes longer, is more involved, more passionate. We don't do it too often, maybe once a week, or once every two weeks, so when we do it's a treat. There is a red light somewhere, music playing, special clothes . . . the works.

Joel Block, in *The Magic of Lasting Love*, suggests yet another way to introduce variety, and through it emotional arousal, into sex. His recommendation focuses on changing sex roles (masculine is rough and tough; feminine, soft and sweet). Breaking those sex roles (especially for couples who are boxed into them and for couples who feel that sex has become a boring routine) increases the mates' ranges of sexual satisfaction. One way to do this is by reversing roles:

> If you are a male and conceive of a woman as being gentle and seductive, cuddly or sexually passive, be that way yourself. If you are female and view men as aggressive, initiatory, active, you may be that way. Be true to form in coming "out of role" in your sex play. For instance, if the female partner usually lies on her back and is mounted by the male, reverse this; if the male partner usually fondles his lover's nipples, she is to fondle his. (Block 1982, 86)

Barbara and Michael, a San Francisco couple committed to keeping the spark alive in their twenty-year-old marriage and to helping other couples bring it back to their relationships, developed a successful board game called *An Enchanted Evening*. The instructions for playing the game include creating a special time, place, and atmosphere: the time—when there are no children around, no telephone calls and no other interruptions; the place—comfortable and pleasant; the atmosphere—romantic, preferably with candlelight, soft music, a pleasant area to lie on, sensuous lounging clothes, tantalizing edibles, and good wine. At the beginning of the game each player takes a blank "wish card" and writes down a secret wish that the player wants fulfilled by or with his/her partner. The wish has to be one that can be completed the same night. Then, without disclosing the wish, they place the cards in a special "wish box." The goal of the game is to be the first to reach that box. The "loser" is obliged to make the "winner's" wish come true.

During the game, players in alternating turns roll two dice. The dice have only 1 or 2 on them, to assure that the game progresses very slowly and takes a long time to finish. After each move, the person who threw the dice has to respond to cards corresponding to the design on which he or she landed. The cards start with less erotic questions such as: "In what way is your partner supportive of you?" and progresses to more daring instructions such as: "Gently fondle something your partner has a pair of" or "The scene is a theater balcony, back row; give your partner a 'matinee' kiss." The game, which is recommended by couple and sex therapists, is valuable because it provides a break from the routine, a way to be totally focused on each other in a relaxed, sensuous, and entertaining way.

The game is most useful for couples who want variety in their sex life but don't know how to go about creating it. Other couples may find the idea of a board game artificial and boring. Couples like that can be challenged to create their own version of *An Enchanted Evening*, which will be more relevant to them and, of course, more exciting.

Security, according to my research findings, is yet another important component of good sex.[15] A sixty-year-old Catholic woman, married almost forty years, says she has never had such good sex in her life. Having five children, she and her husband had to make an effort to be quiet during lovemaking. She was always nervous that the sounds they made might be heard through the thin walls separating the children's bedrooms from their own. Not believing in the use of contraceptives, she was also nervous about the possibility of getting pregnant. The rhythm and withdrawal methods they used to prevent pregnancy never seemed safe enough to enable either of them to relax completely. Now that the children have finally left home and she has gone through menopause, they can, for the first time in their lives, really relax and enjoy sex. So they do it all over the house. Their favorite place is the floor next to the fireplace. They do it any time they feel like it, day or night. And they make as much noise as they like.

The security that comes from living with another person for many years provides for some people (such as Mimi and Bill) a relief from the burdensome pressure to perform sexually. It gives them the freedom to enjoy their bodies unabashedly. Because of this welcome relief from the pressure and awkwardness that sometimes hamper the early stages of a sexual relationship, for them sex tends to get better with time.

In order to feel secure in their sexuality, it is important for couples to know themselves and each other. It is important for them to be comfortable with their and their partners' bodies and be able to express openly (which is to say, without fear, embarrassment, or guilt) likes and dislikes, "turn-ons" and "turn-offs." Yet it is knowing themselves and each other and feeling comfortable with their own and their partner's bodies that is going to make them feel more secure. How can they break the cycle?

The answer (both from the perspective of the couple and that of the couple therapist) is that it doesn't really matter where you start. Open communication about such things as sexual fantasies and erogenous zones, for example, helps couples know each other's sexual preferences. Talk about such things is not only sexually arousing in itself, it also increases the bond of trust between mates. Reading sex-education literature can also increase knowledge and, with it, a sense of security.[16] Reading such literature together is both educational and sexually exciting when it gives partners permission to experiment with their bodies in ways they did not know about or had not considered.

The same experiences, however, can be anxiety provoking rather than security enhancing if they are used for establishing new norms for sexual performance. "Sensate focus," a favorite among sex and couple therapists, is a technique aimed at being sexually arousing without being threatening. In it mates take turns touching each other nonsexually, without making demands that the caressing lead to sexual performance. (The couple is given a specific instruction to avoid intercourse.)

Instead of the traditional approach, which viewed sexuality as a climb to the top of the mountain (each partner focuses on his own journey, and the goal is to reach the peak), modern approaches view sexuality as a couple's fun trip to the mountain, where they may reach the peak eventually, but that is not the ultimate goal. The goal is for the couple to have fun—together. So, if they discover an interesting cave along the way, they can stop and explore it leisurely. And if they feel so relaxed that they just want to lie down on the grass and take a little nap, they can do that and then go on the top of the mountain—where the view is so breathtaking—or decide that they have had enough for the day and climb down. When couples feel secure in the knowledge that whatever happens is fine, as long as they both enjoy it, no trip to the mountain is likely to be the same as the one before.

When the Sexual Spark Is Dead

Being overanxious about the sexual spark is one of the best ways to kill it. In every relationship there are times when one or both mates is either uninterested in sex or unable to perform sexually. In those relationships sex usually deteriorates rapidly. A Catholic couple provides a sad example. For twenty-three of their years together, sex had been one of the most satisfying aspects of the relationship and one that compensated for many annoyances. Then one night the husband couldn't perform sexually, which the wife took as a personal insult and a testimony to her diminishing attractiveness. Her shocked response made their next attempt at lovemaking a nerve-wracking experience. Performance anxiety made the husband's next "sexual failure" a near certainty. Thus, an incident that should have been taken very lightly (especially in light of their long history of good sex) ended up destroying their sex life altogether.

This brings me to the question: What do you do (as a couple or a as couple therapist) when the sexual spark is dead? Unfortunately, in my experience when the spark is gone completely (or in those cases when it was never there to begin with), it is extremely difficult, almost impossible, to revive it. Sometimes that means the end of the relationship but not always. People differ in their sex drives and the importance they give to sex. Some couples feel like brother and sister: they are each other's best friend but have no sexual interest in each other. Other couples have never had sex as the major component of the relationship (I will describe two such cases when discussing split romantic images). This chapter has been written with a view toward the majority of couples in long-term relationships: couples who value passionate sex and who still have at least a spark of it left.

A Note to Therapists: On Split Romantic Images

Split romantic images (when a romantic image of a lover has two contradictory elements) are very important for understanding certain patterns of sexual behavior that are very destructive for intimate relationships and *very hard to treat*. One pattern involves continuous affairs ("The first was on our honeymoon"). The other pattern involves a long term affair ("I am married thirteen years, and my relationship with the other man has been going on for fifteen"). In both cases, the outside relationships reflect an internal split in the romantic image.

The first pattern—the whore/madonna complex—tends to characterize men who had a very close symbiotic relationship with their mother and whose father was absent, invisible, or weak. Rick is an example. He came to see me after his wife of twenty years kicked him out of the house because she discovered he had an affair with her best friend. He seemed quite cheerful and pleased with himself, telling me with great pride of his sexual conquests (ever since the honeymoon). The only thing that troubled him was the chance that his wife might not want him back. He "loves her very much," he said, she is "a wonderful mother" and his "best friend." He has never loved another woman the way he loved her. But he is not attracted to her sexually and never was. He *never* loved any of the women he was sexual with, he emphasizes. It seems that for men like Rick, an incest taboo is activated when a relationship moves from being strictly sexual to an emotional connection. Such a woman (like Rick's wife) becomes "a mother," a madonna, and cannot be an object of sexual desire.

The second pattern—of a long-term extramarital involvement—can be seen in either men or women and usually is a reenactment of a childhood trauma. Angie fell in love with her husband when she saw him coming down the stairs she was climbing. She decided right then and there that this was the man who would be the father of her children. And indeed, he is "a wonderful father and husband and friend." When I asked her to describe him she said all that and added that he is "kind, loving, and trustworthy." Unfortunately, he is "not exciting" her sexually. Her lover, with whom she has a relationship that is longer than her marriage, is an "untrustworthy son of a bitch." She would never be in a relationship with him, even if he got out of his marriage. Despite all his terrible qualities, she finds him "extremely exciting sexually" ("I can come just thinking about the feel of his skin"). When I asked her to describe herself in this triangle, she describes herself as "torn" between the two men. After identifying the three points in this triangle, I asked Angie if these traits fit some other triangle of people in her childhood. As is always the case, it turned out that her mother was the "good parent," "loving, kind, trustworthy," and "unexciting." Her father, on the other hand, was "a real son of a bitch" who was unfaithful to her mother and eventually left her for another woman. Angie was told not to keep in touch with her dad, because if she did she would be betraying her mother. She was torn as a child, and is reenacting the split in her love relationships.

Needless to say, in all such cases therapists should also ask themselves what is the other partner getting from the relationship. And it almost always turns out that the partner is also working through the relationship an unresolved childhood issue. In the case of Angie's husband, Dick, for example (it may be worth noting that Dick is tall and skinny, his head full of curly grey hair, and is far better-looking than her lover), it turns out that his mother (who was a beautiful, powerful, and charismatic woman much like Angie) also had a long-term lover. The man (her piano instructor) was in the house often, and Dick called him "uncle." Only as an adult he figured out what the true nature of the relationship between his mother and the "uncle" was. His identification with his weak and powerless father pushed him to reenact this childhood triangle in his marriage.

7

Is Couple Burnout Inevitable?

The only way to conquer love is to run away from it.
—Napoleon Bonaparte

Preventing Couple Burnout
by Forsaking Romantic Love

Among the people I interviewed, two groups had an important thing
in common: They did not experience any burnout in their intimate
relationships whatsoever. Both groups assured me that they never
burned out and could not imagine ever burning out in the future.
The first group consisted of Orthodox Jews living in one of the most
religious neighborhoods in Jerusalem. The second group was com-
prised of the members of a very unorthodox San Francisco commune
I mentioned once before—Kerista Village.[1]

One Orthodox Jewish wife I interviewed said:

> I simply don't understand the concept of marriage burnout.
> When I was introduced to my husband, I didn't fall madly
> in love with him. But I knew right away that he was some-
> one I could share my life with, someone who had the same
> values and world view that I did. I don't expect either one of
> us to change our basic value system, so what is there that
> could possibly burn out?

This woman was saying, in effect, that since her religion gave her life its sense of meaning, she did not expect her marriage to do that. Consequently, she was not going to be disappointed in the marriage.[2] I would wager that I might find similar ideas about marriage in Amish communities, in Mormon communities, among evangelistic Christians, and among the devoutly religious all over the world. The deeply religious seek a connection with something larger than themselves in God. Thus, they are far less likely than nonreligious people to idealize romantic love and use it as the most important element in the selection of a mate. Instead, they are likely to seek someone who shares their religious beliefs.

In other conversations I had with Orthodox Jewish couples, I was told that an additional reason they are not likely to burn out is that they are better prepared for marriage than are nonreligious people. Schooling in the holy scriptures includes discussions of the proper relationship between husband and wife and the prescribed behavior for both. Secular schooling does not provide such (much needed) preparation for marriage. As different as members of Kerista Village were from the Orthodox Jews in their life style, the reason they gave to explain why they could never burn out is very similar. (I must add that the comparison was very distasteful to the Orthodox Jews.)

The eight men and eleven women of the commune termed their relationship "polyfidelity"—a coined word describing "a group of best friends living together with sexual intimacy occurring equally between all members of the opposite sex, no sexual involvement outside the group, a current intention of lifetime involvement, and an intention to raise children together with multiple parenting" (Pines and Aronson 1981, 374). Kerista Village resembled a traditional marriage in that members did not become sexually involved with each other until they had made the mutual commitment to lifetime involvement, and once that commitment was made, they were faithful to each other. It differed markedly from a traditional family in the assumptions that a long-term relationship doesn't need to be limited to two people and that a person is capable of loving many people equally and simultaneously. Sexual relationships within the commune were supposed to be nonpreferential (everyone loves everyone else equally) and happened within a rotating sleeping cycle.

The commune started over twenty years ago as an alternative life style with both personal and global goals (for example, overcoming sexual jealousy and working toward world peace). Jud, one of the founding members of the commune, explained: "Working on a vision together provides the basis for nonpreferential love in a group. In our group people don't draw security from each other. They draw it from their shared ideals."

All members of the commune described themselves as having been drawn to the group because of its ideals and lifestyle. They, like the Orthodox Jews, did not believe in romantic love as the most important basis for mate selection. They considered such love flimsy and short-lived because it is based on the shallow foundation of physical attraction. Since they didn't believe in romantic love, and they didn't make the commitment to the group marriage because of it, they argued there is no chance they will ever burn out.

In their book *Habits of the Heart,* sociologist Robert Bellah and his coauthors contrast two images of love: "Love as a spontaneous inner freedom, a deeply personal, but necessarily somewhat arbitrary, choice" and "love as a firmly planted, permanent commitment, embodying obligations that transcend the immediate feelings or wishes of the partners in a love relationship" (Bellah, et al. 1985, 93). The authors find that the second view of love is held most strongly among certain evangelical Christians for whom "emotion alone is too unstable a base on which to build a permanent relationship," who "must subordinate or tame their feelings so they follow the mind's guidance." Howard Crossland, a scientist from a rural background and an active member of an evangelical Christian church, is given as an example. Although Crossland and his wife of twelve years had a fairly good marriage, according to his own testimony, without the Christian faith he "probably would have been divorced by now" (Bellah, et al. 1985, 95).

Only in the Christian faith is it "logical" to say "till death do us part." Otherwise, "if the relationship is giving you trouble, perhaps it is easier to simply dissolve the thing legally, and go your way, than it is to maybe spend five years trying to work out a problem to make a lasting relationship." In any relationship there will be crises. The Christian faith allows you to "weather the storm until the calm comes back. If you can logically think through and kind of push the emotions to the back, I guess the love is always there. Sometimes it's blotted out." Crossland's definition of love is not very romantic: "when another's needs are greater than your own" (Bellah, et al. 1985, 95).

Like the Orthodox Jews and the polyfidelitous Keristans, the evangelical Christians reject romantic love as an important form of love and as the best basis for the foundation of a permanent relationship.

These three examples, as different as they are, draw our attention to the importance of shared ideals you can identify with, ideals you can get excited about, ideals that enable you to make a connection with something larger than yourself, something that makes your life matter in the larger scheme of things. Unfortunately, ideals are in pitifully short supply in our pragmatic and materialistic culture. (Making money and acquiring things don't quite make it as ideals.) In the absence of other ideals and ideologies, some relationships acquire a great value, and too much is expected of them.

Shared ideals have the same positive effect on couple relationships that are based on romantic love that they have on relationships based on a shared religious or political belief. The shared ideology provides roots of a deep emotional bond and a strong commitment, together with wings of joint opportunities for spiritual growth. In a life devoted to a religion, to working for world peace, or working for political change, where two people also love each other passionately, love is only one of the things that bind them, rather than being the only one. When love wanes temporarily—as it almost always does—the bond of their shared ideal keeps them together. In addition, the emotional arousal they both feel from working toward their ideal helps keep their romantic spark alive.

Walter and Betty are both in their fifties, and even after three decades of marriage are still very happy together. They have a satisfying sex life and a strong emotional and spiritual bond. In their youth, both of them were active members of a socialist group. They were excited about socialism and believed that socialist politics would make the world a better place. It was wonderful to be in love and share such ideals. Several times they were arrested together and it actually brought them closer and kept their relationship alive. Walter and Betty didn't get married because of their socialist ideology, but because they were "in love." Both the marriage and the ideology gave their life meaning.

Is Couple Burnout Inevitable?
Some Theoretical Answers

While relationships that are based on a shared religion or a shared ideology can be very satisfying, the couples in them are not struggling with the challenge to keep a romantic spark alive, since that spark wasn't important to them to begin with. Like Napoleon, they conquer love by running away from it. For those unwilling to forsake the ideal of romantic love, the knowledge that rejecting it can guarantee against burnout is not much of a comfort. Furthermore, even if we can conclude with certainty that burnout does not happen in relationships not based on romantic love, that doesn't tell us whether it is inevitable in relationships that *are* based on love.

Throughout this book I have argued that people who believe in romantic love expect it to give life a sense of meaning. Otto Rank describes modern man as fixing on his beloved his "urge to cosmic heroism" (Rank 1958, ch. 4; 1961, ch. 4). The love partner becomes the divine ideal within which to fulfill one's life. Ernest Becker expanded on Rank's ideas:

> As we know from our own experience this method gives
> great and real benefits. Is one oppressed by the burden of
> his life? Then he can lay it at his divine partner's feet. Is
> self-consciousness too painful, the sense of being a sepa-
> rate individual, trying to make some kind of meaning out
> of who one is, what life is, and the like? Then one can wipe
> it away in the emotional yielding to the partner, forget
> oneself in the delirium of sex, and still be marvelously
> quickened in the experience. . . . But we also know from
> experience that things don't work so smoothly or unam-
> biguously. The reason is not far to seek: it is right at the
> heart of the paradox of the creature. Sex is of the body, and
> the body is of death. (Becker 1973, 162)

The fact that romantic love has an erotic component, which is related to a sexual function of a mortal body, is according to Rank and Becker "central to the failure of romantic love as a solution to human problems, and is so much a part of modern man's frustration" (Becker 1973, 162–63). The procreative function of sex may assure the continuation of the species, but not the continuation of the unique individual. This is why sex is a "disappointing answer to life's riddle," and why the sexual partner does not and cannot represent a complete and lasting solution to the human dilemma (Becker 1973, 164–65).

The romantic solution, according to Rank and Becker, may be ingenious and creative, but because it is still an attempt to deny the mortal body by spiritualizing it, it is a lie that must fail. The failure of romantic love to give meaning to people's lives explains its "historical bankruptcy." "It is impossible to get blood from a stone, to get spirituality from a physical being." No human being can be "everything" to another. No human relationship can bear this burden, "and the attempt has to take its toll in some way on both parties" (Becker 1973, 166).

However much we may idealize and idolize our beloved, he or she can never be perfect because he or she is human and real. If that person is "everything" to us, then any shortcoming becomes a major personal threat to us. Like Augustine and Kierkegaard, Rank and Becker believe that since man cannot fashion an absolute from within his human and mortal condition, "cosmic heroism" must transcend human relationships and come from a belief in God.

Scott Peck is also sure that love must fail, but for a different reason. Peck defines love as "an effortful act of will." It is "the will to extend one's self for the purpose of nurturing one's own and another's spiritual growth" (Peck 1978, 81). According to this definition, as Peck notes, falling in love is not real love because it is not an act of will, and it is effortless. The proof for that is the annoying observation that "lazy and undisciplined individuals are as likely to fall in love as energetic and dedicated ones" (89). Also, falling in love is not real love because "the experience of falling in love is specifically a sex-linked erotic experience" (84). In addition, "the experience of falling in love is invariably temporary" (Peck 1978, 84).

> No matter whom we fall in love with, we sooner or later
> fall out of love if the relationship continues long enough.
> This is not to say that we invariably cease loving the
> person with whom we fell in love. But it is to say that
> the feeling of ecstatic lovingness that characterizes the
> experience of falling in love always passes. The honey-
> moon always ends. The bloom of romance always fades.
> (Peck 1978, 84)

To understand the nature of the phenomenon of falling in love and the inevitability of its ending, according to Peck, it is necessary to understand the nature of "ego boundaries"—the internalized images of our physical and psychological selves that define our individual identity as separate from the rest of the world. According to Peck, the essence of falling in love is:

> a sudden collapse of a section of an individual's ego
> boundaries, permitting one to merge his or her identity
> with that of another person. The sudden release of oneself
> from oneself, the explosive pouring out of oneself into the
> beloved, and the dramatic surcease of loneliness accompa-
> nying this collapse of ego boundaries is experienced by
> most of us as ecstatic. We and our beloved are one!
> Loneliness is no more! (Peck 1978, 87)

The collapse of ego boundaries is temporary and partial:

> Sooner or later, in response to the problems of daily living
> . . . reality intrudes upon the fantastic unity of the couple
> who have fallen in love . . . both of them, in the privacy of
> their hearts begin to come to the sickening realization that
> they are not one with the beloved, that the beloved has
> and will continue to have . . . desires, tastes, prejudices and
> timing different from the other's. One by one, gradually or
> suddenly, the ego boundaries snap back into place; gradu-
> ally or suddenly, they fall out of love. Once again they are
> two separate individuals. (Peck 1978, 88)

Once he has excluded falling in love from his definition of true
love, Peck has an easy time arguing that with will and discipline love
can remain in relationships indefinitely—but only in those relationships based on what he calls "real love," which is to say, a spiritual
rather than a physical love. Unfortunately, by excluding failing in
love from his definition, Peck excludes what is for many people the
most intense and significant emotional experience in their lives.

Social psychologist Elliot Aronson has another explanation for
why people fall out of love:

> In the words of the well-known ballad, "You always hurt
> the one you love." That is, once we have grown certain of
> the rewarding behavior of a person, that person may
> become less potent as a source of rewards than a stranger.
> (Aronson 1995, 393)

Because they have learned to expect love, favors, and praise from
their mate, after a while people start taking these for granted. Things

can't get any better than unqualified praise and adoration; but they can get worse. Therefore, with the passage of time, mates increase their power to hurt but lose the power to reward. An example Aronson presents helps clarify this point:

> After fifteen years of marriage, a doting husband and his wife are getting dressed to attend a formal dinner party. He compliments her on her appearance—"Gee, honey, you look great." She hears his words, but they do not fill her with delight. She already knows that her husband thinks she's attractive; she will not turn cartwheels at hearing about it for the thousandth time. On the other hand, if the doting husband (who in the past was always full of compliments) were to tell his wife that he had decided that she was losing her good looks and that he found her quite unattractive, this would cause her a great deal of pain, because it represents a distinct loss. (Aronson 1995, 395)

The longer the history of love, esteem, and reward, the easier it is to get used to them, and the more devastating is their withdrawal. A vivid description of this process appears in Marilyn French's novel *The Women's Room*:

> Marriage accustomed one to the good things, so one came to take them for granted, but magnified the bad things, so they came to feel as painful as a grain in one's eye. An opened window, a forgotten quart of milk, a TV left blaring, socks on the bathroom floor, could become occasions for incredible rage. (French 1977, 558)

Nathaniel Branden also describes the painful process of disillusionment in love in *The Psychology of Romantic Love*:

> Many persons begin a relationship genuinely in love and with good will and high hopes for the future, and then, across time, tragically, painfully, and with a good deal of bewilderment, watch the relationship deteriorate and ultimately collapse. They think back to the time when they were deeply in love, when so much seemed right and good and rewarding, and they are tortured by not knowing how

and why they lost what they had. If that love could die, they find themselves feeling, can any love last? Is romantic love possible for me at all? Or for anyone? (Branden 1983, 2)

Otto Rank, Ernest Becker, Scott Peck, Elliot Aronson, and Nathaniel Branden—all of them men—seem to be saying the same thing: Romantic love ends and burnout is inevitable. Depressing isn't it? Couples in love are almost universal in their desire to believe that burnout is not inevitable. Their response to the skepticism (backed, as we saw, by mountains of theory) is to insist that theirs is one of the rare exceptions.

Is Couple Burnout Inevitable? Research Evidence

If burnout is inevitable and a function of the time a couple has lived together, then it can be expected that the longer a relationship has lasted, the more burned out it will be. To find out if that is true, I conducted two studies. In the first, I tried to select people who varied as much as possible in terms of relationship length and style. The one hundred women and men who took part in the study included married, cohabiting, and living separately but seriously involved couples, in various traditional and nontraditional arrangements. The length of relationships varied from four months to forty-one years, with an average of seven years and seven months. By contrast, the second study included as homogeneous and traditional a bunch of married couples as I could find. For all but six of the one hundred couples in the study, this was the first marriage. Most couples had two or three children still living at home. The average length of the marriages— 15.1 years—was almost twice the average of the first study, and ranged from one to over thirty-four years.

Analysis of the data in both studies indicated that there was no correlation at all between the length of the relationship and burnout! If the mere passage of time produces burnout, there should be a strong correlation between the two. This, most definitely, was not the case. The correlation between time and burnout was virtually zero in both studies.[3]

Apparently, a long-term relationship has as good a chance of being vital and alive as a short-term one does of being dead. Sometimes mar-

riages that survived the test of time consisted of couples who had discovered how to stay not only married but also in love. Other times,
long-term marriages consisted of couples who could barely stand the
sight of each other, who stayed together for economic reasons (this
was particularly true for women), for the sake of the children, for lack
of a better alternative, or for fear of the unknown. A computer man in
his forties explained why he was staying in his burned-out marriage of
fifteen years:

> I don't expect anything from my marriage anymore, which
> suits me just fine. I don't get anything, but I also don't give
> anything, and I can invest myself in my work, where I feel
> I can make a significant contribution that will be recog-
> nized and appreciated. To get a divorce at this stage of the
> game would be too much hassle. I simply can't afford the
> waste of time and energy.

The data from the two studies seem to violate common sense and
disconfirm many people's personal experiences. Indeed, it is hard to
accept that time, together with the mundane problems of living, does
not facilitate disillusionment, boredom, and taking the other for
granted. The unequivocal nature of the findings, however, forces us
to search for a different explanation for burnout than the passage of
time. Even if most people will agree that the marriages that defy
burnout and remain vital over many years are the exceptions that
need analysis and explanation, we need to look for something other
than time to explain their rarity.

The study of these "abnormal" marriages was one of the most fascinating parts of my research. The fact that some couples stay married
for years, for decades, without falling out of love demonstrates why
burnout is not correlated with time. It also suggests, contrary to all the
theoretical arguments presented earlier, that burnout is not inevitable.

In many of the books and articles that have appeared in recent years
on staying together in an age of divorce, the focus has not been on
these "abnormal" couples (who are still in love even after many years)
but rather on the far larger group of couples who merely stay married
for twenty, thirty, fifty years, and more. The main question researchers
have addressed in their studies of these long-term marriages has been:
Why do some couples stay married? The far more interesting question,
in my opinion, is: Why do some couples stay in love?

These long-term couples-in-love seem to violate all the theoretical explanations for the inevitability of burnout. They continue to find "cosmic significance" in their relationships, even though it is with another mortal who is imperfect and is aging in front of their very eyes. They describe their sex life as exciting even though the arousal of the infatuation stage is long gone. And they have a strong sense of togetherness even though their ego boundaries are snapped securely into place.

Couples in Love

All couples would like to remain in love forever, but they go about preserving their love in very different ways. One of those ways was described by Robert Johnson in his book *We: Understanding the Psychology of Romantic Love.* It involves transforming the emotional arousal of falling in love into "stirring-the-oatmeal love," which, according to Johnson,

> symbolizes a relatedness that brings love down to earth . . .
> [and] represents a willingness to share ordinary human
> life, to find meaning in the simple, unromantic tasks. . . .
> To "stir the oatmeal" means to find the relatedness, the
> value, even the beauty, in simple and ordinary things, not
> to eternally demand a cosmic drama, an entertainment, or
> an extraordinary intensity in everything. . . . It represents
> the discovery of the sacred in the midst of the humble and
> ordinary. . . . The real relatedness between two people is
> experienced in the small tasks they do together: the quiet
> conversation when the day's upheavals are at rest, the soft
> word of understanding, the daily companionship, the
> encouragement offered in a difficult moment, the small
> gift when least expected, the spontaneous gesture of love.
> When a couple are genuinely related to each other, they
> are willing to enter the whole spectrum of human life
> together. They transform even the unexciting, difficult,
> and mundane things into a joyful and fulfilling compo-
> nent of life. (Johnson 1983, 195–96)

In a "stirring-the-oatmeal love," people find meaning in the little joys of day-to-day living with an intimate partner. For some people, however, leading a "down-to-earth" existence pales in comparison with the thrill and ecstasy of falling in love with a new person. For such people, falling in love is the most fulfilling part of the relationship. It is the quality of this experience, rather than the quality of the particular relationship, that they want to preserve. They are players in a "cosmic drama," and love is a magical experience that they have no control over. They want to be open to the possibility that love will "strike" them at any moment because, for them, it is the most significant experience in life and the highest "high." So they stay in a relationship only as long as the intensity and passion are there and leave when they wane, waiting to be struck by love again with another person. Alan Watts describes this "divine madness" and says that "making it the basis for marriage is an extraordinarily dangerous thing to do" (Watts 1985. 21):

> Falling in love is a thing that strikes like lightning and is,
> therefore, extremely analogous to the mystical vision. . . .
> We do not really know how people obtain [them], and
> there is not as yet a very clear rationale as to why it hap-
> pens. If you should be so fortunate as to encounter either
> of these experiences, it seems to me to be a total denial of
> life to refuse it. (Watts 1985, 23)

It is interesting that Alan Watts describes as a "denial of life" the same experience that Ernest Becker describes as "a denial of death." Both authors see the denial as motivated by fear. Thus, they seem to suggest that the fear of life and the fear of death are flip sides of the same experience. Both authors note that one person who in the eyes of everyone else is a perfectly plain and ordinary person, can appear to be a god or goddess incarnate to someone smitten with love. For both, the deification of the beloved shows that romantic love gives ordinary people a vehicle for cosmic heroism.

The "stirring-the-oatmeal love" described by Robert Johnson emphasizes the roots of a relationship. The "divine madness" described by Alan Watts emphasizes its wings. A third kind of love relationship involves, of course, both "roots and wings." People enter the three kinds of relationships with different expectations, face in each one different dangers, and when their expectations are not met, they are disappointed differently.

In a "divine-madness" love, they expect an ecstatic bonding with a beloved who represents the whole world. There are two dangers in this kind of love, both related to the collapse of ego boundaries characterizing it. One danger is that one would be lost in the love, unable to regain one's sense of self. The other danger is that with each successive series of such temporary mystical experiences there will be no ego growth, and when it's over, because such a state can't last indefinitely, the feeling is of disappointment and betrayal by the unmet promise of love.

In a "stirring-the-oatmeal" love, people expect permanence, security, stability, and understanding. Love is reduced to what can be controlled by acts of will, and the ego boundaries are all in place. There are two dangers in this kind of love as well. One danger is that the love will die because of the lack of emotional intensity. The other danger is that despite the commitment, one mate will still fall in love with someone else and leave. In both cases, the disappointment and betrayal are related to the failure of security to give meaning to life.

In a "roots and wings" love, the expectations are highest and seemingly contradictory—namely, to get the relatedness, the permanence, and the security of the oatmeal, with the emotional, physical, and spiritual intensity of the divine madness. In such a relationship, mates' ego boundaries are partially collapsed permanently. While there is both a danger of losing one's sense of self in the relationship, *and* a danger of betrayal by the mate and the subsequent loss of security—the two are contradictory and can balance each other out. In relationships with roots and wings mates live a contradiction: they lose their ego in the unification with each other, and at the same time strengthen their egos and sense of self—because the roots enable them to develop wings. Despite the difficulty involved in balancing these contradictory expectations, some couples succeed in achieving the balance and thus assure that their relationship will remain exciting yet still provide the gentle comfort of security.

Since the romantic solution can't solve the existential dilemma, every version of that solution is going to fail in some way. While relationships with roots and wings are just one such solution, some couples seem able to live with this particular compromise quite happily, looking at their relationship as a creative challenge. The intensity of such a relationship does not derive from the hope that it will give meaning to life, but from the realization that it actually does, and that one's mate is indeed "the one." Instead of the promise of a relationship, it reflects the joy of having the promise come true. Instead of fears about the future, there are certainties based on years of life together. This was articulated by the Italian sociologist Francesco Alberoni in his book *Falling in Love*:

Falling in love, when all goes well, ends in love; the movement, when it succeeds, produces an institution. But the relationship between falling in love and love itself, between nascent state and institution, is comparable to that between taking off or flying and landing, between being in the sky above the clouds and firmly setting foot on the ground again. Consider another image, that of the flower and the fruit. The fruit issues from the flower, but they are two different things. When there is fruit, there is no longer any flower. And there is really no point in asking if the flower is better than the fruit or vice versa. By the same token, there is no point in asking whether the nascent state is better than the institution. One does not exist without the other. Life is made up of both. Still, there is no point in confusing them, because they are distinct. (Alberoni 1983)

Falling in love involves the romantic images people have before being confronted by the realities of daily life, the images that draw them to a particular person. Those who dismiss falling in love as not "the real thing" miss out on extremely important data that affect couple's expectations. Couples who believe in romantic love, and do not have a shared religious or political belief, can make that dream their shared ideal.

Is Couple Burnout Inevitable? The Romantic Answer

When Rank and Becker argue that sex, which is a bodily function, can't possibly give spiritual significance to life, they are right. Yet the conclusion they reach—that as a result, the burnout of love is inevitable—is not. Why? Because sex is only the basis on which we impose our ideology of romantic love. That ideology itself is spiritual, and as such capable of giving life a sense of significance. The ecstasy generated by the fulfillment of a romantic ideal can replace sexual arousal, which diminishes with time.

Rollo May discusses in *Love and Will* the difference between sex and love (eros) and argues that, in our society, some people use sex as a way to avoid involvement with eros. He writes:

Eros is the drive toward union with what we belong to—union with our own possibilities, union with significant other persons in our world in relation to whom we discover our own self fulfillment. Eros is the yearning in man which leads him to dedicate himself to seek arate, the noble and good life.

Sex . . . is the mode of relating characterized by tumescence of the organs (for which we seek the pleasurable relief) and filled gonads (for which we seek satisfying release). But eros is the mode of relating in which we do not seek release but rather to cultivate, procreate, and form the world. In eros, we seek increase of stimulation. Sex is a need, but eros is a desire.

The ancients made Eros a "god," or more specifically a daimon. This is a symbolic way of communicating a basic truth of human experience, that eros always drives us to transcend ourselves. . . . The ancients, taking sex for granted simply as a natural bodily function, saw no need to make it into a god. (May 1969, 72–73)

What about the argument that burnout is inevitable because our beloveds are mortal human beings and as such incapable of giving indefinitely a sense of cosmic significance to our lives?

The best answer to this argument comes from those couples who continue to get a sense of meaning from their relationships despite their beloveds' humanness. For these couples, romantic love may be a more appealing answer to the existential dilemma than any other belief. Other people—who feel that they don't have control over romantic love, who do not feel that romantic love could answer the central question of life's meaning, or who cannot make the "leap of faith" required to make a commitment to one person—commit themselves to God, to a political ideology, or to the modern alternative of work. People who are willing to make this leap of faith in romantic love, on the other hand, see themselves as having control over their love. These people seek romantic love, and some of them find it.

For such people, as noted earlier, a certain part of the ego boundaries is permanently collapsed. There is a sense of "we," a shared identity that coexists along with their individual identities. Such people do not become "as one" in everything. Simply, a certain part of themselves has blended with their mate, even after the stage of falling in love is over. The sense of "we-ness," the bonding, the togetherness, are associated with feelings of safety and security that are counterbalanced by openness to growth.

The reader may recall Aronson's example of Mr. and Mrs. Doting who have, with the passage of time, growing power to hurt each other but diminished power to provide each other with meaningful rewards. This pessimistic future can be avoided, but only when mates are willing to take responsibility for creating an open, honest, and authentic relationship in which they are able to share their true feelings with each other and to grow:

> Although Mr. Doting has great power to hurt his wife (by telling her that she is losing her looks), Mrs. Doting is apt to be very responsive to such criticism and will likely strive to gain his interest. It goes without saying that the reverse is also true: If Mrs. Doting suddenly was to change her high opinion of Mr. Doting, he could—and chances are that he would—take action to regain her approval. A relationship becomes truly creative and continues to grow when both partners strive to grow and change in creative ways—and in all of this "authenticity" assumes great importance. Carrying this reasoning a step further, the more honest and authentic a relationship, the less the possibility of reaching the kind of dull and deadening plateau on which the Dotings appear stuck. (Aronson 1995, 393)

Creativity and striving to grow and change are the wings of the relationship. They also increase a couple's ability to reward each other. In a closed relationship, mates are far less likely to change, or improve, or reward each other:

In a closed relationship, people tend to suppress their annoyances and to keep their negative feelings to themselves. This results in a fragile plateau that appears stable and positive but that can be devastated by a sudden shift in sentiment. Unfortunately, this may be a common kind of relationship in this country. In an open, honest, authentic relationship, one in which people are able to share their true feelings and impressions (even their negative ones), no such plateau is reached. Rather, there is a continuous zigzagging of sentiment around a point of relatively high esteem. (Aronson 1995, 394)

When couples suppress their negative feelings, there is no way for them to deal directly with those feelings, and no way to grow as individuals and as a couple. Honesty, of course, is not always motivated by a desire for communication and for growth. Sometimes people use honesty as a weapon against each other. This kind of honesty can be cruel and damaging. Its use is one of the ways in which couples increase their power to punish each other. But the nondefensive, aimed-at-self-growth exploration of negative feelings and taboo subjects (which was discussed in chapter 6) also characterizes what Aronson terms "open, honest and authentic relationships."

So all a couple needs to make a love relationship work is to "strive to grow and change in creative ways," right? Sounds simple, doesn't it? If it is so simple, why do so many couples who get married because of love, who desperately want the marriage to work, end up trapped in dead relationships? One place to look for an answer, once again, is the environment. If the life circumstances that a couple has to face are extremely stressful, it is reasonable to assume that they will take their toll on the relationship. Yet the experiences of couples who have survived wars and natural disasters and whose relationships were not weakened but actually strengthened by the experience suggest that this is not always the case.

Burnout is not inevitable even in the most stressful of situations because it depends on the way the stress is perceived by people. One of the happiest couples I interviewed had been married over fifty years, had escaped Nazi Germany, and had gone through the long and hard years of the war together. This stress did not break their spirit or their marriage. On the contrary, it made them stronger, more appreciative of each other, and more committed to each other. Both of them felt that having the other was the only thing that kept them going—even when hungry, sick, and exhausted. Together, they felt united in a struggle against a cruel and hostile world.

What is it, then, that makes some people stronger and others weaker as a result of the same stress? According to personality psychologist Susan Kobasa, the answer is "hardiness" (Kobasa, 1979). "Hardiness" defines a particular personality structure that is resistant to illness even in situations of great stress. In her studies, Kobasa looked at groups that were similar in terms of background and work and life stresses yet different in terms of vulnerability to illness. Under the same conditions of stress one group got sick, while the other one, which was later termed "hardy," did not. What differentiated people in the hardy group from those in the nonhardy group were:

• Involvement—as opposed to alienation—and curiosity about the environment, which they perceived as interesting and significant.

• Control—as opposed to helplessness—and belief in their ability to influence their environment with ideas, words, and actions.

• Challenge—as opposed to indifference—and an assumption that change is natural, necessary, and important for growth.

People in the hardy group were interested in and cared about everything around them. Whenever they were involved in an activity, they were all-absorbed by it. They felt they were leading rich and meaningful lives. They felt in control of their environment, and believed that they had a significant impact on it. They took responsibility for creating the kind of lives they wanted to live. When things did not work out for some reason, they confronted obstacles directly and actively, and saw them as a challenge. They loved change and looked for it in their work and in their intimate relationships.

People in the nonhardy group were far less interested in their environment, which they tended to see as insignificant, boring, or threatening. They felt alienated from the people around them, and helpless against what they saw as hostile, all-powerful forces. They disliked change and were fearful of it. They believed that life is best when not threatened by change, and did not consider growth possible or important. They were passive and pessimistic, always expecting the worst, and because of that, only willing to give the least of themselves.

Kobasa came to a not very startling conclusion: It is better to be hardy than to be nonhardy. This kind of statement may be nice for the naturally hardy person to hear, but it is not of much value for the nonhardy person. It is possible, however, to view hardiness not as an inborn attribute but as a way of interacting with the environment that is often learned in childhood, but that can be learned in adulthood as well.

From this perspective, the hardy person can be seen as more likely to make situational attributions in dealing with the world, the nonhardy person as more likely to make dispositional attributions. When we transfer the concept of hardiness from an individual to a couple, we can see that its three components—involvement, control, and challenge—are as important for couples as they are for individuals. While hardy couples see a certain stress as a challenge within their control that provides an opportunity for growth, the nonhardy couples are likely to feel alienated, threatened, and powerless, thus enhancing their burnout.

Shifting from the dispositional attribution of hardiness as a personality structure to hardiness as a set of attitudes that is learned, and thus can be unlearned and relearned, leaves some hope even for those people unlucky enough to have been raised nonhardy or to have created a nonhardy relationship. How does one learn to be hardy? Culture, it turns out, has a lot to do with it. Different cultures socialize people to perceive the world around them differently and to cope with it differently. In some cultures (such as Israel), there is an emphasis on direct and active coping; in others (such as Japan), indirect coping is valued more. These cultural differences have a big influence on the likelihood of burnout, above and beyond the effect that cultures have on people's expectations from their intimate relationships and from their life in general. The comparison between Israelis and Americans is an example.

As anyone who has spent time in both countries knows, life in Israel is considerably more stressful than life in the United States. There are physical and emotional stresses of ongoing warfare with Arabs within and around Israel and compulsory military service (which for women is two years, for young men is three years and for men on reserve duty is one month a year until they are fifty-five). There are economic stresses, and there are tensions between groups of different cultural origins, religious beliefs, and political affiliations. It is natural to expect that burnout would be higher in Israel than in America. The data, however, show Israelis reporting lower levels of burnout than Americans.[4] It is noteworthy that the same results were found in all the studies in which samples from the two countries were compared. These studies—which involved comparable groups in terms of sex, age, and profession—investigated burnout both on the job and in marriage. Their data confirmed the same unexpected result There are several reasons why this might be so:

• Israelis have more realistic expectations of life, work, and marriage because the Israeli culture does not build in as many unrealistic expectations as the American culture does; they are therefore less likely to be disappointed.

• Israelis expect, more than Americans, that their marriages will last forever, and have a stronger commitment to them than Americans have.

• Israelis' coping tends to be more confrontational (active and direct) than Americans' (Americans' coping tends to be more avoidance-based and more dependent on crutches such as drugs and alcohol), and as such is more likely to produce changes (Etzion and Pines 1986; Etzion, Pines, and Kafry 1983).

• The existential problems in Israel, on both the personal and the national levels, are so immense that marital problems and other personal problems seem trivial by comparison. Americans live in a fairly benign culture, where one's marital and personal problems loom large.

• The social structure in Israel provides more support for individuals and couples, and Israelis' social support networks are more stable and protect them better from stress.

• The one-month-a-year military service gives the Israeli couple an important yearly vacation from each other, a vacation that helps reaffirm the significance of their relationship and reestablish their commitment to each other.

• There are stronger social norms against admitting to personal or marital problems among Israelis. Because of such cultural sanctions Israelis are less likely than Americans to admit it to themselves and to others.

• Israelis experience less burnout than Americans, not in spite of their greater stress, but because of it. When an American fails, either on the job or in marriage, the focus of the blame is most often dispositional ("How could I be so dumb!"). When an Israeli fails, on the other hand, the blame is assigned most often to the situation or the system ("the lousy government," "the crazy economy"). Israelis are much less likely to blame themselves for failure. Their networks of family and friends also tend to reinforce that outward-directed focus of blame.

Since there is no reason to think that Israelis are constitutionally different from Americans, we can assume that Israeli couples, either because of their situation or because of the way they have learned to deal with problems, have learned how to cope with burnout better.

The comparison between Israelis and Americans, combined with the discussion of the individual differences mediating between the environment and burnout, leads again to the conclusion that burnout depends on the interaction between people and their subjective environment, and thus is not inevitable. This ought to be good news not only for married couples who are struggling with burnout in their relationships but also for people who have shunned serious relationships because they fear that "there is no hope. If every marriage ends unhappily, why bother?"

The implication from the conclusion that burnout is not inevitable is not always eagerly drawn or accepted, however, because it implies that couples have more power to influence the quality of their relationship than some care to admit. The power results from the fact that couples are actually providing part of the "subjective environment" for each other. In other words, each mate is part of the environment of the other. Couples are not only affected by the environment in which they live; they also influence and affect it. A science fiction story I read as a child demonstrates that effect.

> Two scientists wish to discover the origin of an ancient god symbolized by a winged lightning bolt. According to legend, the mysterious god visited earth and then vanished. Using a time machine, the scientists go back in time and experience many thrilling adventures. At the end of their last adventure, they are pursued by a group of angry warriors and barely make it back to the time machine to escape the past and return to their own time. Once safely back home again, the scientists recount their adventures, noting that they have failed to find the origin of the winged-snake god. Suddenly they notice that there is a sign of lightning on their safety helmets. They realize that they themselves, visiting the ancient people and later disappearing in their time machine amid clouds of smoke and fire, must have been the origin of the legend.

Like the scientists back in time, we all play an active part in creating our relationships. And like those scientists, we often don't notice our own impact. Yet our influence is very powerful. It derives in part from the power of self-fulfilling prophecies, which was demonstrated in a fascinating experiment by social psychologist Mark Snyder and his colleagues (Snyder 1979). In the experiment, pairs of unacquainted male and female students participated in what they thought was an investigation of the processes by which people become acquainted.

Participants in the study were told that they would engage in a brief telephone conversation with a person of the opposite sex and that they were to get acquainted with that person. Male subjects received a snapshot of what they believed was the female they were about to talk to. The snapshots were actually chosen previously because they received either very high or very low ratings of attractiveness. The decision whether a man would get a picture of a very attractive or unattractive woman was made randomly and had nothing to do with the actual woman he talked to. Female subjects did not get snapshots and knew nothing about them being given to the men.

Each twosome then engaged in ten minutes of unstructured conversation by means of microphones and headphones ("Where are you from?" "What's your major?" etc.). A tape recorder recorded each participant's voice on a separate channel of the tape. Raters, who knew neither the subjects nor the true purpose of the study, listened only to the track of the tape containing the women's voices. They rated those voice recordings on dimensions such as animation, flirtatiousness, enthusiasm, intimacy, and friendliness.

The results of the study showed that those women who (unbeknown to them) were perceived by the men they were talking to as very attractive actually talked in a more flirtatious, friendly, and likable manner. Those women who spoke with men who thought them unattractive, on the other hand, were more cool and aloof.

Similarly in intimate relationships, people who perceive their mates as unattractive behave toward them in a way that helps bring out their mates' more unattractive qualities and thus fulfills their negative prophecy. Such people can be surprised to discover that their mates are much more attractive—flirtatious, friendly, warm—in outside social encounters. This surprise is especially painful and disturbing when it happens after a divorce that was initiated because of the mate's supposed unattractiveness. A man who divorced his wife because he saw her as homely, unattractive, and asexual was shocked to discover that, after the divorce, his wife had blossomed into the sexy, elegant, and interesting woman she was when they first met—the kind of woman he was now searching for.

The same person, depending on the situation, can be sexual or asexual, flirtatious or reserved, warm or cold, exciting or boring. Being treated as physically attractive by your mate is likely to bring out more of your physically attractive behavior. That behavior, in turn, will reinforce your mate's perception of you. Both partners have the power (even if not an equal power) to influence the quality of their relationship. A couple's ability to avoid burnout depends, in large measure, on both mates' willingness to take (at least some) responsibility for what happens in the relationship. Some couples avoid taking this responsibility because they are socialized by romantic myths to expect the romantic spark to remain in the relationship all by itself—effortlessly, spontaneously—by magic.

This socialization to passivity is akin to a training toward nonhardiness of people whose approach to the world and everything else can be active and direct. The negative effects of such training for passivity are compounded by the effects of socially sanctioned, unrealistic expectations that are bound to disappoint, as well as by the erosion caused by everyday living.

There is another reason people avoid taking action in love relationships—fear:

> The old myths and symbols by which we oriented ourselves are gone, anxiety is rampant . . . we do not will because we are afraid that if we choose one thing or one person we'll lose the other, and we are too insecure to take the chance. The bottom then drops out of the conjunctive emotions and processes—of which love and will are the two foremost examples. (May 1969, 13)

Earnest awareness of the dangers of burnout is not enough. In order to avoid burnout one needs to take action. Couples who take action don't need awareness of what they are doing right to have a vital relationship. Still, awareness is a good first step. As with any problem, it is important to be aware and to desire change, but much more direct action is needed to reverse a problem once it has occurred.

While it is definitely true that one human is incapable of fulfilling all of another's needs, some couples manage to live with this reality quite successfully. That is not to say that they don't have problems, disagreements or disappointments. But they take responsibility, and use problems, disagreements, and disappointments as opportunities to learn more about themselves and each other.

Their success can be attributed, at least in part, to an environment that is supportive, challenging, and relatively stress-free. Their success can also be attributed to positive childhood experiences that enabled them to develop romantic images that are compatible, achievable, and growth enhancing. Another important part is a cluster of attitudes that includes:

• A high degree of commitment to the relationship as opposed to a "take it or leave it" attitude.

• A sense of control over the relationship as opposed to an "it doesn't matter what I do" attitude.

• A love of challenge as opposed to an "it can't be done anyway, so what's the point of even trying" attitude.

Armed with this set of attitudes, these couples channel their creative energies into creating a love relationship that satisfies their most important physical, emotional, spiritual, and intellectual needs. Having committed themselves to what Erich Fromm calls "the art of loving" (Fromm 1956), they build their relationships with the energy and creativity that an artist puts into building an important work of art.

A Note to Therapists

A therapist's attitudes, values, and beliefs—whether acknowledged or not—have a powerful impact on the therapeutic process. If a therapist believes that a certain procedure will work, chances are that the people undergoing that procedure will believe it too. All things considered, it is best for couples and for couple therapists to believe that burnout is not inevitable.

8

High and Low Burnout Couples

To be loved, be lovable.

—Ovid, *The Art of Love*

Ovid, the Roman poet, in his counsel for lovers seeking romantic success, suggested that love be seen as an art to be mastered. A similar suggestion was made nineteen centuries later by Erich Fromm in *The Art of Loving*:

> There is hardly any activity, any enterprise, which starts with such tremendous hopes and expectations, and yet which fails so regularly, as love. If this were the case with any other activity, people would be eager to know the reasons for the failure, and learn how one could do better—or they would give up the activity. . . . The first step to take is to become aware that love is an art; if we want to learn how to love we must proceed in the same way we have to proceed if we want to learn any other art. . . . The process of learning an art can be divided conveniently into two parts: one, mastery of the theory; the other, the mastery of the practice. . . . But, aside from learning the theory and practice, there is a third factor necessary to becoming a master in any art—the mastery of the art must be a matter of ultimate concern. (Fromm 1956, 45)

How does one master the art of love? Does mastering the art guarantee no burnout? One way to answer these questions is to look at couples who did burn out and couples who did not, which is just what I did. In examining the descriptions couples gave about their relationships, it was possible to identify what differentiated between those who burned out and those who, after the same number of years, had relationships that were vital and passionate.

In one study involving one hundred couples, I compared the 17 percent who had the highest scores on the Burnout Measure (see Appendix 1) with the 17 percent who had the lowest burnout scores.[1] The two groups were similar in terms of age, number of children, and length of the marriage. In analyzing the data, I found ten variables that best accounted for the differences in burnout between them. The ten variables are discussed in this chapter in order of their significance as burnout correlates. Each one of these variables touches, in one way or another, on issues discussed throughout the book. In that sense, this chapter represents a summary as well as a translation of the abstract ideas expressed in the book into the actual life experiences of couples. While the variables will be presented separately, it is important to emphasize that they never operate in isolation. They are all dynamically interrelated, affecting and being affected by each other in all relationships and at all times.

Because it can be cumbersome and confusing to compare the way these variables operate in the lives of different men and women in the high and low burnout groups, I use two couples as examples, both of whom were mentioned several times throughout the book. One couple—Dona and Andrew—is my yardstick for burnout; the other—Ellen and Anthony—is an example of a loving couple.

Looking Positively at the Relationship as a Whole

The biggest difference between the high and the low burnout groups was in a couple's ability to look positively at the relationship as a whole (as opposed to focusing on a particular annoyance or trait).[2] Ellen, in the low-burnout group, explains:

> I am careful about money, and Anthony is casual, even
> wasteful. I like to plan what I'm going to do with our
> money, and to spend money on things that we both value,

and he just lets it run through his fingers without knowing what he spent it on. I often look on his attitude toward money with complete bewilderment. . . . There is something else too. . . . He burns pots. Not just once, or twice, or three times. He burns pots about once a month. He puts the kettle on the stove, or puts on a pot of soup, and then he starts reading and the next thing you know the whole house is full of smoke. . . . But every time I get furious with him, I stop short of saying "That's it, I've had it" because I remember what a good thing we have going between us; how lucky I feel to have a husband who is my best friend, with whom I can talk about everything, who is loving and supportive even after all these years.

Ellen can keep her composure over little things, like scorched pots, and big things, like money, because she knows that Anthony is right for her, her best friend. What about a guy who burns pots and can't or won't communicate with his wife, a guy who isn't her best friend? Dona, in the high-burnout group, explains how her husband's annoying habits make her feel toward him and toward their marriage:

What really gets me are the things he does repeatedly, things that seem to be motivated by nothing else but a desire to drive me crazy . . . like putting away in the garage all my beautiful cups, because he thinks it's enough to have two cups in the house. . . . Or like his habit of not paying parking tickets till they've tripled the fine . . . Or not carrying insurance.

Andrew sees things differently:

I am not a very organized person, but I have my own priorities and my own order. I am very careful about things I consider important, and I take care of things in my own way and in my own time. But that was not good enough for her. She wanted me to do things the way she wanted it done and when she wanted it done. When I wouldn't she would have a fit.

When people are able to look positively at the relationship as a whole, burned pots, parking tickets, and tidying up can be seen in context. But when love has gone out of a relationship, little annoyances can become the focus of incredible rage. Anger out of proportion to the crime is perhaps the clearest sign of the disappointment in love. On the other hand, if a relationship continues to provide a sense of meaning, couples are able to turn aside anger and remember how much joy the relationship provides. Such couples are less likely to burn out.

While a correlation does not tell us about causality, so it is not clear whether burnout causes the focus on the little irritations of a relationship or whether focusing on these little irritations causes burnout; one thing is clear: the two are closely related. Dona even kept track of these irritations:

> A lot of things took place on symbolic occasions, which made them easy to remember. One of the things that in fact cemented my decision to get a divorce was my birthday. I got a phone call at six o'clock in the morning from Europe, from a cousin, wishing me a happy birthday. Here was someone far away, taking the trouble. And Andrew just sat there listening. He didn't even say "Happy birthday!"
> ... I'd given him a lot of opportunities to get me a present because it is also symbolic. And I said I'd like a book, maybe a book certificate. And here's what he said when I got home from work that night: "I went to look for a book, but then I decided that a book or a book certificate wasn't a good idea. Why don't you just go to the bookstore and pick out a book you want?" Which I haven't done, obviously. I suddenly realized that here are all these people who love me, and here is my husband who doesn't even appreciate me. He doesn't value me. He doesn't love me. If he did he wouldn't treat me the way he did. He would want to do something special for me.... I kept a hate book all these years. Whenever I've been depressed or upset I've written it down. I've got in this book fourteen years worth.

Keeping the hate book helped Dona focus on the negative and remember all the bad times she had experienced in her fourteen years with Andrew. We can assume that if she had kept a love book instead, she might have been able to remember the good times. Whenever something happened that bothered her, she could have looked in her love book and remembered what was good about her marriage. Ellen describes keeping track of the good:

> I don't like to carry grudges. I don't like harping on the past or on things that I can't do anything about. I imagine myself standing on a bridge, throwing whatever troubles me down and seeing it flowing away with the "water under the bridge." I remember getting very upset with Anthony on my birthday. My family and friends gave me a big party, which was very touching, and made me feel loved. The only one who did not give me a gift was Anthony. I was very hurt. After everyone else was gone, and after some hesitation, I asked him why he hadn't bothered to get me a gift. He said he was obsessing about it for weeks, knowing how important such things were for me. But as hard as he tried, he couldn't come up with something that he felt sure would make me happy. By the day of the birthday he said he was in a real panic. He finally decided just to wait and ask me what I wanted to get from him. I can't say it really made it all right. Birthdays, anniversaries—all those occasions are very important to me. I wished he had given me something . . . anything. . . . I told him that, just as I tell him all my feelings. And as I was doing that I was thinking how lucky I am to be able to tell him I am upset. It was something I had never been able to do with my first husband. Anthony and I talked for quite a while about the birthday and at the end I just sent the rest of my bad feelings with the water under the bridge.

While it is possible to argue that the difference between Dona and Ellen in their handling of "the birthday issue" reflects a basic difference in personality, and that Dona's personality type is more prone to burnout, I can state unequivocally that Ellen's way of looking at the problem can be learned.

Jeannette and Robert Lauer studied three hundred couples in marriages that lasted at least fifteen years. Their goal was to identify the characteristics of long-term happy marriages. They found that:

> Couples in a happy marriage genuinely like and respect each other. Husband and wife consider their spouse to be

their best friend and generally would rather be in their company than anyone else's.

Happy couples had their major conflicts over the years, but always kept in mind that "the relationship was more important than any issue that came up." Happy couples argue by focusing on the issue rather than the person. Happy couples spend most of their leisure time together. Happy couples realize that marriage is rarely a 50–50 proposition. They seem to know that sometimes you have to give 80 percent and get only 20 percent and realize that over time it tends to balance out. (Lauer and Lauer 1985)

All four of these characteristics reflect, in one way or another, an ability (willingness?) to look positively at the relationship. When your mate is your best friend, annoyances are kept in perspective. When your best times are together, bad times are seen within that positive context. When, as you tackle problems, you can keep the relationship foremost in your mind, minor conflicts are not likely to become major destructive fights. When you are willing to give more than your "fair share," this is likely to be reciprocated and become the norm.

Similar findings were reported by Florence Kaslow and Helga Hammerschmidt in a study in which they tried to identify the essential ingredients in long-term "good" marriages. The study, which was based primarily on data from mailed questionnaires, also emphasized the importance of friendship, commitment, and shared values in keeping marriages happy over time (Kaslow and Hammerschmidt, 1992).

John Gottman, in his recent book *Why Marriages Succeed or Fail*, describes the results of a landmark investigation including 20 different studies and 2,000 couples. Goffman and his many colleagues analyzed three videotapes of couples both during conversation and during viewing sessions in which they described what they had been thinking and feeling during certain moments of their filmed interaction. The tapes' data were correlated with electronically measured physiological responses and with questionnaires and interview data. The main conclusion Gottman reports is that it is possible to actually quantify the ratio of positive to negative interactions needed to maintain a marriage in good shape. Satisfied couples, it turns out—whether they are conflict avoiders, conflict seekers, or validators—are those couples who maintain a five-to-one ratio of positive to negative moments. Relationships thrive on, proportionately, a little negativity and a lot of positivity. The total amounts can vary, argues Gottman, but the proportion between the pluses and minuses must remain the same. With a five-to-one ratio, I would argue, couples maintain an overall positive evaluation of their relationship (Gottman 1995).

Another recent book by Judith Wallerstein and Sandra Blakeslee, addresses the question of what are the makings of *The Good Marriage: How and Why Love Lasts*. The book is based on an in-depth study of fifty couples who consider themselves happily married. The men and women interviewed by Wallerstein readily admitted that even the best relationships require hard work and continuing negotiation. Nevertheless, for almost all of them the marriage was perceived as the single greatest accomplishment; in other words, the relationship gave their life a sense of meaning.

> Each person felt strongly that on balance their marriage
> had a goodness of fit in needs, wishes, and expectations. . . .
> They spoke movingly, often lyrically, about how much they
> valued, respected, and enjoyed the other person and how
> appreciative they were of the other's responsiveness to their
> needs. (Wallerstein and Blakeslee 1995, 328)

Many times, people at social gatherings asked Wallerstein what she discovered in her study about what makes a good marriage. Since she did not have a one-line answer, she often turned the question back to the asker. Her all time favorite is a response she got from a woman who said laughing: "Do I know what makes a happy marriage? A bad memory." "She had a point" writes Wallerstein. "Surely, being able to forget the day-to-day disappointments and keep one's eyes on the big issues is what is needed to make a marriage go, . . . separating the trivial from the important" (Wallerstein and Blakeslee 1995, 328). This is the power of looking positively at the relationship as a whole.

Quality and Quantity of Communication

"How much time do you and your spouse spend daily in direct communication with each other? This does not include time spent together doing things that do not require talking, or time spent together talking to other people. How satisfied are you with the quality of your communication with your spouse? How many taboo subjects do the two of you have—subjects that affect the relationship but are never talked about (such as attraction to other people or feelings toward inlaws)?" The second highest difference between the low- and the high-burnout groups was the difference in quality and quantity of their communication.[3]

Happy couples described themselves as talking "all the time" and as being able to talk about "absolutely everything." Burned-out couples described great difficulty in talking to each other, even about trivial issues. Their communication tended to be curt, mechanical, and kept to the bare minimum. Ellen attributes much of the success of her second marriage to "the magic of passionate words":

> My first husband and I were not really honest with each
> other. There were so many subjects that were taboo, that
> he would raise hell if I dared bring up. Toward the end of
> our marriage all we ever talked about were things like who
> would pick the kids up from piano lesson. We never talked
> about being attracted to someone else. That was simply
> unacceptable. But, of course, in the ten years of our mar-
> riage it did happen. So we had to deny it, which made us
> lie to ourselves and to each other. After doing it for so
> long I didn't know whether it was even possible to untan-
> gle this gigantic tangle of lies, half-truths, and things
> unspoken. This is why I value so much my relationship
> with Anthony. We share everything with each other. It is
> such a relief not to have to worry about what can and
> can't be said, to be able to share every thought and feel-
> ing. Of course, it also means feeling a pang of jealousy
> when he tells me another woman looks sexy. But experi-
> ences like that also add spice to life.

As part of my research on couple burnout, I asked people what were the major stresses in their marriages and how they coped with them. I presented them with a list of twelve coping strategies (see coping grid, pg. 198) including: I try to change the source of the stress; I ignore the source of stress (or my spouse); I talk about it with a supportive friend; I drink, take a tranquilizer or a drug; I confront my spouse directly; I avoid the source of stress (or my spouse); I try to find the positive aspects in the situation; and so forth. These twelve strategies were identified in previous research as the primary ones (Pines and Kafry 1981a).

	Active	**Inactive**
Direct	• Changing the source of the stress • Confronting source • Adopting a positive attitude	• Ignoring source of the stress • Avoiding source • Leaving
Indirect	• Talking about the source of stress • Changing self • Getting involved in other activities	• Alcohol or drugs • Getting ill • Collapsing

Coping Grid

To my surprise I discovered that "talking to a supportive friend" was highly correlated with burnout. In other words, the more people speak to their best friend (or their therapist) about the problems with their spouse, the more burned out they are likely to be in their relationship.[4]

When I first saw this result I went back to the computer printouts, sure there was an error. There wasn't. Looking further I discovered that confronting one's spouse directly had the opposite effect—the more direct confrontation, the less burnout.[5] I also found that talking directly to one's spouse about problems had far greater power to prevent burnout than talking to one's best friend had power to cause it. What these findings are telling us is that the best person to talk to about a relationship problem is one's spouse, not one's best friend (or therapist). The best friend is on one's side, and this one-sided support is not likely to help understand the mate's side. And it is understanding the other side that makes it possible to change. (Needless to say, talking to a best friend doesn't help one's mate understand what the trouble is either.)

Like all generalizations, however, this one is not true in all cases. Talking to a good and trusted friend (or to a good therapist) can help rather than hurt a relationship if the friend understands the full complexity of the problem and can help understand the mate's point of view. This is what should also happen with a good therapist.

It is, of course, possible that people start confiding in a friend not before but after communication has broken down within the relationship. They turn to the friend because they feel lonely and have no emotional or verbal contact with their mates. The friend provides emotional support, helps clarify confused feelings, and helps affirm one's view of reality.

Many books have been written in recent years detailing for couples the "how tos" of communication, training that is always part of the behavioral approach to couple therapy.[6] The reason: none of the behavioral techniques will work if the couple doesn't have communication skills. Couples are trained to express feelings and wishes assertively and are given rules (such as: be specific; don't attack; limit the discussion to one problem and to the present or future; let your partner finish a thought before responding; respond to a complaint directly, not with your own complaint; address only observed behaviors, not intentions or personality traits). The best advice for couples interested in improving their communication, however, is to spend more time talking. A middle-aged couple told me that their communication improved tremendously when they got a dog. Their nightly walks with the dog increased significantly the amount of time they spent talking to each other. When couples spend time together, chances are they will start talking.

Having more time to talk (quantity) means that it is more likely that something of real importance (quality) will be discussed. Discussing issues of actual or potential conflict increases couples' ability to look positively at the whole relationship. Ellen explains how working on a communication problem in her marriage affected her feelings about the marriage as a whole.

> In Anthony's family, both the parents and the four siblings are all very verbal, very opinionated, and very very loud. To be heard you need to scream louder than everyone else and be persistent, so they'll quiet down long enough to let you speak. In my family, on the other hand, people rarely raise their voices. This difference presented a real problem for me at the beginning of our relationship. Whenever there was a disagreement between us, Anthony would start

screaming, which would make me withdraw as fast and as
far away as possible. I even considered breaking up with
him because of it. But there were enough good things in
the relationship to make us want to solve this problem. I
made myself stay in conversations even when the urge to
withdraw was overwhelming. And I explained to him each
time that the volume of his voice intimidated me. Tony
tried to suppress his urge to raise his voice, knowing that if
he did we will be dealing with the volume of his voice,
rather than with the content of what he was trying to say.
The fact that we were able to overcome this major hurdle
made us feel good about the whole relationship and gave
us a lot of faith in it.

For simplicity, I will discuss the last eight variables in three clusters
of related variables (such as physical attraction, sex, and variety)
that influence each other. I will discuss the interaction between the
variables in each cluster, and mention briefly the interaction between
the clusters.

Physical Attraction, Sex, and Variety

The degree of physical attraction couples experience and express
toward each other was the third highest difference between the high-
and the low-burnout groups.[7] Burned-out couples talked about feeling
anything from a little attraction, through no attraction at all, to
absolute revulsion toward each other. Dona describes her feelings:

When we were first married I used to look at Andrew's
body, when we were on the beach for example, with admi-
ration. He is tall, and at that time was trim, in great physical shape. Now there is nothing left of this attraction. I
look at him sometimes and I feel revulsion. My physical
reaction to him tells me, against all my logical protestations, how burned out I really am in this marriage.

Andrew describes similar feelings:

There is nothing left of the physical interest that was there
at the beginning of our marriage. Even if I get sexually

aroused sometimes—I am a normal, healthy man with normal sexual needs—her coldness and hostility are enough to
kill any desire or romantic ideas I may have. It's a shame,
because we had a good thing going. Now there is nothing.

Ellen in the low-burnout group, feels quite differently:

When I look at Anthony sometimes, after all these years
together, I still find him exquisitely beautiful. Even when I
get mad at him, I can't stay mad for long because there he
is with those gorgeous eyes, and hair, and lips that I love.
. . . My anger just melts away.

Anthony sounds similar when he talks about Ellen:

I never believed physical attraction could last. But even
after more than a decade I still find Ellen one of the sexiest
women I know. Her sexual energy, her body, the touch of
her skin, are even more exciting to me today than they
were when we first met.

Which comes first: burnout or finding your mate no longer physically appealing? The answer to that question is less important than
what we can learn from the question itself: If you change one, you can
change the other.[8]

Even couples who are aware of how much physical attraction
means in a romantic relationship may defeat themselves by saying:
"We both look older, we're never going to be teenagers again, what's
the use? What's gone is gone." This is simply not so. It is easy to "let
yourself go" around the house. Couples that take each other for
granted stop making an effort. But if there is any message in this chapter it is that couples have to make the effort and break the downward
spiral; otherwise burnout is just around the corner.

And what if a couple is simply no longer attracted to each other?
William James, the father of American psychology, said that the best
way to get out of a bad mood is to whistle a happy tune. By whistling,
you are "behaving as if" you are in a good mood. The whistling
makes you change your posture, which changes your mood. This
technique works in relationships too. If a couple acts "as if" they are
attracted to each other, they will not only find themselves more

attracted, they will also increase the other's attractiveness and attraction to them. And when they feel more attractive, they are more attractive. What "behaving as if" means depends on each couple. Fortunately, couples have a pretty good idea where to start if they simply recall how they behaved when they first fell in love. This, like many other behavioral techniques, may sound artificial, silly, and even impossible to pull off, but it works. The challenge, in most cases, is for couples to decide to try it.

Behaving toward one's mate as if he or she were physically attractive is likely to bring out the mate's more attractive qualities in the way that a positive self-fulfilling prophecy does. This is most clearly evident when a couple is in love. Similarly, thinking that with time and domesticity one's mate has become unattractive, and behaving in accordance with that, is likely to bring out the mate's most unattractive qualities in the way that a negative prophecy does. This is most clearly evident when a relationship burns out. In both cases, people's own behavior helps reaffirm their preconceived notions about their mate.

Sex Life

It should come as no surprise that couples in the low-burnout group reported significantly better sex than couples in the high-burnout group.[9] The quality of sex affects the physical attraction between mates, and is affected by it.[10] Dona describes the downside of sex:

> Most of the time either I would go to bed early and he
> would stay up late or, if he went to bed early, I would stay up
> late—so the issue of sex often didn't come up at all. I really
> didn't want to make love to him. I didn't even want to kiss
> him. When we had sex I just wanted to get it over and done
> with. He was actually much better at it than I was. In fact,
> he gave more to me sexually these last few years than I gave
> to him. I had already tightened up inside, and wasn't able to
> give. He lost all physical attraction to me.

Ellen, on the other hand, describes sex that is exciting and enriching:

> Sex colors everything pink. I keep being surprised that
> things can be so intense even after doing basically the same

thing so many times. . . . Every time we make love a part of
me expects to be ever so slightly disappointed. But it never
happens. I wonder sometimes whether it is not blinding me
from seeing problems in the relationship. But you know
what? I don't care. This is what being alive is about.

The relationship between poor sex and burnout can mean two
things: that burnout causes sex to deteriorate, or that when sex gets
boring it facilitates the process of burnout.[11] But, as couple therapists
know, poor sex means a bad prognosis for a relationship.

Sex is clearly important. Yet, it ranked only fifth in the list of variables that separate the high- and low-burnout groups. This probably
tells us that—even after a couple studies all the sex education books
and practices well all the possible positions—if there is no love in the
relationship, sooner or later sex cannot help but become disappointing. Sex manuals and how-to books have value, especially in providing information. They are less helpful for the growing numbers of
couples who know all the positions, all the erogenous zones, and the
various ways to stimulate each zone, but who are nonetheless bored
with their sexual partner. Rollo May talks about the disappointment
with technique:

Sex, as rooted in man's inescapable biology, seems always
dependable to give at least a facsimile of love. But sex, too,
has become Western man's test and burden more than his
salvation. The books which roll off the presses on technique in love and sex, while still bestsellers for a few
weeks, have a hollow ring: for most people seem to be
aware on some scarcely articulated level that the frantic
quality with which we pursue technique as our way to salvation is in direct proportion to the degree to which we
have lost the salvation we are seeking. (May 1969, 14)

Passionate sex is a by-product of emotional arousal. Romantic love is
a chronic state of an emotional arousal. While the intensity of sex may
go down with time, the overlay that love imposes on the biological
drive makes it possible for sex to remain exciting and fulfilling. This is
especially true in those relationships in which mates continue to grow
and get from their love a sense of meaning. Variety is one of the ways
these couples continue to grow.

Variety

After eighteen months in solitary confinement as a suspected spy in Nazi-occupied France, Christopher Burney wrote that he soon learned that variety is not the spice but the very stuff of life (Burney 1952). Earlier in the book I noted that variety buffers against burnout. Boredom, on the other hand, fosters burnout, especially in men. Thus it should not be surprising to discover that variety made the top ten.[12]

A prerequisite for variety is change, what Joel Block calls "the deliberate breaking out from accustomed patterns, in other words, changing one's own behavior" (Block 1982, 20). Block notes that

> change requires a kind of flirting with inadequacy, the courage to fumble, a willingness to open ourselves to a degree of pain in the present in the hope that greater satisfaction will be delivered in the long run. . . . This, of course, is not easy. (Block 1982, 20)

Richard Stuart, a noted behavioral couple therapist, describes the "Fear-of-Change Principle" (Stuart 1980, 370). Joel Block elaborates:

> Although we may want to change our responses and behaviors, we do not necessarily welcome the change. In most areas of our lives, we put a premium on security and resist change even if the novel behavior is toward the relief of pain and the promise of pleasure. (Block 1982, 20)

Block believes that there are three common obstacles to change in long-term relationships: pride, inertia, and fear:

> Both partners typically decide to withhold positive changes on the basis of pride; they feel that "giving in" implies they have been wrong all along. In essence, they adopt a "change second" rather than a "change first" attitude, which results in a hopeless deadlock. Just as false pride makes progress more difficult, inertia comes into play. This is the tendency for an established pattern to remain unaltered. In order for us to move forward, an extra push is needed. Once the initial energy is exerted and

change is well under way, less effort will be required. But it
is often onerous to exert this extra energy. It is fear,
though, that exerts the most powerful influence in the
change process. Fear is the feeling that engulfs us when we
seriously consider altering a pattern that is well established, even if it is dysfunctional. (Block 1982, 20–21)

In order to overcome these obstacles, couples need to be gradual, to
persist, expect resistance, and remain positive. The rule of thumb for
those who want variety is—whatever you do, at times do it differently.
In the sexual arena, couples can change not only what they do, but
when they do it, where, and how. These, and similar, recommendations are based on the assumption that people want their need for variety fulfilled within their marriages, which is not always true. As we
know, some people believe that the best way to get in sexual variety is
through a different sexual partner. In order to get that kind of variety
they go outside their marriages. They get security from marriage and
variety from the affairs.

One group tried to get both variety and security from the primary
relationship—Kerista Village. Lil, one of the members of the commune, explained:

Asking one person to satisfy all of our needs for sexual,
emotional, intellectual, and spiritual fulfillment is, after
all, a tall order. Polyfidelity is an attempt to find a way out
of this quagmire without sacrificing the depth of intimacy.
It combines the best features of monogamy with the best
features of the open lifestyle. Since intimacy is shared, and
since the base of security is broadened, no one feels pressured by an expectation to be all things to each person.
People look to different partners to share with them different things. Since variety gives each person plenty of exciting nooks and crannies to explore in each partner,
relationships refuse to get dull.

Variety makes lovemaking more exciting, which improves the
quality of sex, which makes mates more physically attractive to one
another. Physical attraction, sex, and variety represent the wings of a
relationship. The next variables represent its roots.

Appreciation, Security, and Support

People in the low-burnout group felt more appreciated than people in the high-burnout group did.[13] Andrew knows Dona doesn't appreciate him:

> She always put down my work. She said it was pedestrian, not artistic like her work. . . . I have never been in love with accounting, but I still don't like having her put it down. Her ankle-biting, derogatory references to accounting got pretty repetitive . . . kinda old. It was like chipping at a stone.

Dona feels both unappreciated and unappreciating:

> I began to find myself feeling hopeless, feeling locked in a situation I could do nothing with. I thought it was obvious that neither of us could change and that, in fact, we would both be better off if we found someone who liked us for who we were and appreciated the good qualities we both have. Andrew really does have some lovely qualities. . . . I feel like I'm a special kind of person—someone with enthusiasm, exuberance, joy of people—and Andrew doesn't care about all that. He doesn't like any of that in me.

Ellen, on the other hand, knows she is appreciated:

> I guess that in part it's because my ex-husband was so critical of me that Anthony's appreciation is so important. To my ex-husband everyone in the humanities was a "soft head," and anything they had to say was by definition trivial. He once read a paper I wrote, muttering all the while to himself, "What nonsense." He was also critical of me as a mother and as a woman. Anthony, on other hand, appreciates me both as a professional and as a woman. I know he respects my mind, likes my personality, and loves my looks. And it feels wonderful. My self-concept has improved tremendously as a result of being with him.

Even people who realize full well how important it is to show appreciation at work forget how important it is to show appreciation at home. And, the data clearly show that the more appreciation, respect, and recognition you get from your spouse, the less likely you are to burn out in your marriage.[14] Similarly, Judith Wallerstein discovered in her study of happy couples that for both husbands and wives, happiness in marriage meant feeling respected and cherished (Wallerstein and Blakeslee 1995).

Some people give these positive rewards generously and easily to other people, yet have great difficulty giving them to their mates. While speaking to an acquaintance they feign attentiveness, sympathy, and respect. When speaking to their mates, however, whom they supposedly love, they are often rude, impatient, or openly critical. Their assumption, conscious or unconscious, is that since they "have" their mates, they don't need to exert effort. The high correlation between feeling unappreciated and the incidence of burnout shows just how wrong that is.

What about people who stay in relationships with people who constantly criticize them, put them down, and give them little or no appreciation? Such people often have a very negative self-image to begin with, which they suppress and deny. By being with someone who criticizes them and puts them down, they can externalize the source of their bad feelings; it is not themselves that they dislike but rather the critical mate who is making them feel bad about themselves. It is easier to deal with—and blame—an outer critic than to confront an inner critic. The solution for this problem, according to the psychodynamic approach, is for these people to develop a more positive self-concept, which can be done most effectively in the context of individual therapy. My own experience leads me to believe that it can be done even more effectively in the context of a couple relationship and couple therapy.

According to the social psychological approach, which I suggest as a valuable addition to the three clinical approaches (presented in chapter 3), focusing on the pathology of the individual is not the best way to understand or treat a couple problem. Instead, the social psychological approach focuses on the couple's "romantic schema." With time and the routine of daily life, the "romantic schema" that operated when a couple fell in love has changed to a far less romantic "marital schema."

"Schemata" are frames of reference for understanding the social world that are built through experience. They are scaffolds within our minds that help provide order, structure, and organization for incoming information. We almost never receive information in a passive manner. Instead, input is usually filtered, organized, and interpreted through those existing frames of reference, through schemata (Baron and Byrne 1991, 88–97).

Romantic relationships start out with both partners sharing the romantic role schema of "lover." With time, the schemata of "husband and wife," "father and mother," or "housewife and breadwinner" replace it. In order to reinstate the lover schema, the behaviors and atmospheres that were part of it need to be recreated. One way couples can do this is to think, when responding to something nice the other has done or said, how they would have responded if this very thing was said or done by their lover—rather than by their husband or wife of twenty years. Positive action is reinforcing. If a little gesture such as bringing in the morning paper is recognized with a smile and thanks, it is much more likely to happen again.

Security

While burned-out couples described little or no security in their relationships, for happy couples security provides a very positive and important reward.[15] Ellen explains:

> In my work I am always "on." I have to be on top of things,
> with perfect control and a perfect smile. When I come
> home I can take off my shield and my masks. I am com-
> pletely myself. And I feel loved and accepted. My marriage
> is my foundation. From here I can go anywhere and do any-
> thing—knowing I will always be supported.

Anthony adds:

> I think that the success of our relationship is a result of two
> things: making the commitment to stay together and let-
> ting each other develop as individuals. To me this commit-
> ment, and the security that derives from it, provide the
> opportunity to experience life to the fullest.

Knowing that security helps prevent burnout still does not tell couples how to make their own relationships more secure. Unfortunately, one of the most threatening topics of conversation for a couple is what things make them feel insecure. In addition, the people who feel most insecure in their relationships are the ones least likely to talk about it. In short, while threats to security are the topic most couples are least likely to talk about, it is possibly the topic couples should talk about most.

Security gives a relationship its roots, its depth, and its strength. For some of the people I interviewed, security was the most positive aspect of a long-term relationship, and one that more than compensated for the loss of excitement and the rush of expectations in new love. For others, however, too much security was stifling; security implied stagnation, and boredom, lack of challenge. Andrew has this negative notion about emotional and financial security:

> She always talks about security. Security, security, security.
> It became oppressive. I mean, I'm only just now beginning
> to think about security. I've still got lots of time. And I have
> lots of confidence in my ability to earn money and provide
> for that. It's just a question of when. But with her it is the
> overriding concern—and that was very oppressive to me.

Women tend to perceive security in an intimate relationship as more important than do men. Jeanne H. Block, a developmental psychologist, argued that in our society we encourage boys to develop only wings, and girls to develop only roots—to the detriment of both (Block 1984).

Support

The physician Sidney Cobb defines social support as the knowledge that you are cared for, loved, esteemed, and valued, and that you belong to a network of people who communicate and share mutual obligation. Cobb reviews an extensive literature showing that social support protects against the negative health consequences of life stresses: from arthritis through tuberculosis to depression, alcoholism, and emotional breakdowns (Cobb 1976). In my own work, I have found that social support provides a buffer against burnout (Pines 1982a). The comparisons between the high- and the low-burnout couples showed that burned-out individuals feel less supported by their mates than do those in happy marriages.[16]

Support, which is essential to psychological well-being, can be condensed into six basic functions: listening, professional appreciation, professional challenge, emotional support, emotional challenge, and sharing social reality:

> Everyone needs someone who will *listen,* especially in times of crisis. People appreciate someone who listens actively, without immediately giving advice or making judgment. They want someone who will share their pain and frustration as well as their joy and pride, their major conflicts as well as trivial incidents.
>
> At work, people need *professional appreciation* from someone who is an expert in their field and whose integrity they trust. They want positive feedback from someone who is expert enough to understand the work they do, and whom they trust to be honest.
>
> If they are not challenged in their work, people run the risk of stagnation and boredom. A good boss or a talented colleague can keep them from growing stale. A good critic can *challenge* their way of thinking and encourage them to stretch themselves.
>
> Everyone, when in a difficult situation, needs to have someone on their side, even if he or she is not in total agreement with what they are doing. At least on occasion they need to have someone who is *unconditionally support-ive*. This can be vital in stressful situations. When under stress, people need someone who will support them "come hell or high water." This person does not have to be an expert in their field, only a friend.
>
> An *emotional challenge* can stretch people psychologically by forcing them to question if they are really doing their very best to fulfill their goals and overcome obstacles. Most people can delude themselves into thinking they are doing their best when they are not. It is comforting to convince oneself that all avenues have been explored when they have not. It is easy to blame someone else rather than take responsibility. An emotional challenger can help by forcing people to question their excuses.
>
> Having someone who shares their *social reality,* who views the world the way they do, and who has a similar value sys-

tem is important when people think they are losing the ability to assess accurately what is happening. In a room full of people all agreeing enthusiastically with something that sounds like utter nonsense, it's enough to exchange understanding looks with this one person to know that one's perception is valid. (Pines and Aronson 1988, 160–68)

A moment's reflection makes it clear that a spouse cannot fulfill all six of these functions. For example, the functions of professional appreciation and challenge are best provided by a coworker or a superior familiar with the intricacies of one's work. For people to be disappointed in their mate for not supplying every kind of support they need (and the kind of support that cannot reasonably be expected from him or her) is terribly unfair. People can expect their mates to listen and to give unconditional support, at least occasionally. (Even if the mate told them not to do it, but they went ahead and did it anyway and now they're sorry, they want to know that their mate still loves them, and is on their side.)

The third form of support that can be expected from a mate is emotional challenge. Mates can encourage each other to examine defenses, question excuses, and explore what seems like impassable roadblocks. And mates can share social reality—thus helping to affirm each other's world view and perspective on reality.

Unfortunately, many people, especially when they are under stress at work, do not make the effort to discriminate between the various forms of support. They want their mates to be all things to them and then are disappointed when they can't or won't. Frequently, this disappointment is not verbalized but becomes associated with home life. The atmosphere of regret and disappointment begins to erode the marriage; the result is burnout at work that spills over to burnout in the marriage.

Support, security, and appreciation interact with each other at all times, and the results of their dynamic interaction influence the likelihood of burnout in a relationship. Feeling listened to and supported unconditionally increases the sense of security in the relationship. Feeling secure and appreciated makes it easier to be challenged emotionally and to grow. Sharing social reality increases security and mutual appreciation. Conversely, when these support functions are not available in a relationship, their combined negative impact is intensified. Dona describes it:

> I get a lot of appreciation for my professional skills, my
> skills as a homemaker, and just the way I am, from most
> of the people I come in contact with. But I never get
> support or appreciation from Andrew. It's as if he is afraid
> to pay me a compliment because it will take something
> away from him. Since I don't get support from him, I
> don't give it back either. Besides, I don't think he would
> appreciate my support anyway. Feeling unappreciated
> pushes all my insecurity buttons. And no one does it as
> well as Andrew.

Since Dona feels unappreciated, and unsupported, she is unwilling
to provide Andrew with support. Andrew feels similarly unsupported
and unappreciated, and consequently is unwilling to provide Dona
with the support he knows she needs. Thus both of them are stuck in
a negative cycle where neither one gets their needs met. Since they
are not communicating, there is no way to break this negative cycle.

Self-Actualization and Intellectual Attraction

Intellectual attraction together with self-actualization, the highest
in the hierarchy of needs according to Abraham Maslow (Maslow
1962), give relationships their wings.

Self-actualization, reaching one's full potential, and continuous
growth are important for individual mates as well as for relationships. The more people are able to actualize themselves in their intimate relationships, the less burned out they are.[17]

If self-actualization is so good, why does it cause so much stress in
some relationships and end others? Andrew explains:

> Dona and I were developing in different directions. She
> was spending a lot of time with her intellectual friends and
> preferred to spend her free time in ways that did not
> include me. So I also started developing interests and
> friends that did not include her. Eventually we had almost
> nothing left in common. We had no shared interests, no
> mutual friends, nothing of any significance we enjoyed
> talking about together or doing together. We were two
> strangers sharing a household.

Anthony, on the other hand, attributes the success of his marriage to the fact that he and his wife each continued to grow:

> While we have a very strong bond between us, we still let each other grow and develop as independent individuals. We both have our own interests that we don't always share. So I go to football games and I play golf with my friends, and she goes folk dancing and attends poetry readings with her friends. And that's okay because we share with each other the high points of our individual interests. Besides, we share so many other things.

The difference between Anthony and Andrew has to do with the balance between roots and wings. Couples who grow powerful wings when the relationship has no roots (of a deep commitment) end up flying away from each other because there is nothing to hold them together. On the other hand, couples who grow only powerful roots (of deep commitment and security) without developing wings (of self-actualization and growth) end up locked in a stifling relationship, feeling trapped, hopeless, and helpless—in other words, burned out.

In order to keep the romantic spark alive, couples have to grow both roots and wings, which is to say grow as individuals and strive to reach self-actualization without sacrificing their commitment to the relationship and without losing the foundation of trust and security. It is important that mates take at least some interest in each other's activities, because any activity that involves other people can ultimately represent a threat to the relationship.

The first step in achieving self-actualization is finding out such essentials as what is it that gives, or could give meaning to one's life, and how it can (if it can) be achieved within the relationship. A helpful exercise for either couples or individuals is to imagine meeting a good fairy who can grant only one wish. What would their wish be? Can it be achieved without the help of a magic wand?

Intellectual Attraction

Intellectual attraction was the tenth variable found to differentiate between the high- and the low-burnout groups.[18] People in the high-burnout group often complain that they are intellectually bored with their mates, even when those mates seem an intellectual challenge to most other people. Dona, who is aware of the respect Andrew gets from others, says:

> I know he is a very bright man. He must be, to be as suc-
> cessful as he is in the work he does. But in terms of those
> things that matter to me he is anything but bright. He
> doesn't understand—and doesn't seem to care—about the
> areas that mean the most to me such as aesthetics and
> human emotions. In these areas he is simply dumb.

Mates in the low-burnout group, on the other hand, describe intellectual attraction as a very important and stimulating part of their relationship. Ellen says:

> In all my years with Anthony, I don't think I have ever
> been bored with him, not for one moment. I love talking
> to him about books, movies, people, and everything else.
> He is a very well-read man, and I love it when he tells me
> things. I love to hear his analysis of events. I always feel
> enriched by his knowledge. Mutual learning is a very
> important component of our relationship.

Intellectual attraction, like self-actualization, is part of the wings of the relationship. Couples who have independent minds and interests are better able to challenge each other and to maintain an intellectual spark in the relationship. Such personal interests, when brought back to the relationship, enhance growth. They stretch the couple and the relationship.

There were other things that differentiated between the high- and the low-burnout groups, but the ten presented in this chapter differentiated between the two groups best.[19]

Sharing Chores

It is interesting to note a variable that, in spite of all expectations to the contrary, did not keep couples from burnout: sharing chores. It appears that when couples are able to look positively at their relationship as a whole, when they feel heard and cared for, and when the relationship gives their lives a sense of meaning, the exact sharing of chores is seen as trivial in comparison. Ellen, talking about her first marriage, describes the diminishing value of her husband's help with household chores:

> Only when things got really bad, and I began to consider getting a divorce, did he started helping around the house. After a dinner party for his business associates, he would help me do the dishes. But it was too little and too late. I was so furious at the idea of laboring over this dinner party for hours that I was no longer able to appreciate his help as much as I would have if he had pitched in earlier in our marriage. Then he did absolutely nothing around the house.

Despite the development of labor-saving devices, there is more housework today than there was fifty years ago. (Yes, we have electric washers and driers, but we also have more clothes that need to be washed separately.) While couple-speak praises the idea of sharing chores, women still carry most of the household burden. Ellen explains (talking about her second marriage):

> It's not that Anthony doesn't want to help. He simply doesn't notice that things need to be done, obvious things that I couldn't ignore if I wanted to. We're both trying to cope with the problem and to change. He tries to pay attention to the things I point out, such as a dirty kitchen counter left after he's supposedly "finished" washing the dishes. And I try to ignore such things as dirt on the carpet until the cleaning lady comes once every two weeks. But it's an effort for both of us.

The findings of a national survey concluded that wives most often complain about their husbands' messiness and husbands most often complain about their wives' nagging about their messiness. Yet in studies on couple burnout, household chores never came out significantly correlated with burnout.[20] Women reported carrying significantly more of the burden of housework. Husbands felt unappreciated for what they did around the house and for their effort. In both cases it was not housework that made or broke the relationships. Complaining about housework served as a barometer of other stresses in the relationship. When other things—especially communication and sex—were good, housework was considered unimportant and often became the focus of jokes.

A Dynamic System

All ten of the variables I have discussed (and many others I did not mention because of space limitations) interact with one another. This means that, in addition to their own effects, they also influence each other, thus multiplying their combined impact. In this way, improved communication improves sex life, which improves physical attraction, which improves the ability to look positively at the whole relationship, which improves communication, and so forth and so on. Because the variables interact dynamically with each other, making a positive move in any area can start an upward spiral, while making a negative move can start a downward spiral whose final stage is burnout.

This "domino effect"[21] makes the task of changing a burned-out relationship into one with roots and wings seem very simple. All a couple needs to do is to adopt a positive attitude toward the relationship, or perhaps improve the quality and quantity of communication in it. Yet we all know that this kind of advice is easier to give than to execute. Most couples know what they should do; their problem is that they can't make the "shoulds" happen in their relationship.

Psychodynamically oriented couple therapists believe that unconscious motives compel some people to destroy their intimate relationships. Because of traumatic experiences in their early childhood, such people don't believe that they are lovable or that love can last, so they actively destroy them, thus making their worst fears come true.

While it is true that such unconscious destructive forces operate in some relationships, they are not what destroys most. Daily hassles, stresses, habit, and routine erode love and passion. Couples don't need to destroy their relationships actively; all they need to do is watch passively as they slip away. Once this process of love's erosion starts, it is very difficult to stop and even harder to reverse.

Change is never easy. The greatest block against it is inertia, and it is primarily because of inertia that people cannot make the "shoulds" happen in their lives. This is especially true when those shoulds involve changing themselves or their partners: "I should be more patient"; "He should be more open about his feelings"; "She should be less demanding." Change is easier when it involves changing the situation, not people. When a couple spends a romantic evening together, it is usually easier for him to be more open and for her to be less demanding. Yes, reigniting a relationship that has lost its spark is not an easy task; it requires commitment and the combined effort of both mates. When only one mate decides to change things, the task can be overwhelming. But when both mates are committed to the change, couples can change their lives in important ways.

Many of the recommendations for preventing couple burnout, and for coping with it once it has started, that have been presented throughout this book have been made as general as possible. It is my experience that most couples—both homosexual and heterosexual—are able to translate such generalizations into recommendations that are best suited to their particular circumstances. In order to do this it is helpful for couples to know that their problems (in most cases) are not pathological; that what they experience as the most difficult problem in the relationship is related to unresolved childhood issues as well as unrealistic expectations and situational stresses; that working on these problems in the context of a couple relationship is the best way to resolve them and to achieve both personal and couple growth; that they have the power to change their relationship and that this is easier than trying to change either themselves or their mates. They also need the desire, the time, and the energy to apply these recommendations. The most difficult task, in most cases, is the first step—breaking the negative cycle. After that, once a positive cycle has started and is set in motion, all the next steps are smaller and easier.

It is always easy to put off making changes by telling ourselves "It won't work" or, even if it does work, "I can't do it" or, even if it works and we believe we can do it, "the time isn't right." The anticipation of change almost always produces some anxiety. Yet, if a certain change is an important one to make, it is unlikely that there will be a better time than now. As Rabbi Hillel said in *Ethics of the Fathers*, "If I am not for myself, who will be for me? If I am only for myself, what am I? And if not now, when?" (ch. 1, verse 14, 44).

9

Couple Burnout Workshops

In a couple burnout workshop, the material presented in the preceding chapters is brought together and applied. This material is most effective when presented in the context of experiential learning. Workshop participants not only learn what couple burnout is, but they are also given the opportunity to become more aware of the role they themselves play in the stresses they experience in their relationships, to understand the origin of these stresses, and to learn new and positive ways to overcome them in a highly personal and individualized manner. As noted in chapter 3, the presence of other couples has a great advantage in helping people break their fallacy of uniqueness—they discover that their problems are not unique, but shared by other normal and loving couples.

Another of the great benefits of a workshop is that it enables couples to take time out from their usual activities and to concentrate on the problems they are experiencing as a couple in a supportive environment, and to do so with other couples who have similar problems or have had similar problems in the past. The view of couples' problems as normal, the emphasis on these problems as opportunities for growth, the individualized guidance, and the social support, are the hallmarks of couple burnout workshops.

There is nothing magical about the actual activities in a couple burnout workshop. These workshops are effective because they represent a focused and concrete attempt to deal with couples burnout in a growth-enhancing way. The activities presented in this chapter can be used in a workshop context or in the context of either individual or couple therapy.

In the last fifteen years I have conducted hundreds of such workshops throughout the United States and abroad. Some of them were on marriage burnout (how to keep the spark alive in a long-term intimate relationship) and some were on job and marriage burnout (how to balance a job and an intimate relationship when you love both). These workshops ranged in size from a minimum of eight to over one hundred participants, with most groups numbering about twenty. Some workshops were open to the general public, others were offered during professional conferences for training purposes. Some were homogeneous, with couples of a similar age, background, and issues attending. Others were heterogeneous, with couples of different ages, social and economic backgrounds, and presenting problems. The length of such workshops varied from half a day to a week. Some workshops included only couples, others both couples as well as married and single individuals who wanted to figure out what went wrong in a current or a past relationship. A workshop can be structured as an intensive weekend or week-long residential program, as several consecutive two to three hour meetings, or as a semester-long course.

The box below is an example of the way one of these workshops was advertised. In this particular case the intended audience was couples in long-term marriages.

Keeping the Spark Alive and Preventing Marriage Burnout

The way we look at a problem can often be a major factor in resolving it. Marital discord and disillusionment should not be looked at as individual pathology and failure, but as normal responses to stress.

The conceptual framework of marriage burnout assumes that enormous pressures and stresses are built into the process of two people sharing a life together. It is almost inevitable that these stresses will become intense and at times even unbearable. Contrary to the clinical approaches to couple therapy—the psychodynamic, systemic, and behavioral approaches—the conceptual framework of marriage burnout assumes that marital stress is universal and

(continued)

---

normal and best treated in the context of couples' groups. This conceptual framework, which is based on research as well as clinical work with couples, helps eliminate guilt and blame, and thus frees energy for better coping. Couples in long-term relationships learn how to rekindle their romantic spark.

In the workshop, the psychodynamic, behavioral, and systems approaches to couples' therapy will be discussed briefly, and the conceptual framework of marriage burnout presented as a valuable addition. Several experiential exercises—that derive from the conceptual framework of marriage burnout—will be presented. These exercises help couples cope in a positive and constructive way with the burnout-causing stresses in their marriage and open their hearts to each other.

Tentative outline

What is marriage burnout?
How burned out are you in your marriage?
Causes of marriage burnout
The clinical approaches to couple therapy and the conceptual framework of marriage burnout
Attraction predicts stress
The building blocks of our romantic image
Changing marital stresses into opportunities for growth
From marriage burnout to "roots and wings"
Toward a career-marriage balance
Gender differences in marriage burnout

Recommended reading:
Pines, A. M. (1996) *Couple Burnout*. NY: Routledge.

A Workshop Description

When the participants in a workshop first get together, whether it is the first hour of a one-day workshop or the first session of a five-day workshop, it is important to take as long as necessary to have all of them introduce themselves to the group. In turn, they tell about their relationship status (have they been married many years, are they newlyweds, living together, dating, recently divorced, or never married);

what problem is it in this relationship, or with relationships in general, that has brought them to this workshop; and what are their expectations for the workshop.

Another version of self-introductions is to have each participant describe what his or her partner would have said about them, and what the partner would have described as the main problem or issue in the relationship. To make sure that this is a positive experience, the instruction should be for the group members to describe "something positive" they think their partner would have said about them. (This perspective reversal can also be used during the first session of couple therapy.) This method has the advantage of having people focus on their partner's perceptions of them and of the problem, instead of being focused on their own perspective.

The self-introductions can be put forth as serving two purposes. First they give an idea of the particular needs of the group, so the group leader can direct the workshop as much as possible to fulfill those needs. Second, they give participants an idea of the human resources available to them in the workshop in addition to the group leader. The interaction among group members is a very important part of the workshop. The deepest work in the workshop is done in foursomes. Listening carefully to the introductions enables group members to choose at least one (and preferably all three) of the people most appropriate for them to work with. In addition to these two purposes, the group leader's responses to the self-introductions provide an opportunity, without explicitly saying so, to establish the norms of the group (for example, that honesty and openness are respected and welcome but criticisms, judgments, and attacks are not).

Soon after the first few people tell their relationship story, it usually becomes abundantly clear that the workshop is a place where fallacies of uniqueness will be challenged. The statement "I have a story/problem similar to the one described by. . ." is repeated in different versions over and over again. Often it is voiced by people who are in a similar kind of a relationship. Other times it is echoed by people who are at a different stage of life or in a different relationship who have experienced that same problem in the past. In all cases it is obvious to the group members that they are not alone—that there are other people struggling with similar problems.

After all the group members have introduced themselves and told their relationship stories, if it is a weekend or a week-long workshop, it is best to engage them in a nonverbal activity that will remind them how nurturing a couple's relationship can be. In a place such as the Esalen Institute in Big Sur, California, where rooms are covered with thick carpets and participants sit on large pillows, I have couples give each other a foot massage, a head massage, or a head lift. I prefer to avoid activities that may have a sexual connotation for the benefit of couples who may have a problem with that kind of intimacy as well as for single people attending the workshop. When the room has only chairs, couples can still give each other a back-and-shoulders massage, with the receiver sitting on a chair facing its back.

If it seems that the group will be uncomfortable with any kind of physical contact, another nonverbal activity that may be appropriate is to have group members use colored crayons to draw on large drawing paper (which it is always good to have around) a symbol of their relationship. After each partner has drawn a symbol, the couple can be asked to draw one together. These drawings can then be posted on the walls for the remainder of the workshop. The drawings can be—but do not need to be—analyzed. Each group member should have an opportunity to explain the meaning of his or her symbol. Other group members can give feedback, as long as it is not pathologizing. Couples should also have an opportunity to describe the process of drawing together (how did they decide what to draw, who did what, etc.). All these exercises, with the sole exception of the "couple drawing," can be done by singles who are participating in the workshop.

The next day (in a half-day workshop this is the first part) starts with a formal definition of couple burnout, its symptoms and danger signs (chapter 1), and with a discussion of the two paths leading either to burnout or to "roots and wings" (chapter 2). Following this presentation, participants are usually very curious to discover their own levels of burnout. They can do it by responding to the Couple Burnout Measure (see Appendix 1), which has twenty-one items and takes about fifteen to twenty minutes to fill out. After all the group members have calculated their couple burnout score, they should be told what the score means (4 = burnout, etc.). It is important for the group leader to invite people with a score of 4 or higher for a talk during one of the breaks. These are people who are severely burned out, and if their score is 5 and higher they may be clinically depressed and needing professional help for their depression.

In a five-day workshop (or if the group seems interested), the next session can be devoted to a discussion of the three clinical approaches to couples' therapy and the importance of integrating them within a nonpathologizing conceptual framework such as burnout (chapter 3). Group participants are usually fascinated with this material, especially if it includes many examples they can relate to.

Clearly, the theoretical material covered in a couple burnout workshop corresponds to the material covered in this book (especially the first three chapters). The difference between reading the book and receiving the information in a workshop is that in a workshop participants are not simply exposed to it but rather have an opportunity to experience its relevance to their own lives. For the remainder of this chapter I will describe some ways in which this experiential learning occurs. The exercise I will describe next has a large number of parts. (The first three parts were mentioned in chapter 3.) Some of the parts take place in the large group, some take place in foursomes, some in couples, and some alone. In a half-day workshop, it is possible to do only the first three parts.

To avoid the anxiety associated with choosing and being chosen, group members are reminded of the introductory session in which they identified people who seemed to share their concern. They are asked to choose one of these people to be a member of their support group. Next, each pair is instructed to choose another pair that shares their issue and form a foursome. Foursomes should never include husbands and wives; if at all possible, they should not include people who know each other well; and they should include at least one member of each sex. The reason for this last suggestion is that often couples' issues are gender related, and it is an extremely valuable experience for a man to hear another woman talk about an issue with her husband that his wife complains about to him.

Once the foursomes have formed (even if there are only two foursomes in a four couples workshop), they are asked to tell, in turn, how they met their partner, what were their lives like at that time, and, most importantly, what was it that most attracted them to their partner. People should be encouraged to try to avoid generalities such as "good looks" and try to be more specific in describing what was it about the good looks that they found attractive. Was he rough and masculine or gentle and intelligent looking? Was she ladylike and sweet or sexy and flirtatious? Group members should be cautioned that they have only five minutes each (one member in each foursome can be designated timekeeper) and that they should only describe the "falling in love" stage of the relationship and avoid the later stages of the relationship and today's problems. I should add that this part of the exercise is my favorite. I always join one of the foursomes and listen with great delight to their wonderful stories of falling in love.

It is often difficult to stop the foursomes after about twenty to twenty-five minutes because they are having so much fun. Now that they know about the wonderful qualities of each other's partners, they are likely to feel more free to talk about problems. Being told that problems are normal in couple relationships also helps people feel comfortable talking about the most stressful aspects of their relationship or of their partner's behavior—which is the task in the next stage of the exercise.

Once people have permission to "complain," they do it with great enthusiasm. Again, it is usually difficult to stop them after twenty minutes, when they are told that the next (third) part of the exercise is actually the most important. Their task now is to find the relationship between whatever it was that attracted them to their partner and what is now most stressful. Examples are most useful in clarifying this point: a husband who was attracted to his wife because she seemed so strong and independent and now complains that she always has to have her own way; a wife who was attracted to her husband because he was "the strong silent type" and now cannot stand that he doesn't talk (see chapter 3 for other examples).

Some people, especially if not accustomed to psychological thinking, may find this task difficult. This is when the support group can take on the role of an emotional challenger and help them find the connection. Recognizing the connection between what attracted a couple to each other and what is now most stressful for them in each other is as important for couples in therapy as it is for couples in a burnout workshop.

Once the connection has been identified by all members of the group (with the help of the group leader, when necessary) they need to do some individual work that will serve them in the next part of the exercise. The work requires paper and pen and about ten to fifteen minutes. The task is to summarize in two lists (on one page) the most attractive and the most burnout-causing traits of their partner and the relationship. This is actually a written summary of the information that was brought up in the first two parts of the exercise.

The next parts of the exercise have to do with romantic images (discussed in chapter 2). After a relaxation exercise (such as focusing on the breath or gradually relaxing all parts of the body from the facial muscles to the toes) group members are asked to recall an event that happened in their childhood that involved their parents. If this is a five-day workshop, they can tell their support group about this event. Next, group members are asked to take their papers and pens and make, once again, two lists. One list should include all the positive characteristics of their mother and father (or step-parent or grandparent, if they were the significant parental figures in their childhood). The second list should include all their negative traits. These two lists are then shared with the support group; the activity should run about twenty to thirty minutes.

The next connection that group members are asked to make is likely to be the most important one for their relationships. It is the connection between the two lists they have made: of the traits (positive and negative) of their partner, and those of (both) their parents. A star put next to each of the traits of the partner that are either the same or the exact opposite of the parents results, in most cases, in a page full of stars.

The reason for putting a star next to traits of the partner that are either the same or the exact opposite of the parents' traits is a well-known psychological phenomenon: whether we choose a mate who is exactly like the parent with whom we have an unresolved childhood issue (cold and rejecting or intrusive and suffocating), or whether we choose a mate who is the exact opposite of that parent, we are still dealing with the same unresolved issue. The proof (which can be checked by a show of hands) is that most group members have at least three stars. Such is the power of the romantic image on mate selection. This part of the exercise is very appropriate for couple therapy.

In the next part of the exercise, couples are asked to translate the insights they have each gained into concrete suggestions for improved coping with relationship burnout. Once again, the first part of the exercise is done alone. Group members are asked to look at the list of the most stressful traits of their partner, compare it to the list of the negative traits of their parents, and see if they can deduce from the comparison between the two lists a notion of what is the most important thing that they need to get in the relationship—their "core need." This core need is likely to be something that they did not get from their parents and don't get from their partner, and which is manifested in the burnout-causing stresses they experience in the relationship. Core needs tend to be such "simple" things like a need to be loved, to feel safe, to feel special, to feel respected, to be the one and only. Not getting that need met is almost always related to the major stresses in the relationship (e.g., "The fact that he is always late shows that he doesn't respect me and my time"; "The fact that she spends time with her girl friends on the phone when I'm around means that I'm not that special to her").

Once group members have identified their core needs, they are ready for the difficult task of translating these needs into concrete and specific requests from their mate. Instead of asking their mate to be more loving, more understanding, or more respectful—which addresses their need, but may be responded to by their mate in a way that will not be appropriate for them—they need to make a list of things that their mate can do, say, or give, that will have that meaning for them. This tends to be a difficult task for many people, so suggestions from their support group can be very helpful. In the foursome, people have a chance to describe the core need that they have identified and the requests they would like to present to their mate that address that need. Since the group members know what attracted and stresses them in their mate and how both are related to their romantic image (the parents' characteristics), they can provide feedback about the core need (does it make sense given all that information?) and help with suggestions for requests that address that need. Since most people's core needs are similar (especially if they have chosen to be in the same foursome because they felt that they have similar issues), group members often inspire each other to have more and more creative requests.

It is a good idea to have as many requests as possible (at least seven) to allow the partner some choice. In order to generate as many creative ideas as possible, in the presence of all the workshop participants, each foursome is asked to share the most creative, fun sounding, and growth-enhancing ideas that came up in their group. Everyone is encouraged to add to their list ideas that seem good and likely to answer their core need.

Up to this point, most of the work done by group members has been done in foursomes, and a small part of it has been done individually. Only during breaks do couples have a chance to talk about what goes on for each one of them. This makes for lively discussions about relationship issues, which for some couples is a new experience and for others an experience they once had and have long forgotten. Now, however, the work unit is the couple. Couples are asked to take their lists of requests and sit together. Single people who attend the workshop can sit in dyads and do the same task.

The couples tell each other what they identified as their core need and explain how that need is related to their stresses in the relationship and to their romantic image, and how they are manifested in each of the requests they are about to make. They take turns presenting their requests (each presents the entire list in his/her turn) and discussing the meaning and importance of each request. After one presents a request, the other responds with feelings about the request and how difficult or easy they seem to fulfill. Often, couples are amazed to discover that they came up with similar requests (for example, a romantic dinner once a week, with both alternating the responsibility for discovering the special place to have that dinner). After exchanging their requests (not demands!), couples make a written contract (one that can be posted somewhere so it is not subject to memory distortions). In the contract, both describe in detail their commitment to fulfill these requests. (As noted in chapter 3, such contracts are very common in behavioral marital therapy.)

The next and last part of the exercise is done in the large group; it is inspired by the work of Kurt Lewin, the father of American Social Psychology who discovered that people are most likely to change their behavior if they commit themselves to it in front of a group. Each group member, in turn, describes what he or she is committed to do. This process is similar in structure to the one that took place in the introductory session, but is very different in content. Rather than describe what burns them out in each other, couples now talk about what they take as their responsibility to change in order to improve the relationship.

Taking responsibility for being in the relationship and for shaping it is a reflection of an important concept: "self-focus." It is hard for people to accept the idea that they chose very carefully, even if unconsciously, who to fall in love with and that they are equally responsible for what happens in our relationships. But with self-focus comes a sense of power.

Another important concept is "mutual selection." People's choice of each other is mutual. It is not by accident that the very rational man chose the very emotional woman. She fell in love with him at the same time, and for the same reason—he represented a split-off part of herself. Both of them saw in the other an opportunity to receive something they did not receive in their childhood. For him, the unresolved childhood issue may have to do with a hysterical mother he had to protect himself from. For her, the unresolved issue may have to do with a highly intellectual and distant father she felt unable to reach. They chose each other because each resembled the parent they had an unresolved issue with, but what they want most of all is for their partner to be different from that parent toward them. When they realize the connection between what attracted them to each other and what is most stressful for them in the relationship, and the connection of these to their romantic image, they can ask each other for what they need. Not surprisingly, these needs tend to be related (control your emotions vs. express your feelings; give me more space vs. come closer). These conflicting needs *between* the partners reflect an internal conflict *within* each one of them. Therefore, responding to their partner's request is the best thing they can do *for themselves,* for their own growth.

While the advantage of a couple burnout workshop is the presence of other people (both in the large group and in the foursomes), this entire process can be done in the context of couple counseling. Many therapists, even those who are very skilled and comfortable in individual therapy, find themselves unsure about what to do when they have to work with a couple. Often, they work with one member of the couple then with the other. For an inexperienced couple therapist, the multi-step exercise presented here can provide a structure that is sure to bring about a very therapeutic process.

The complete exercise can take anywhere between two and five days to do properly. Another exercise—*role play*—makes use of the presence of other people in the group and can be used whenever a couple asks for work on an individual issue, or when it becomes apparent, during the cycle of introductions, that there is an issue that is shared by several couples in the group.

The couple that volunteers to work on their issue is asked to sit in the center of the group and present their problem. Each partner describes the problem from his or her perspective. When it is clear that both have said everything they had to say and are starting to repeat themselves, they are asked to stop. Now the group is asked whether there is anyone who identifies with either one of the couple. When two such people have raised their hands, (they don't need to be a couple, and most often are not) they are asked to sit in the center next to the first couple and continue the discussion exactly where it was interrupted. In most cases, the new couple has no problem continuing the argument as if it was theirs.

This process can be repeated until there are at least four couples in the center of the room or until the entire group takes a position on one or the other side of the issue. This exercise helps the couple break their fallacy of uniqueness by making it clear that other couples share their problem. In addition, it enables the couple to listen to their issue being discussed by other people and in that way get a more objective perspective on it. The rest of the group can also see how universal couples' issues are, which encourages them to bring up their own issue for group discussion. In a week-long workshop it is usually possible to go through this process with most of the couples in the group. In a weekend workshop there is usually time to do it with only a few. But since most of the group members take part in these role plays, they learn the process vicariously.

Another exercise that can be used in a couple burnout workshop is a *sociodrama*. When a normative issue comes up in the group, especially one that tends to be divided by gender (e.g., is it better for couples to be monogamous or is it better to have open relationships), this is a valuable technique that can help address the issue. I start this exercise by drawing an imaginary line across the room. On each end of the line is one extreme position (only a monogamous relationship can offer true intimacy and allow the development of true love, vs. only by allowing your partner to be free can you be truly loving). I ask two volunteers to present convincingly these two extreme views, even if they are more extreme than their own views. Once they have done so convincingly, I ask for other volunteers who will add information that can reinforce these extreme positions. After the two extreme positions have been completely clarified, I ask other group members to place themselves on that part of the imaginary line that seems to best reflect their position on the issue. I invite people to move along the line if they discover that their position changed during the discussion.

I also use a sociodrama for a group exploration of "roots and wings" (discussed at the end of chapter 2). The two extreme positions (on the two ends of the imaginary line) are: the advantage of "roots" (commitment, security, intimacy) vs. the advantage of "wings" (freedom, self-actualization, excitement). I ask one couple for whom this is a conflictual issue to defend the two extreme positions. After they have done so convincingly, I ask other couples to join them. Once the two extreme positions have been clarified, I ask the rest of the group members to place themselves along the continuum between these two positions. In the group discussion following this exercise, couples usually arrive at the conclusion that it is important for them (as individuals and as couples) to have both "roots" and "wings." They understand that it is important not to divide those roles so that one member of the couple (usually the wife) is the spokesperson for the "roots" while the other member (usually the husband) is the spokesperson for the "wings." As I noted in chapter 2, the happiest, least burned-out, couples are those in which both partners have both "roots" and "wings."

The final segment of the workshop can be devoted to plans for the future. One way to start is by using guided imagery to lead group participants to imagine (in great detail) a typical day in their lives five years into the future. It is best to start the guided imagery on Friday morning, five years from today, the minute they wake up, and continue with the details of the day until they fall asleep at night, emphasizing activities and feelings related to their partner (for example, how do they feel about their partner when they wake up, do they reach to touch their partner, etc.). The advantage of starting the guided imagery on Friday is that it enables exploration of plans for weekend activities. This use of imagery in projecting the future provides couples with the opportunity to use what they have learned in the workshop to reconstruct their relationship and reprioritize their lives in order to bring their relationship in line with what they now believe is best for them. Later, based on their projections, they can be asked to make, as a couple, a concrete plan that will make the future more likely to unfold in the way that they both envision it.

The workshop ends with time for final feedback and leave-taking. By the end of the workshop, participants who started out as strangers part—with hugs and deeply felt and expressed emotions.

When couples in the workshop live close by, they often exchange phone numbers and plan to continue meeting as a couples' support group.

Appendix 1
The Couple Burnout Measure

The Couple Burnout Measure is a self-diagnosis instrument. It is presented here as part of a couple burnout questionnaire. A brief discussion of the scoring system at the bottom of the measure explains how the burnout score is calculated and how it should be interpreted. Appendix 2 includes a detailed discussion of the measure and some data that were obtained using it; chapter 9 describes how to use the questionnaire in the context of a couple burnout workshop.

The Couple Burnout Questionnaire

What attracted you to your mate when you first met?

What were your hopes and expectations when you decided to make a commitment to this relationship?

What is your image of the ideal relationship?

Appendix 1

What three things do you find most stressful about your partner or about the relationship?

1.

2.

3.

How do you usually cope with these stresses?

1.

2.

3.

How successful are you in your coping?

1	2	3	4	5	6	7
not at all successful			moderately successful			very successful

If you found someone else you could be intimate with, would you leave your mate?

1	2	3	4	5	6	7
definitely not			not sure			definitely yes

Please explain your response.

The Couple Burnout Measure

You can compute your burnout score by answering the following questionnaire as it relates to your marriage or intimate relationship.

How often do you have any of the following experiences? (Insert the number that most closely matches your experience.)

1	2	3	4	5	6	7
Never	Once in a great while	Rarely	Sometimes	Often	Usually	Always

1. Being tired _____
2. Feeling depressed _____
3. Having a good day _____
4. Being physically exhausted _____

 5. Being emotionally exhausted ____

 6. Being happy ____

 7. Being "wiped out," whole body hurts ____

 8. Feeling like you "can't take it anymore" ____

 9. Feeling unhappy ____

10. Feeling rundown, susceptible to illness ____

11. Feeling trapped ____

12. Feeling worthless ____

13. Being weary, nothing left to give ____

14. Being troubled ____

15. Feeling disillusioned and resentful about mate ____

16. Feeling weak, having sleep problems ____

17. Feeling hopeless ____

18. Feeling rejecting of mate ____

19. Feeling optimistic ____

20. Feeling energetic ____

21. Feeling anxious ____

How to figure out your burnout score:

Step 1. Add up the numbers you wrote next to these items:
1, 2, 4, 5, 7, 8, 9, 10, 11, 12, 13, 14, 15, 16, 17, 18, 21. Total: ____

Step 2. Add up the numbers you wrote next to these items:
3, 6, 19, 20. Total: ____

Step 3. Subtract the answer for Step 2 from 32: 32 – ____ = ____

Step 4. Add the number in Step 1 to the number in Step 3:
____ (Step 1) + ____ (Step 3) = ____

Step 5. Divide the answer in Step 4 by 21:
____ ÷ 21 = ____

This is your burnout score.

How to evaluate the burnout score:

A score of 4 indicates a state of burnout. A score of 3 may be seen as a danger sign of burnout. A score of 5 defines a crisis. A score above 5 defines a need for immediate help. A score of 2 or below means that the relationship is in very good shape.

The same test (with slight modifications) can be used to evaluate career burnout. To do that one needs to respond to the measure as it relates to one's work and the people involved in it (boss, employees, service recipients, etc.). Comparing the levels of burnout at work and in the couple relationship can be both interesting and valuable.

Of course, as is the case with almost all self-diagnostic instruments, the value of both these burnout scores depends on people's honesty in responding to them. If the respondent is dishonest (either in trying to make things appear better or worse than they really are), the test scores will be of little diagnostic value as far as burnout goes.

Appendix 2
Research on Couple Burnout

Burnout is a state of physical, emotional, and mental exhaustion that occurs as a result of long-term involvement in emotionally demanding situations. Such situations are typically caused by too great a discrepancy between expectations and reality. The most significant expectation people have is to find something that will give meaning to their lives. When they look to find it in their intimate relationship and fail, the result is couple burnout.

In order to evaluate their levels of couple burnout, people are asked to respond to a twenty-one–item measure representing its three components: physical exhaustion (e.g., feeling tired, run-down, and having sleep problems; weak and susceptible to ill-ness), emotional exhaustion (e.g., feeling depressed, trapped, hopeless), and mental exhaustion (e.g., feeling worthless, disillu-sioned, and resentful about mate). All these items are responded to on seven-point frequency scales. Respondents are asked to indi-cate how often they have these experiences in their intimate rela-tionship (with 1 = never, 4 = sometimes, and 7 = always). The burnout score is calculated by averaging the responses given to the individual items (see Appendix 1).

Test-retest reliability of the measure was found to be .89 for a one-month interval; .76 for a two-month interval; and .66 for a four-month interval. Internal consistency was assessed by the alpha coefficients for most of the samples studied; the values of the alpha coefficients ranged between .91 and .93. All correlations between the individual items and the composite burnout score were statistically significant at the .001 level of significance in all the studies in which it was used. In a study involving one hundred men and women (the San Francisco study), for example, all the correlations between the individual items and the composite couple burnout score were statistically significant at .001 level of significance, ranging from $r = .53$ (being physically exhausted) to $r = .86$ (feeling weary).

The measure's high face validity can be seen in the close correspondence between the items and the theoretical definition of burnout, as well as in respondents' positive reactions to it as defining their own level of couple burnout.

A factor analysis done on the responses of two hundred men and women (the Haifa study) gave evidence supporting the notion that the measure is primarily assessing a single meaningful construct. (The analysis was done using the Initial Factor Method with a Principal Axis.) As can be seen in Table 1, Factor 1 (the emotional exhaustion factor) accounted for most of the variance in the composite couple burnout score. Factor 2 (the physical exhaustion factor) explained far less of the variance.

Construct validity of the couple burnout measure (CBM) was examined by correlational analyses with several theoretically relevant variables. For example, in a study involving fifty-eight men and women, it was found that the correlation between burnout and desire to leave one's mate was: $r = .56$, $p < .0001$. In a study involving one hundred couples, burnout was found to be significantly and negatively correlated to satisfaction from life ($r = -.52$); from the marriage ($r = -.53$); from the spouse ($r = -.49$); and from self ($r = -.45$) (all r values are smaller than .0001). Burnout was also found to be negatively correlated to one's emotional state ($r = -.41$, $p < .0001$); and to one's physical condition ($r = -.35$; $p < .0001$). Self-diagnosis of burnout was correlated ($r = .42$,

Table 1

Factor Loadings in the Couple Burnout Measure

Item	Factor 1	Factor 2	Factor 3
Emotionally exhausted	.82	.00	.13
Unhappy	.80	.13	.19
Can't take it	.75	.07	.22
Depressed	.75	.12	.01
Disappointed	.72	.18	.31
Trapped	.71	.05	.20
Happy	.71	.51	.01
Troubled	.68	.10	.15
Rejecting mate	.67	.21	.22
Hopeless	.64	.11	.07
Good day	.64	.35	.20
Inferior	.62	.06	.10
Tired	.60	.04	.34
Nothing left to give	.56	.05	.38
Optimistic	.52	.30	.02
Physically exhausted	.52	.39	.49
Sleep problems	.49	.44	.11
Whole body hurts	.48	.58	.30
Anxious	.45	.38	.13
Energetic	.41	.51	.55
Susceptible to illness	.27	.60	.03
Variance explained:	8.2	2.1	1.3

$p < .0001$) with one's burnout level as seen by one's mate. The significant correlation, in addition to demonstrating that one can recognize burnout in one's mate, also served as instrument validation. It is interesting that couple burnout is more highly correlated to one's emotional state than to one's physical state. This finding fits the burnout profile seen in the factor analysis, in which emotional exhaustion symptoms contributed much more to the composite burnout score than did physical exhaustion symptoms. This was definitely not the case with career burnout.

Table 2
Pearson Correlation Coefficients for Burnout
and Eighteen Relationship Features

	r	p
Positive outlook	−.72	.000
Communication	−.64	.000
Security	−.59	.000
Self-actualization	−.57	.000
Significance	−.55	.000
Emotional attraction	−.54	.000
Sex life	−.54	.000
Growth	−.50	.000
Compatibility	−.50	.000
Variety	−.49	.000
Partner's desirability	−.46	.000
Physical attraction	−.41	.000
Things in common	−.40	.000
Similar goals	−.40	.000
Own desirability	−.36	.000
Intellectual attraction	−.33	.000
Control	−.23	.011
Sharing chores	−.14	.084

For example, in one study in which the burnout profiles of teachers, nurses, and police officers were compared, the highest contributor to their burnout score was feeling tired. (See Pines [1982c] "Helper's motivation," for details.)

Table 2 presents the rank order of Pearson correlations between couple burnout and eighteen relationship features obtained in the San Francisco study (N = 100).

The eighteen relationship features were entered one by one into a step-wise multiple regression in order to isolate a subset of the predictor relationship features that would yield an optimal prediction equation of burnout with as few independent variables as possible. As can be seen in Table 3, one relationship variable alone (namely, positive outlook on the relationship as a whole) accounted

Table 3
Stepwise Regression Analysis of Burnout
with Relationship Descriptors

Relationship Descriptions	Steps Entered	Multiple R	R^2 (all p<.001)	F
Positive outlook	1	.70	.50	90.4
Communication	2	.75	.56	57.7
Partner's desirability	3	.77	.60	43.5
Security	4	.79	.62	36.4
Sharing of chores	5	.79	.63	29.9
Emotional attraction	6	.80	.64	25.4
Things in common	7	.80	.65	22.4
Variety	8	.81	.65	19.9
Significance	9	.81	.66	18.0
Control	10	.81	.66	16.2
Own desirability	11	.82	.67	14.8
Sex life	12	.82	.67	13.7
Intellectual attraction	13	.82	.67	12.7
Compatibility	14	.82	.68	11.7
Similarity in goals	15	.82	.68	10.8
Physical attraction	16	.82	.68	10.0
Self-actualization	17	.82	.68	9.3

for 50 percent of the variance in the dependent variable couple burnout (R^2 = .50; F (1, 92) = 90; p<.000). The three top-ranking variables (positive outlook, communication, and partner's desirability) accounted for 60 percent of the variance in relationship burnout (R^2 = .60; F (3, 90) = 43.5; p<.000). The highest level of explained variance (68 percent) was accomplished by including fourteen variables in the regression analysis, which is to say 68 percent of the variation in burnout can be explained by linear dependence on fourteen independent relationship variables, while 60 percent of it can be explained by dependence on only three relationship variables operating jointly.

Table 4
Pearson Correlation Coefficients for Burnout and Marriage Descriptors for Men and Women

	Men		Women		Rank order (women)	Rank order (men)
	r	p	r	p		
Positive outlook	−.60	.0001	−.56	.0001	1	1
Communication	−.58	.0001	−.46	.0001	4	2
Appreciation	−.50	.0001	−.42	.0001	8	3
Sex life	−.49	.0001	−.41	.0001	9	4
Overload	.51	.0001	.48	.0001	3	5
Boredom	.48	.0001	.23	.02	16	6
Conflicting demands	.46	.0001	.56	.0001	1	7
Success	−.45	.0001	−.38	.0002	11	8
Physical attraction	−.44	.0001	−.40	.0001	10	9
Variety	−.44	.0001	−.45	.0001	5	9
Security	−.43	.0001	−.42	.0001	8	10
Compatible personality	−.39	.0001	−.35	.0001	12	11
Support	−.37	.0001	−.33	.002	13	12
Guilt and anxiety	.37	.0002	.44	.0001	6	12
Commitments' pressure	.37	.0002	.50	.0001	2	12
Things in common	−.36	.0003	−.25	.01	15	13
Self-actualization	−.35	.0005	−.42	.0001	8	14
Emotional attraction	−.34	.0008	−.33	.0007	13	15
Intellectual attraction	−.34	.0008	−.32	.001	14	15
Demand to prove self	.31	.002	.22	.03	17	16
Feedback	−.29	.004	−.43	.0001	7	17
Similar goals	.25	.01	.43	.0001	7	18

Table 4 describes the rank order of the correlations men and women had between various relationship features and burnout. The correlations were obtained in the Haifa study, in which 200 men and women took part. Due to space limitations, only the statistically significant correlations are presented.

The most interesting findings in Table 4 are the gender differences in the rank ordering of the relationship features as burnout correlates.

Tables 5 and 6 present the rank ordering of positive and negative features as burnout correlates, for women only.

Table 5
Correlations between Burnout and Positive Marriage Features for Women Only

(N = 100 Women)

	r	p
Positive outlook	−.56	.0001
Communication	−.46	.0001
Variety	−.45	.0001
Feedback	−.43	.0001
Similar goals	−.43	.0001
Appreciation	−.42	.0001
Security	−.42	.0001
Self-actualization	−.42	.0001
Good sex life	−.41	.0001
Physical attraction	−.40	.0001
Success	−.38	.0001
Compatible personality	−.35	.0001
Emotional attraction	−.33	.0007
Input into decisions	−.33	.0008
Support	−.33	.002
Intellectual attraction	−.32	.001
Independence	−.27	.007
Things in common	−.25	.01
Significance	−.25	.01
Self-expression	−.21	.04

Table 6
Correlations between Burnout and Negative Marriage Features for Women Only

(N = 100 women)

	r	p
Conflicting demands	.56	.0001
Commitments pressure	.50	.0001
Overload	.48	.0001
Guilt and anxiety	.44	.0001
Exploitation	.32	.002
Work-home conflict	.29	.005
Stressful environment	.24	.02
Boredom	.23	.02
Demand to prove self	.22	.03
Housework	.03	NS

Table 7
Correlations between Burnout and Various Social Relationships

	Spouse	Family	Friends	Coworkers	Supervisor	Subordinates
205 Americans	−.32*	−.25*	−.28*	−.26*	−.23*	−.24*
118 Canadians	−.25*	NS	−.22*	−.12*	−.23*	−.17*
81 Israelis	−.32*	−.37	−.18*	−.39*	−.25*	NS

*p<.05.

Table 8
Means and Correlations with Burnout of Home and Work Conflict

	Mean	Correlation
205 professional men and women	4.2	.36
277 professional women	3.6	.22
724 human-service professionals	3.6	.33
294 undergraduate students	4.1	.26
118 Canadian human-service workers	4.1	.38
55 Israeli male managers	3.7	.28
21 Israeli men and women managers	4.0	.24

Note: for all correlations, p<.05.

Table 7 presents the correlations between burnout and various social relationships at home and at work in an American, an Israeli, and a Canadian sample.

Table 8 presents the mean values and correlations with burnout of the conflict between home and work in seven different samples.

Table 9 presents the mean values and correlations with burnout for a variety of home and work features in two samples, one involving 205 professionals, the other 724 human-service professionals.

Table 10 presents mean values and correlations with burnout of home and work features for 205 professional men and women.

Table 9
Means and Correlations with Burnout
of Home and Work Features

| | 205 Professional Men and Women | | | | 724 Human Service Men and Women | | | |
| | Home | | Work | | Home | | Work | |
	Mean	r	Mean	r	Mean	r	Mean	r
Variety	5.2	−.23*	5.0	−.21*	5.2	−.22*	4.8	−.20*
Complexity	4.9	−.11	5.1	−.20*	4.9	−.09*	5.2	−.03
Autonomy	5.7	−.15*	5.0	−.28*	5.8	−.19*	4.7	−.19*
Overextension	4.1	.22*	4.2	.23*	3.8	.23*	4.4	.31*
Overload	3.8	.13	4.0	.13	3.9	.27*	4.5	.35*
Underload	3.2	.29*	3.3	.15*	3.3	.22*	3.5	.20*
Decision load	3.4	.21*	3.9	.19*	3.2	.18*	4.1	.30*
Innovation	4.7	−.15*	4.7	−.17*	4.9	−.12*	5.0	−.08*
Significance	5.2	−.22*	5.3	−.21*	5.7	−.18*	5.9	−.15*
Feedback	4.9	−.23*	4.7	−.15*	5.0	−.21*	4.4	−.15*
Success	5.2	−.48*	5.2	−.24*	5.4	−.28*	5.2	−.17*
Negative consequences	4.3	−.07	5.0	−.19*	4.6	.00	5.3	.04
Self-expression	5.6	−.31*	4.9	−.22*	5.7	−.15*	4.9	−.20*
Self-actualization	5.5	−.28*	4.7	−.22*	5.4	−.24*	4.7	−.20*
Self-worth demand	3.6	.11	4.2	.00	3.8	.08*	4.6	.17*
Guilt	3.2	.51*	3.1	.29*	3.3	.41*	3.6	.42*
Physical danger	2.0	−.03	1.9	−.06	2.2	.10*	2.9	.12*
Enviromental pressures	2.5	.26*	2.8	.27*	2.4	.19*	3.3	.21*
Comfortable environment	5.6	−.35*	4.6	−.29*	5.5	−.20*	4.4	−.24*
Bureaucratic pressures	3.0	.20*	4.2	.11	2.7	.10*	4.6	.24*
Administrative hassles	2.8	.20*	4.5	.06	2.5	.10*	5.1	.26*
Policy influence	5.2	−.24*	4.0	−.15*	5.5	−.16*	4.1	−.18*
Rewards	5.0	−.41*	4.4	−.33*	4.9	−.17*	4.0	−.17*
Opportunity to take off	4.4	−.18*	4.2	−.11	4.5	−.16*	4.3	−.09*
Social Overextension	4.4	.28*	4.2	.16*	3.7	−.33*	3.9	.38*
Support	5.0	−.29*	4.5	−.27*	5.1	−.12*	4.6	−.17*
Personal relations	5.7	−.32*	5.5	−.27*	5.9	−.26*	5.6	−.25*
Sharing	4.7	.28*	4.4	.13	5.1	−.20*	4.9	.23*
Conflicting demands	3.8	.38*	3.9	.27*	3.5	.30*	4.0	.31
Appreciation	5.0	−.31*	4.6	−.32*	5.1	−.13*	4.3	−.16*
Responsibility	4.4	−.12	4.1	−.06	4.3	−.01	4.3	−.07*
Emotional reciprocity	5.2	−.29*	4.5	−.18*	5.2	−.22*	4.2	−.18*

*p<.05.

Table 10
Means and Correlations with Burnout of Home and Work Features for 205 Professional Men and Women

		Men		Women		Men/Women
		Mean	r	Mean	r	Mean Comparison t
Variety	Life	5.4	−.17	5.0	−.22*	1.98*
	Work	5.3	−.19	4.8	−.20*	2.10*
Complexity	Life	5.1	−.04	4.9	−.11	.035
	Work	5.4	−.02	4.9	−.30*	2.52*
Autonomy	Life	5.8	−.02	5.7	−.18	.040
	Work	5.4	−.20*	4.7	−.30*	2.99*
Underload	Life	3.1	.19	3.2	.32*	−0.63
	Work	3.1	.03	3.5	.21*	−1.75
Overload	Life	3.9	.17	3.9	.12	0.25
	Work	4.3	.21*	3.9	.10	1.57
Decision load	Life	3.5	.14	3.3	.30*	1.44
	Work	4.1	.22*	3.8	.17	1.20
Overextension	Life	4.1	.20*	4.2	.27*	−0.41
	Work	4.4	.20*	4.1	.25*	1.56
Self-worth demand	Life	3.7	−.05	3.7	.19	0.06
	Work	4.5	−.07	3.9	−.03	2.44*
Innovation	Life	4.7	−.14	4.7	−.12	0.04
	Work	5.2	−.02	4.4	−.25*	2.97*
Significance	Life	5.1	−.22*	5.3	−.21*	−.1.20
	Work	5.3	−.24*	5.3	−.22*	0.15
Success	Life	5.3	−.41*	5.2	−.48*	0.48
	Work	5.3	−.22*	5.1	−.23*	0.76
Feedback	Life	4.7	−.29*	5.0	−.17	−1.34
	Work	4.8	−.17	4.6	−.11	0.75
Self-expression	Life	5.5	−.09	5.6	−.42*	−0.51
	Work	5.2	−.09	4.6	−.28*	2.62*
Self-actualization	Life	5.5	−.18	5.5	−.29*	0.27
	Work	5.1	−.15	4.5	−.24*	2.49*
Guilt	Life	3.0	.43*	3.5	.57*	−2.28*
	Work	3.0	.30*	3.2	.25*	−0.64

Appendix 2

		Men		Women		Men/Women
		Mean	r	Mean	r	Mean Comparison t
Environmental	Life	2.3	.15	2.6	.33*	−1.60
pressures	Work	2.6	.11	3.0	.37*	−2.04*
Bureaucratic	Life	3.0	.22*	3.1	.18	−0.27
pressures	Work	4.2	.08	4.3	.13	−0.23
Administrative	Life	2.9	.20*	2.8	.18	0.44
hassles	Work	4.7	.06	4.5	.03	0.50
Comfortable	Life	5.7	−.42*	5.5	−.30*	−1.28
environment	Work	4.9	−.25*	4.2	−.31*	2.97
Responsibility	Life	4.3	.05	4.3	.16	−0.34
	Work	4.1	−.19	4.2	.00	−0.44
Policy	Life	5.2	−.22*	5.3	−.28*	−0.61
influence	Work	4.5	−.13	3.7	−.12	3.16*
Rewards	Life	5.1	−.34*	5.0	−.44*	0.18
	Work	4.7	−.24*	4.2	−.36*	1.96*
Opportunity	Life	4.5	−.14	4.3	−.21*	0.78
to take off	Work	4.5	−.09	3.8	−.05	3.08*
Support	Life	4.8	−.31*	5.2	−.31*	−2.13*
	Work	4.4	−.28*	4.6	−.27*	−0.93
Appreciation	Life	5.0	−.34*	5.1	−.27*	−0.47
	Work	4.8	−.25*	4.4	−.33*	1.56
Emotional	Life	5.1	.31*	5.4	.30*	1.74
reciprocity	Work	4.4	−.20*	4.5	−.13	−0.43
Sharing	Life	4.6	−.27*	4.9	−.30*	−1.05
	Work	4.1	−.20*	4.6	−.11	−2.19*
Personal	Life	5.6	−.21*	5.9	−.42*	−1.96*
relations	Work	5.4	−.24*	5.6	−.30*	−1.10
Social	Life	4.0	.16	4.7	.34*	−2.76*
overextension	Work	3.9	.04	4.6	.21*	−2.16*
Conflicting	Life	3.7	.30*	3.9	.44*	−1.38
demands	Work	4.0	.29*	3.8	.25*	1.05

*p<.05.

Appendix 2

Table 11
Means of Frequency and Success of Coping Strategies
for 220 Professional Men and Women

	Frequency		Success	
	Men	Women	Men	Women
Direct-Active				
Changing the source	3.5	3.4	3.5	3.3
Confronting the source	4.3	4.1	4.5	4.4
Finding positive aspects in the situation	4.5	4.5	4.4	4.1
Direct-Inactive				
Ignoring the source	3.7	3.1	3.2	2.6
Avoiding the source	3.4	3.6	3.2	3.1
Leaving the source	3.5	3.3	4.2	3.7
Indirect-Active				
Talking about the source	4.7	5.3	4.8	5.3
Changing self	3.8	3.6	3.9	3.5
Getting involved in other activities	4.4	4.6	4.6	4.9
Indirect-Inactive				
Drinking or using drugs	2.5	2.6	3.0	3.0
Getting ill	1.8	2.8	2.5	2.4
Collapsing	1.5	2.3	2.3	2.5

Table 11, the last table, presents mean values of frequency and success in the use of various coping strategies for 220 professional men and women.

Notes

Chapter 1

1. Walster and Walster (1978), 9. There are different kinds of love. Erich Fromm discussed love between parent and child, brotherly love, motherly love, erotic love, self-love, and love of God (see Fromm 1956). Others have talked about such things as love of a mate, love of a friend, love of ideals, love of freedom, love of nature, love of beauty, and love of humanity. Greek philosophers and modern scholars discoursed on six different styles of love: storge (best friends), agape (unselfish), mania (possessive), pragma (practical), lodus (playful), and eros (romantic) (Lasswell and Lobsenz, 1980). My own assumption is that while there may be differences between people in their styles of love, these are only differences in emphasis, and that all lovers would like to have all the positive aspects of love combined in their own relationship.

2. It is important to note that since the mid-eighties, divorce rates in the United States have been declining. After rising sharply between 1970 and 1980, the divorce rate has leveled off and even begun to decline. In 1986 it was 4.8 per 1,000 people, 2 percent below 1985 and the lowest since 1975. At the same time, the median length of marriage has been increasing from 6.5 years in 1976 to slightly more than 7 years in 1986. In the mid-nineties, data suggest that more than half of all first marriages and 60 percent of second ones end in divorce, while a full 67 percent of all recent first marriages dissolve (Gottman 1994 as well as 1995).

3. I found, for example, that the more people believed that "true love is forever," the less burned out they were. On the other hand, the more they

believed that "marriage kills love," the more burned out they were. But since a correlation does not indicate causality, the same findings can be interpreted as suggesting that the more burned out people are, the more they believe that marriage kills love; and conversely, the less burned out they are, the more they believe in true love. I am indebted to Dr. Ofra Nevo of Haifa University in Israel for her contribution to the ten romantic truisms.

4. The 1981 U.S. Census reported 2,422,000 marriages and 1,213,000 divorces, which constitutes slightly over 50 percent. "Marital dissolution in the United States is at an all-time high" (Moles and Levinger 1976, 1). Similarly, James and Janice Prochaska note that "the United States now has the highest rate of divorce in the world. Trends between the seventies and the eighties also indicated that the divorce rate was higher than ever before in history and for a whole decade was climbing at an unprecedented pace" (Paolino and McCrady 1978, 3). In Blumstein and Schwartz (1983), demographers are quoted as projecting that half of all first marriages would end in divorce and that 41 percent of all American adults will at some time in their life experience a divorce.

5. Troubled marriages were identified in several studies as precipitants of suicide attempts. See, for example, Kessel (1965).

6. Framo also quotes marriage counselors Whitaker and Keith: "Marriages end up driving some people mad, pushing others into homicidal and suicidal acts, producing hateful demons out of perfectly nice people" (p. 133). [(C. Whitaker and D.V. Keith [1977] Counseling the Dissolving Marriage, in R.F. Stahmann and W.J. Hiebert (Eds.) *Klemer's Counseling: Marital and Sexual Problems*, Baltimore: William and Wilkins, p. 69.]

Chapter 2

1. Studies that documented the effects of proximity on mate selection include: Bornstein, et al. (1987); Bossard (1932); Burgess and Wallin (1953); Clarke (1952); Festinger (1951); Kellerman, Lewis, and Laird (1989); Newcomb (1961); Segal (1974); Thelen (1988); White and Shapiro (1989); and Zajonc (1968).

2. Studies that document the effects of emotional arousal on romantic attraction include: Allen, et al. (1989); Berscheid and Walster (1978); Clore and Byrne (1974); Dutton and Aron (1974); Gouaux (1971); Kaplan (1981); May and Hamilton (1980); Schachter (1964); Schachter and Singer (1962); Stephan, Berscheid, and Walster (1971); Valins (1966); Veitch and Griffitt (1976); and White, Fishbein, and Rutstein (1981).

3. Writings on unconscious mate selection include: Ainsworth, et al. (1978); Bowen (1978); Dicks (1967); Fisher (1992); Hazan and Shaver (1987); Hendrix (1992); Money (1986); Reik (1964); and Winch (1958).

4. Studies demonstrating the effects of similarity on mate selection include: Boyden, Caroll, and Maier (1984); Buss (1985); Byrne (1969); Caspi and Harbener (1990); Feingold (1988); Folkes (1982); Galton (1884); Hinsz (1989); Locke and Horowitz (1990); Mehrabian (1989); Merikangas, et al.

(1988); Nagoshi, Johnson, and Ahern (1987); Neimeyer (1984); Parnas (1988); Phillips, et al. (1988); Rushton (1988); Rushton and Nicholson (1988); Schafer and Keith (1990); Taylor and Vandenberg (1988); White (1980); Wilson (1989); and Zajonc, et al. (1987).

5. These studies were reported and analyzed by Bersheid and Walster (1978), and Breem (1992).

6. This kind of "need compatibility," "reciprocal arrangements," "interlocking collusion," or "unconscious deals" have been noted by a number of writers including: Bowen (1978); Dicks (1967); Framo (1982); Hendrix (1992); Kreckhoff and Davis (1962); Mittelman (1948); Papp (1990); and Sager (1976).

7. The importance of smell in romantic attraction is also emphasized by Helen Fisher (1992).

8. The research involved asking people to describe various aspects of their relationships and correlating those with their responses to the burnout measure (see Appendix 2). Since the results were consistent in the different samples studied, it seems sufficient to present here only those generated by one of these studies. The study involved one hundred couples. The average length of their marriage was fifteen years, ranging all the way from several months to thirty-four years.

It should be noted that all the participants were asked openly and directly to describe their relationships and their feelings about those relationships. All the data presented are based on self-reports and consequently may be influenced by such factors as the honesty of the respondents or their desire to say things in order to put themselves in a more favorable light. My best guess is that these factors account for only a small part of the findings. This "best guess" is an informed judgment based on corroborating evidence from in-depth interviews with a subsample of the subjects.

9. In the study of one hundred couples, the correlation between overload and marriage burnout was $r = .54$ $p<.0001$ (r indicates the level of the correlation, p indicates the probability of it happening by chance).

10. In the same study, the correlation between conflicting demands and marriage burnout was $r = .49$ $p<.0001$.

11. The correlation between the pressure of family commitments and burnout in marriage was $r = .48$ $p<.0001$.

12. The correlation between variety and burnout in marriage was $r = -.44$ $p<.0001$.

13. The correlation between boredom and burnout was $r = .35$ $p<.0001$.

14. The correlation between appreciation and burnout was $r = -.43$ $p<.0001$.

15. The correlation with self-actualization was $r = -.39$ $p<.0001$.

Chapter 3

1. In a study involving interviews with hundreds of couples, 80 percent indicated that they had seriously considered divorce at one time or another. Many said that the primary factors that kept them from divorce were eco-

nomics and concern for their children. The researchers' conclusion: marriage is in a state of calamity. See Lederer and Jackson (1968).

2. See Paolino and McCrady (1978); and Segraves (1982).
3. See Meissner (1978) and Nadelson (1978).
4. For example: Sluzki (1978); Haley (1977); and Minuchin (1974).
5. Paradoxical interventions are most closely associated with the Mental Research Institute (MRI) and Communication Theory including such people as Don Jackson, Gregory Batson, Paul Watzlawick, James Weakland, Carlos Sluzki, and Jay Haley. See, for example, Fisch, Weakland, and Segal (1982); Haley (1976); and Watzlawick, Weakland, and Fisch (1974).
6. The feminist writers who criticize the systems approach include: Goldner (1985); Goodrich, et al. (1988); Hare-Mustin (1978); and Walters, et al. (1991).
7. The conference provided the basis for a book by Chasin, Grunebaum, and Herzig (1990): *One Couple Four Realities: Multiple Perspectives on Couple Therapy.*
8. For similar reasons why existential psychotherapy is not applied to couples, see Yalom (1980).
9. For a further discussion of this point as it relates to jealousy, see Pines (1992); and Pines and Aronson (1983).
10. See White and Epston (1990); and Alexander and French (1946).
11. I am indebted to Arie Kruglanski for his contribution to the conceptual development of this part of the research. As for the study's results: The hardworking Joe and his wife Judith received an average of 5.3 in one study (n = number of subjects = 200) and 5.1 in the second study (n = 100). Tina, with her four young children, and her husband Tom received an average of 5.1 in one study and 5.0 in the second. The newlyweds Gary and Gina received the lowest burnout scores: 1.6 in one study and 2.0 in the second. The compatible Mark and Mary were seen as less burned out, averaging 2.3 in one study and 2.7 in the other, than the incompatible David and Dalia, who averaged 3.7 in one study and 3.6 in the other. The effect of the difference in compatibility was much smaller than the effect of the difference in the quality of the environment—2.3 vs. 3.7 as compared with 5.3 vs. 1.6 in the one study and 2.7 vs. 3.6 as compared with 5.1 vs. 2.0 in the second study.

Chapter 4

1. For example, in one study involving 384 subjects, when asked what was their favorite day, 29 percent said Saturday, 26 percent said Friday, and 17 percent said Sunday.
2. The three studies in which the stresses in work and at home were compared, were presented in Kafry and Pines (1980).
3. In the second of the three studies, for example, the average (negative) correlation between overall work satisfaction and burnout was $r = -.38$ (r = correlation) as compared to an average of $r = -.52$ for life satisfaction.

4. See, for example, Cantril and Roll (1971). The similarity between the process of job and marriage burnout was discussed in Pines (1987).

5. The motivational model of job burnout is detailed in Pines and Aronson (1988); and in Pines (1985). The effects of supportive vs. stressful environments are presented in Pines (1982). The existential perspective on burnout is discussed in Pines (1993).

6. See for example, Basow (1992); Block (1984); Chodorow (1978); Gilligan (1982); and Hochschild (1989).

7. Studies that have showed women reporting higher levels of burnout include: Aryee (1993); Caccese and Mayeberg (1984); Etzion (1987); Etzion and Pines (1986); Fuehrer and McGonagle (1988); Hetherington, et al. (1989); Leiter, Clark, and Durup (1994); Weinberg, Edward, and Garove (1983); Westman and Etzion (1990). Other studies that addressed the issue of gender differences in burnout reported contradictory results. Some studies found no gender differences—e.g., Greenglass and Burke (1988); Greenglass, Burke, and Ondrach (1990); Malanowski and Wood (1984); Maslach and Jackson (1985). And some studies found men to be more burned out than women—e.g. Hiscott and Connop (1989); Maslach and Jackson (1986); Norvell, Hills, and Murrin (1993). The main reason for this inconsistency can be attributed to the measures used. Most of the studies that showed women reporting more burnout used the Burnout Measure (BM) (Pines and Aronson [1988]). Most of the studies that either showed no gender difference or else showed men reporting higher levels of burnout were done using the Maslach Burnout Inventory (MBI) (Maslach and Jackson [1986]).

8. In the Pines and Kafry (1981b) study involving 191 professionals, the mean burnout score for men was $M\bar{x} = 3.1$; for women it was $W\bar{x} = 3.3$ ($\bar{x}$ = mean; $M\bar{x}$ = mean for men; $W\bar{x}$ = mean for women). In the study involving 205 professionals, the mean burnout score for men was $M\bar{x} = 3.1$; for women it was $W\bar{x} = 3.3$. In the study involving 220 professionals, the mean burnout score for men was $M\bar{x} = 3.5$; for women it was $W\bar{x} = 3.8$. In the study involving 118 human service workers, the mean burnout score for men was $M\bar{x} = 3.0$; for women, $W\bar{x} = 3.3$. In the study involving 89 teachers, the mean burnout score for men was $M\bar{x} = 2.7$; for women, $W\bar{x} = 3.2$. In the study involving 66 Israeli managers, men's mean burnout score was $M\bar{x} = 2.8$; women's, $W\bar{x} = 3.1$. See Pines and Aronson (1988).

9. For an excellent review, see Basow (1992), ch. 11.

10. For a review of these studies, see Pepitone-Rockwell (1980).

11. For a detailed description of such a workshop see Pines (1992).

Chapter 5

1. Other writers who have addressed this kind of gender difference from an evolutionary perspective include: Buss and Schmitt (1993); Buss (1994); Feingold (1992); Sprecher, Sullivan and Hatfield (1994); and Weiderman and Allgeier (1992).

2. Women reported feeling more often depressed about the relationship (Mx̄ = mean for men, Wx̄ = mean for women) (Mx̄ = 3.3, Wx̄ = 3.7), emotionally exhausted (Mx̄ = 3.3, Wx̄ = 3.7), wiped out, nothing left to give (Mx̄ = 2.7, Wx̄ = 3.1), and rejecting (Mx̄ = 3.0, Wx̄ = 3.4). Of the 21 burnout symptoms, women experienced 16 more than men in the negative direction, while men experienced only 2 more than women, in the negative direction: feeling trapped (Mx̄ = 3.8, Wx̄ = 3.5), and anxious (Mx̄ = 4.3, Wx̄ = 4.0). Four symptoms were reported with equal frequency by both men and women (a test of a binomial distribution). Using the binomial test, 2 out of 16 is significant at p<.001 (p = the probability of that result happening by chance).

3. Israeli women were more burned out in their marriages than their husbands, and significantly so (Mx̄ = 2.6, Wx̄ = 3.0; t= 4.1, p<.0001) (t test estimates the difference between the means). Out of the 21 burnout symptoms, women experienced 19 more than men in the negative direction; 11 of the 19 were statistically significant: women felt more often depressed (Mx̄ = 2.5, Wx̄ = 3.2; t = 4.7, p<.0001), emotionally exhausted (Mx̄ = 2.8, Wx̄ = 3.5; t = 4.1, p<.0001), unhappy (Mx̄ = 1.8, Wx̄ = 2.4; t = 3.9, p<.0001), physically exhausted (Mx̄ = 3.1, Wx̄ = 3.7; t = 3.8, p<.0002), weak (Mx̄ = 1.6, Wx̄ = 2.2; t = 3.5, p<.0006), and anxious (Mx̄ = 2.5, Wx̄ = 3.3; r = 4.4, p<.0001). Using the binomial test, this difference is significant at p<.001. Men had only one symptom more than women, but the difference was not statistically significant. Only one item was reported with equal frequency by both men and women—energetic.

4. Israeli women reported more anxiety than did Israeli men (Mx̄ = 2.5, Wx̄ = 3.3; t = 4.4, p<.0001), while American women reported less anxiety than did American men (Mx̄ = 4.3, Wx̄ = 4.0; this difference was not statistically significant). It is interesting that Americans (both men *and* women) reported much higher levels of anxiety than did Israelis.

5. These data are also discussed in Pines 1989.

6. The correlation between burnout and home/work conflict for men was r = .02 (n.s.) (n.s. = not significant statistically); for women it was r = .29 (p<.005). When asked what was more important to them, home or work, women indicated that home was more important significantly more than men (Mx̄ = 5.4, Wx̄ = 5.9; t = 2.8, p<.006). Women described their marriages as more significant to them than men did (Mx̄ = 5.6, Wx̄ = 6.1; t = 2.5, p<.01), and women "expressed themselves" in their marriages more than men did (Mx̄ = 5.0, Wx̄ = 5.5; t = 2.7, p<.009). Men felt trapped in the marriage more than women (Mx̄ = 3.8, Wx̄ = 3.5).

7. Responses to the question, "How important are the various aspects of romantic love to you personally?" generated the following sex differences:
Security: Wx̄ = 6.3 vs. Mx̄ = 5.5; t = 3.9, p<.0001
Understanding: Wx̄ = 6.8 vs. Mx̄ = 6.4; t = 4.9, p<.0001
Intellectual interest: Wx̄ = 6.1 vs. Mx̄ = 5.4; t = 4.2, p<.0001
Trust: Wx̄ = 6.8 vs. Mx̄ = 6.5; t = 3.3, p<.0009
Friendship: Wx̄ = 6.5 vs. Mx̄ = 6.0; t = 3.2, p<.001
Shared life: Wx̄ = 5.7 vs. Mx̄ = 5.0; t = 3.0, p<.003
Emotional attraction: Wx̄ = 6.4 vs. Mx̄ = 6.0; t = 3.0, p<.003

It should be noted that in spite of the sex differences in the importance given to the various aspects of romantic ideology, in many cases the rank ordering of these aspects was very similar. Thus, for example, for both sexes, trust, understanding, and friendship ranked highest (for women both understanding and trust: W$\bar{x}$ = 6.8, friendship = 6.5; for men: M$\bar{x}$ trust = 6.5, understanding = 6.4, and friendship = 6.0).

8. The frustration expressed by Ben and Dara is an example of gender differences in verbal communication that are the subject of several recent books, among them the bestselling book by Deborah Tannen (1990), *You Just Don't Understand.*

9. The correlation between the quality of sex life and burnout for men was r = −.49; for women it was r = −.40 (p<.0001). The correlation between physical attraction and burnout for men was r= −.44; for women r= −.40 (p<.0001). The correlation between burnout and boredom for men was r = .48; for women it was r = .23 (p<.0001).

10. The difference between men and women in the importance of physical attraction was noted in many studies. See, for example, Collins and Read (1990); Davis (1990); Ellis (1992); Goodwin (1990); Smith, Waldorf, and Trembath (1990).

11. These kinds of gender differences in attitudes toward sex are discussed by Bernie Zilbergeld in his 1992 book, *The New Male Sexuality.*

12. See Table 4 in Appendix 2. The table presents the rank order of Pearson correlation coefficients between burnout and marriage descriptors for men and the corresponding rank order for women. No distinction was made between positive and negative terms in this analysis. The rank order is only in terms of the size (not the direction) of their correlation with burnout.

13. All these findings are reported in Appendix 2, Table 4.

14. In the study, which was done in collaboration with Ditsa Kafry, the correlation between children's impulsiveness and mother's burnout was r = .49, p<.001.

15. In the study, which was done in collaboration with Teresa Ramirez (at that time a University of California-Berkeley student), the average burnout score of the abusive parents was 4.4 while the average burnout score of 30 other samples totaling 3,659 people was 3.3.

16. In the Haifa marriage burnout study, for example, the correlation between number of children and marriage burnout was r = −.11, p = .11 (not significant). The correlation between marriage burnout and number of children at home was r = −.13, p = .07 (not significant).

17. In recent years there have been calls for fathers to take back their parenting role. An example of this voice is Reuven Bar Levav's 1995 book, *Every Family Needs a C.E.O.*

18. This point is elaborated in Pines 1986.

19. The correlation between burnout and overload for men was r = .51, p<.0001; for women it was r = .48, p<.0001. The mean overload reported by men was M$\bar{x}$ = 2.9; by women, W$\bar{x}$ = 3.7, t = 4.3, p<.0001, which is to say, while the actual overload reported by women was higher than that reported by men, it ranked first for men and third for women.

20.In her 1993 APA address, Janet Hyde reported the results of several meta-analytic studies documenting the fact that gender differences in attitudes toward sex are among the largest gender differences found. For example, the D score (D = the size of the mean difference between the two groups) for attitudes toward sex without love was 1.34; the D score for casual sex was .81.

21.The correlation between burnout and boredom for men was r = .48, p<.0001; for women it was r = .23, p<.02.

22.Men described the communication as better than did women (M$\bar{x}$ = 4.8, W$\bar{x}$ = 4.2); men described more sharing of chores (M$\bar{x}$ = 5.0, W$\bar{x}$ = 4.6), sex life as better (M$\bar{x}$ = 4.6, W$\bar{x}$ = 4.9), and themselves as more desirable sexual partners (M$\bar{x}$ = 5.2, W$\bar{x}$ = 4.9) than did women. Women had only 4 relationship features more positive than men, including intellectual attraction (M$\bar{x}$ = 5.1, W$\bar{x}$ = 5.6), variety, things in common with mate, and overall relationship evaluation. Only 2 relationship descriptors were evaluated equally by men and women: security (x = 4.9) and goal similarity (x = 4.4). Using the binomial test, 4 out of 16 is significant at p<.04.

23.For example, in the Haifa study, women reported being significantly more burdened by housework than men did (M$\bar{x}$ = 3.6, W$\bar{x}$ = 5.8, p<.0001). Women also experienced overload significantly more than men did (M$\bar{x}$ = 2.9, W$\bar{x}$ = 3.7; r = 4.3, p<.0001), as well as a significantly heavier burden of family commitments (M$\bar{x}$ = 3.3, W$\bar{x}$ = 4.0; t = 3.2, p<.002). In addition, as noted earlier, women described their marriages as more significant to them (M$\bar{x}$ = 5.6, W$\bar{x}$ = 6.1; t = 2.5, p<.01), and women "expressed themselves" in their marriages more than men did (M$\bar{x}$ = 5.0, W$\bar{x}$ = 5.15; t = 2.7, p<.009).

24.See, for example, Donelson's "Social Influences on the Development of Sex-typed Behavior," in Donelson and Gullahorn (1977).

25.For a review of studies of women and depression see, for example, Myrna Weissman and Gerald Klerman's chapter, "Sex Differences and the Epidemiology of Depression," in Howell and Bay (1981).

26.This point was elaborated in a paper I presented at the 1987 American Psychological Association convention in New York entitled "Marital Burnout: Love Gone Wrong".

27.In this study, it was found that men confronted the source of their job stress more frequently than women: M$\bar{x}$ = 4.3, W$\bar{x}$ = 4.1; and ignored it more frequently than women: M$\bar{x}$ = 3.7, W$\bar{x}$ = 3.1. Women, on the other hand, used talking to a supporting other as a coping strategy more often than men: M$\bar{x}$ = 4.7, W$\bar{x}$ = 5.3. The study was described in Pines and Kafry (1981a).

28.In the Haifa study, for example, it was found that men used more frequently the direct and inactive strategies of ignoring the stress: M$\bar{x}$ = 3.3, W$\bar{x}$ = 2.9; and of avoiding the stress M$\bar{x}$ = 3.0, W$\bar{x}$ = 2.4; t = 2.9, p<.004. Women, on the other hand, used more frequently confrontation: MR = 4.3, W$\bar{x}$ = 4.8; t = 2.0, p<.05, and talking to a friend: M$\bar{x}$ = 2.4, W$\bar{x}$ = 4.0; t = 6.2, p<.0001.

29.Sex differences in confrontation as a coping strategy for dealing with job stress: M$\bar{x}$ = 4.3, W$\bar{x}$ = 4.1; sex differences in confrontation as a coping strategy for dealing with marital stress: Mx̄ = 4.3, Wx̄ = 4.8. Even though these data come from two different studies, it is interesting to note that men's frequency of using confrontation was identical at work and at home (Mx̄ = 4.3). For women, confrontation in marriage was much more frequent than it was on the job (4.8 vs. 4.1).

30. The average frequency of women's talking to a supportive other as a way to cope with marital stress was Wx̄ = 4.0; for men it was Mx̄ = 2.4. The correlation between the frequency of using this coping technique and burnout was r = .28, p<.02.

Chapter 6

1. The commune is described in detail in: Pines (1987b) and Pines and Aronson (1981).
2. See Pines (1992) and Pines and Aronson (1983).
3. The correlation between burnout and jealousy was r = .51, p<.0001.
4. For example, there was no correlation between the length of the relationship and jealousy, and there was no correlation between age and jealousy. On the other hand, there was a very high correlation between jealousy and a desire to leave the relationship. The correlation between jealousy and length of the relationship was r = .0007 (p = .967). The correlation between jealousy and age was r = .107 (p = .664); between jealousy and a desire to leave the relationship was r = .41 (p = .002).
5. The correlations between the quality of sex and believing that "love is like a good wine, it gets better with time" was r = −.36, p<.0001; "living happily ever after": r = .25, p<.0005; "match made in heaven": r = .20, p<.006.
6. This study was mentioned at length in chapters 2 and 5. The correlation between length of relationship and sex was r = −.25, p<.0003.
7. The correlation between age and the quality of sex life was r = −.24, p<.0009.
8. The correlation between the quality of sex and physical attraction was r=.66; sex and emotional attraction: r = .49; sex and intellectual attraction: r = .46. All p values <.0001. The correlation between quality of sex life and an overall positive evaluation of the marriage was r = .58; sex and relationship with mate: r = .58; as compared to the correlation between sex and the length of the relationship: r = −.25.
9. The correlation between the quality of sex and describing one's mate as the biggest love of one's life was r = .49; between sex and describing one's mate as one's best friend was r = .38. Both p levels <.00001.
10. The correlation between quality of sex life emotional attraction: r = .49, <.0001.

The correlation between quality of sex and an overall positive evaluation of the marriage was r = .58, p<.0001.

The correlation between the quality of sex and the general feeling toward the mate was r = .57; between sex and the quality of the relationship with the mate: r = .58 (not surprisingly the correlation with relationships with both friends and colleagues was zero); the correlation between

sex and the mate's feelings about the respondent: r = .51. All p values
<.0001.

The correlation between the quality of sex and burnout was r = –.41; sex
and partner's burnout: r = –.40. Both p values <.0001.

In both cases of physical attraction and overall evaluation of the relationship, the correlation with quality of sex was r = .66, which is the highest correlation obtained with sex.

11. This is not meant as a criticism of the behavioral approach to sex therapy.
Many of the behavioral techniques used by sex therapists are extremely
effective. Yet few people will be surprised to discover that those techniques
are more effective with couples who love each other and have good communication than with those who don't.

12. In a recent conference entitled "Integrating Sexuality and Intimacy: The
Challenge of Treating Couples in the 90s" held March 3–5, 1995, in San
Francisco, California, practically all the speakers expressed this new, holis-
tic, nonorgasm-directed, approach.

13. The correlation between communication and the quality of sex was r = .56,
p<.0001.

14. The correlation between variety and the quality of sex was also r = .56;
between quality of sex and boredom it was r = .37.

15. The correlation between the quality of sex and security was r = .51,
p<.0001.

16. It is worth mentioning two books—one about male sexuality the other
about female sexuality—that can be recommended to both men and
women: Bernie Zilbergeld's *New Male Sexuality* (1992); and Lonne Barbach's
For Yourself: The Fulfillment of Female Sexuality (1976).

Chapter 7

1. For a more detailed description of Kerista Village, see Pines (1987); and
Pines and Aronson (1981).

2. Growing rates of divorce among Orthodox couples suggest that even religious life does not shield a marriage completely from societal influences
and environmental stresses. In one of the workshops I held in Israel, I was
told, for example, that four of the graduates from one of the most famous
yeshivas (religious graduate schools) in Jerusalem got divorced. While four
out of a whole class may not sound like much, it represents a very sizeable
increase for this group.

3. The findings were obtained in the two studies that were mentioned during
the discussion of gender differences in couple burnout.

The first study involved one hundred men and women from the San
Francisco Bay Area. The correlation between time and burnout was .05.
While the zero correlation between time and burnout was statistically a
very strong finding, it still left some questions. As noted earlier, one could
wonder whether these results are unique to the San Francisco sample. This
town is well-known for being unconventional in its attitudes toward relationships and life styles; perhaps the data were skewed because of that. It

was important to see whether there would be any difference in the results in a different sample. To address these questions, a second study was conducted in San Francisco's sister city, the Israeli port town of Haifa. The assumption was that if any finding can be replicated in two such different samples, they could be considered more reliable and trustworthy.

The Haifa sample was, indeed, very different. Even in Israel, which is generally more conservative in sexual and social matters than the United States, Haifa is considered a quiet, conservative, family-oriented city. The Haifa sample included one hundred suburban married couples. For all but six of the couples this was their first marriage. Most couples had two or three children still living at home. The average length of the marriages was 15.1 years and ranged from one to over thirty-four years. When the data were analyzed, once more, there was no correlation whatsoever between time and marriage burnout. The correlation between burnout and the length of the relationship in the Haifa study was $r = .10$ as compared with $r = .05$ in the San Francisco study.

4. The mean burnout score was 3.4 for the American sample and 2.8 for the Israeli. This difference was discussed in Pines (1989).

Chapter 8

1. The burnout scores of the low-burnout group (LBG) were lower than 2.0 and the scores of the high-burnout group (HBG) were higher than 3.4—representing one standard deviation below the mean and one standard deviation above the mean, respectively.

2. The mean score for looking positively at the relationship as a whole for the LBG was 5.94; for the HBG it was 4.20 ($t = 6.38$, $p<.0001$).

   When the responses of all 200 of the subjects in the study were analyzed to discover the highest correlation of burnout, it was between burnout in the relationship and the ability to look positively at the relationship as a whole ($r = -.53$, $p<.0001$). Half of the variations in burnout could be explained by this one variable.

   Results of the San Francisco study, involving 100 subjects, indicated similarly that the highest correlation was between burnout in the relationship and the ability to look positively at the relationship as a whole ($r = -.72$, $p<.0001$).

3. The mean communication score for the HBG was 4.0; for the LBG the mean was 6.0 ($t = 5.9$, $p<.0001$). The mean time spent in direct conversation with spouse in the HBG was 39 minutes a day; in the LBG the mean was 60 minutes with a maximum of 4 hours ($F = 2.0$ $p<.05$).

   The correlation between burnout and the quality of communication in the Haifa study was $r = -.47$, $p<.0001$. In the San Francisco study the correlation was $r = -.64$, $p<.0001$.

4. The correlation between talking to a good friend about the problem and couple burnout was $r = .25$, $p<.0001$.

5. The correlation between confronting one's mate directly when having a problem and couple burnout was $r = -.53$, $p<.0001$.

6. See, for example, O'Leary and Turkewitz (1978).

7. The mean score for physical attraction to mate for the HBG was 6.5; for the LBG it was 4.9 (t = 6.0, p<.0001).

8. The correlation between physical attraction to mate and burnout was r = −.43 in the Haifa study, and r = −.41 in the San Francisco study.

9. The average evaluation of sex life in the HBG was 4.3; in the LBG it was 5.8 (t = 5.2, p<.0001).

10. The correlation between physical attraction to mate and quality of sex life was r = .66, p< .0001.

11. The correlation between the quality of sex life and burnout in the San Francisco study was r = −.54; in the Haifa study it was r = −.41 (in both cases p<.0001).

   In the Haifa study sex came fifth in the list of variables differentiating between the HBG and the LBG—following the ability to look at the relationship as a whole positively, communication, physical attraction, and mutual appreciation. In the San Francisco study, the quality of sex life came eighth with security, self-actualization, and significance added to the previous list.

12. The mean variety score in the HBG was 3.3; in the LBG it was 4.8 (t = 4.6, p<.0001). On the other hand, the mean boredom score for the HBG was 3.8; for the LBG it was 2.5 (t = −4.6, p<.0001). It is interesting that both t values were equal.

13. The mean appreciation score in the HBG was 3.6; in the LBG it was x = 5.5 (t = 5.9, p<.0001).

14. The correlation between feeling appreciated and respected and burnout was r = −.43, p<.0001.

15. The mean security score of the HBG was 5.1; of the LBG it was 6.4 (t = 4.9, p<.0001).

   The correlation between security and burnout in the Haifa study was r = −.42, p<.0001. In the San Francisco study it was r = −.59 p<.0001.

16. The mean support score for the HBG was 4.3; for the LBG it was 6.1 (t = 4.4, p<.0001).

17. The mean score for self-actualization in the HBG was 4.0; in the LBG it was 5.9 (t = 4.4, p<.0001). The correlation between burnout and self-actualization in the San Francisco study was r = −.57; in the Haifa study it was r = −39 (both p levels <.0001).

18. The mean intellectual attraction in the HBG was 4.4; in the LBG it was 5.9 (t = 4.4, p<.0001).

19. The other variables included, in rank order: feedback from mate; sense of success in the marriage; similarity in goals and expectations from life; emotional attraction to mate; shared decision making; independence, and self-expression.

20. In one study involving 100 women, for example, the correlation obtained between sharing housework chores and reported burnout was r = .03!

21. The "domino effect" refers to the effect of one act on the acts that follow, like the effect of pushing a single domino on a row of dominoes placed behind it—all falling down one following the other.

References

Ainsworth, M.D.S. (1989). Attachment beyond infancy. *American Psychologist* 44: 709–16.

Ainsworth, M.D.S.; M.C. Blehar, E. Waters, and S. Wall. (1978). *Patterns of Attachment: A Psychological Study of the Strange Situation*. Hillsdale, NJ: Elbaum.

Alberoni, F. (1983). *Falling in Love*. New York: Random House.

Alexander, F.; and T.M. French. (1946). *Psychoanalytic Therapy Principles and Applications*. New York: Ronald Press.

Allen, J.B.; D.T. Kenrick; D.E. Linder; and M.A. Mc Call. (1989). Arousal and attribution: A response facilitation alternative to misattribution and negative reinforcement models. *Journal of Personality and Social Psychology* 57: 261–70.

Aronson, E. (1995). *The Social Animal*. San Francisco: Freeman.

Aryee, S. (1993). Dual career couples in Singapore: An examination of work and non-work sources of their experienced burnout. *Human Relations* 46: 1441–68.

Barbach, L. (1976). *For Yourself: The Fulfillment of Female Sexuality*. New York: Doubleday.

Bar Levav, R. (1995). *Every Family Needs a C.E.O.: What Mothers and Fathers Can Do about Our Deteriorating Families and Values*. New York: Parenting, Inc. Press.

Barnett, R.C. (1993). Multiple roles, gender, and psychological distress. In *Handbook of Stress*. 2d ed., edited by L. Goldberger and S. Breznitz. New York: The Free Press.

Baron, R. B.; and D. Byrne. (1991). *Social Psychology: Understanding Human Interaction*. 6th ed. Boston: Allyn and Bacon.

Basow S. (1992). *Gender Stereotypes and Roles*. Belmont, CA: Wadsworth.

Becker, E. (1973). *The Denial of Death*. New York: Free Press.

Bellah, R.N.; R. Madsen; W.M. Sullivan; A. Swidler; and S.M. Tipton. (1985). *Habits of the Heart: Individualism and Commitment in American Life*. Berkeley: University of California Press.

Bengis, I. (1972). *Combat in the Erogenous Zone*. New York: Knopf.

Bernard, J. (1983). *The Future of Marriage*. New York: Bantam.

Berscheid, E.; and E.H. Walster. (1978). *Interpersonal Attraction*. 2d ed. New York: Random House.

Block, J. (1980). *Friendship*. New York: Macmillan.

———. (1982). *The Magic of Lasting Love*. New York: Cornerstone Library.

Block, J.H. (1984). *Sex Role Identity and Ego Development*. San Francisco: Jossey-Bass.

Blumstein, P.; and P. Schwartz. (1983). *American Couples*. New York: William Morrow.

———. (1990). Intimate relationships and the creation of sexuality. In *Homosexuality/Heterosexuality: Concepts of Sexual Orientation*, edited by D.P. McWhirter, S.A. Sanders, J.M. Reinisch. New York: Oxford University Press.

Bornstein, R.F.; D.R. Leone; and D.J. Galley. (1987). The generalizability of subliminal mere exposure effects: Influence of stimuli perceived without awareness on social behavior. *Journal of Personality and Social Psychology* 53: 1070–79.

Bossard, J.H.S. (1932). Residential propinquity as a factor in mate selection. *American Journal of Sociology* 38, 219–24.

Bowen, M. (1978). *Family Therapy in Clinical Practice*. New York: Jason Aronson.

Boyden, T.; J.S. Caroll; and R.A. Maier. (1984). Similarity and attraction in homosexual males. *Sex Roles* 10: 939–48.

Branden, N. (1983). *The Psychology of Romantic Love*. New York: Bantam.

Brehm, S. (1992). *Intimate Relationships*. New York: McGraw-Hill.

Bridges, W. (1977). *The Seasons of Our Lives*. San Francisco: Wayfarer Press.

Bryson, J.; R. Bryson; and B. Lecht. (1976). The professional pair: Husband and wife psychologists. *American Psychologist* 31: 10–16.

Burgess, E.W.; and P. Wallin. (1953). *Engagement and Marriage*. Philadelphia: Lippincott.

Burney, C. (1952). *Solitary Confinement*. New York: Coward-McCann.

Buss, D.M. (1994). *The Evolution of Desire: Strategies of Human Mating*. New York: Basic Books.

Buss, D. (1985). Human mate selection. *American Scientist* 73: 47–51.

Buss, D.M.; and D.P. Schmitt. (1993). Sexual strategies theory: An evolutionary perspective on human mating. *Psychological Review* 100: 204–232.

Byrne, D. (1969). Attitudes and attraction. *Advances in Experimental Social Psychology*, edited by L. Berkowitz. Vol. 4. New York: Academic Press.

Caccese, T.M.; and C.K. Mayeberg. (1984). Sex differences in perceived burnout of college coaches. *Journal of Sport Psychology* 6: 279–88.

Cantril, A.H.; and C.W. Roll, Jr. (1971). *Hopes and Fears of the American People*. New York: Universe Books.

Caspi, A.; and E.S. Harbener. (1990). Continuity and change: Assortive marriage and the consistency of personality in adulthood. *Journal of Personality and Social Psychology* 58: 250–58.

Chasin, C.; H. Grunebaum; and M. Herzig (eds.) (1990). *One Couple Four Realities: Multiple Perspectives on Couple Therapy.* New York: Guilford Press.

Chodorow, N. (1978). *The Reproduction of Mothering: Psychoanalysis and the Sociology of Gender.* Berkeley: University of California Press.

Clarke, A.C. (1952). An examination of the operation of propiquity as a factor in mate selection. *American Sociological Review* 27: 17–22

Clore, G.L.; and D. Byrne. (1974). A reinforcement-affect model of attraction. In *Foundations of Interpersonal Attraction,* edited by T.L. Houston, 143–70. New York: Academic Press.

Cobb, S. (1976). Social support as a moderator of life stress. *Psychosomatic Medicine* 5, 300–314.

Collins, N.L.; and S.J. Read. (1990). Adult attachment, working models, and relationship quality in dating couples. *Journal of Personality and Social Psychology* 58: 644–63.

Congreve, W. (1965). *The Way of the World.* London: E. Arnold.

Davis, S. (1990). Men as success objects and women as sex objects: A study of personal advertisements. *Sex Roles* 23: 43–50.

de Rougemont, D. (1940). *Love in the Western World.* New York: Pantheon, 1983.

Dicks, H.W. (1967). *Marital Tensions,* New York: Basic Books.

Dinnerstein, D. (1976). *The Mermaid and the Minotaur: Sexual Arrangements and Human Malaise.* New York: Harper & Row.

Donelson, E.; and J. Gullahorn (eds.) (1977). *Women: A Psychological Perspective.* New York: Wiley.

Duffy, E. (1962). *Activation and Behavior.* New York: Wiley.

Dutton, D.G.; and A.P. Aron. (1974). Some evidence for heightened sexual attraction under conditions of high anxiety. *Journal of Personality and Social Psychology* 30: 510–17.

Dyer, E.D. (1983). *Courtship, Marriage, and Family American Style.* Homewood, IL: Dorsey Press.

Ehrenreich, B. (1983). *The Hearts of Men: American Dreams and the Flight From Commitment.* Garden City, NJ: Anchor/Doubleday.

Eldridge, N.S.; and L.A. Gilbert. (1990). Correlates of relationship satsfaction in lesbian couples. *Psychology of Women Quarterly* 14: 43–62.

Ellis, B.J. (1992). The evolution of sexual attraction: Evaluative mechanisms in women. In *The Adapted Mind: Evolutionary Psychology and the Generation of Culture,* edited by J.H. Barkow, L. Cosmedes, and J. Tooby, 267–88. New York: Oxford University Press.

Ephron, N. (1983). *Heartburn.* New York: Pocket Books.

Epstein, C.F. (1971). Law partners and marital partners: Strains and solutions in the dual career family enterprise. *Human Relations* 24: 549–63.

Ethics of the Fathers. (English translation, 1964) New York: Judaica Press.

Etzion, D. (1987). Burning out in management: A comparison of women and men in matched organizational positions. *Israel Social Science Research* 1–2; 147–63.

Etzion, D.; and A. Pines. (1986). Sex and culture in burnout and coping among human service professionals. *Journal of Cross-Cultural Psychology* 17: 191–209.

Etzion, D.; A. Pines., and D. Kafry. (1983). Coping strategies and the experience of tedium: A cross-cultural comparison between Israelites and Americans. *Journal of Psychology and Judaism* 8: 41–51.

Farrell, W. (1986). *Why Men Are the Way They Are: The Male-Female Dynamic.* New York: McGraw-Hill.

Feingold, A. (1988). Matching for attractiveness in romantic partners and same sex friends: A meta analysis and theoretical critique. *Psychological Bulletin* 104: 226–35.

———. (1992). Gender differences in mate selection preferences: A test of the parental investment model. *Psychological Bulletin* 112: 125–39.

Festinger, L. (1951). Architecture and group membership. *Journal of Social Issues* 7: 152–63.

Fisch, R.; J.H. Weakland; and L. Segal. (1982). *The Tactics of Change.* San Francisco: Jossey-Bass.

Fisher, H.E. (1992). *Anatomy of Love.* New York: W.W. Norton.

Folkes, V.S. (1982). Forming relationships and the matching hypothesis. *Personality and Social Psychology Bulletin* 8: 631–36.

Framo, J.L. (1981). The integration of marital therapy with sessions with family of origin. In *Handbook of Family Therapy,* edited by T. Paulino and B. McCrady, 131–58. New York: Bruner/Mazel.

———. (1982). *Explorations in Marital and Family Therapy.* New York: Springer.

Frankl, V.E. (1966). *Man's Search for Meaning: An Introduction to Logotherapy.* New York: Washington Square Press.

French, M. (1977). *The Women's Room.* New York: Harcourt Brace Jovanovich.

Fromm, E. (1956). *The Art of Loving: An Enquiry into the Nature of Love.* New York: Harper & Row.

Fuehrer, A.; and K. McGonagle. (1988). Individual and situational factors as predictors of burnout among resident assistants. *Journal of College Student Development* 29: 244–49.

Galton, F. (1884). The measurement of character. *Fortnightly Review* 36: 179–85.

Gilligan, C. (1982). *In a Different Voice: Psychological Theory and Women's Development.* Cambridge, MA: Harvard University Press.

Goffman, E. (1952). On cooling the mark out: Some aspects of adaptation to failure. *Psychiatry* 15: 451–63.

Goldner, V. (1985). Feminism and family therapy. *Family Process* 24: 31–47.

Goodrich, T. J.; C. Rampage; S. Ellman; and K. Halstead. (1988). *Feminist Family Therapy.* New York: Norton.

Goodwin, R. (1990). Sex differences among partner preferences: Are the sexes really very similar? *Sex Roles* 23: 501–513.

Gottman, J. (1994). Why marriages fail. *Networker* (May/June): 41–48.

———. (1995). *Why Marriages Succeed or Fail.* New York: Simon & Schuster.

Gouaux, C. (1971). Induced affective states and interpersonal attraction. *Journal of Personality and Social Psychology* 20: 37–43.

Gove, W. (1972). The relationship between sex roles, marital status, and mental illness. *Social Forces* 51: 34–44.

Greenglass, E.R.; and R.J. Burke. (1988). Work and family precursors of burnout in teachers: Gender differences. *Sex Roles* 18: 215–29.

Greenglass, E.R.; R.J. Burke; and M. Ondrach. (1990). A gender-role perspective on coping and burnout. *Applied Psychology: An International Review* 39: 5–27.

Haley, J. (1977). *Problem Solving Therapy: New Strategies for Effective Family Therapy.* San Francisco: Jossey-Bass.

Hare-Mustin, R. (1978). A feminist approach to family therapy. *Family Process* 17: 181–94.

Hazan, C.; and P. Shaver. (1987). Romantic love conceptualized as an attachment process. *Journal of Personality and Social Psychology* 52: 511–24.

Hendrix, H. (1992). *Keeping the Love You Find.* New York: Pocket Books.

Hennig, M.; and A. Jardim. (1976). *The Managerial Woman.* New York: Doubleday.

Hetherington, C.; M.K. Oliver; and C.E. Phelps. (1989). Resident assistant burnout: factors of job and gender. *Journal of College Student Development* 30: 266–69.

Hinsz, V.B. (1989). Facial resemblance in engaged and married couples. *Journal of Social and Personal Relationships* 6: 223–29.

Hiscott, R.D.; and P.J. Connop. (1989). Job stress and occupational burnout: Gender differences among mental health professionals. *Sociology and Social Research* 74: 10–15.

Hothschild, A. (1989). *The Second Shift.* New York: Avon.

Hyde, J.S. (1993). Sex, Love and Psychology. Paper presented at the annual convention of the American Psychological Association, Toronto Canada.

Jacobson, N. (1991). Keynote address presented at the annual convention of the American Psychological Association, San Francisco, August 16–20, 1991.

Johnson, R. (1983). *We: Understanding the Psychology of Romantic Love.* New York: Harper & Row.

Kafry, D.; and A. Pines. (1980). The experience of tedium in life and work. *Human Relations* 33: 477–503.

Kaplan, M.F. (1981). State dispositions in social judgment. *Bulletin of the Psychonomic Society* 18: 27–29.

Kasl, S.V.; and S. Cobb. (1970). Blood pressure changes in men undergoing job loss. *Psychosomatic Medicine* 6: 95–106.

Kaslow, F.; and H. Hammerschmidt. (1992). Long-term "good" marriages: The seemingly essential ingredients. *Journal of Couples Therapy* 3: 15–38.

Kelleman, S. (1985). *Emotional Anatomy.* Berkeley, CA: Center Press.

Kellerman, J.; J. Lewis; and J.D. Laird. (1989). Looking and loving: The effects of mutual gaze on feelings of romantic love. *Journal of Research in Personality* 23: 145–61.

Kessel, N. (1965). Self poisoning. *British Medical Journal* 2: 1265–1340.

Kierkegaard, S. (1957). *The Concept of Dread.* Translated by W. Lowrie. Princeton, NJ: Princeton University Press, 1988.

264

References

Kishon, E. (1974). *It Was the Lark* [in Hebrew, *Ho, Ho Yulia*]. Tel Aviv: Sifriyat Maariv.

Kobasa, S.C. (1979). Stressful life events, personality, and health: An inquiry into hardiness. *Journal of Personality and Social Psychology* 37: 1–11.

Kobasa, S.C.; and S. Maddi. (1981). Personality and constitution as mediators in the stress-illness relationship. *Journal of Health and Social Behavior* 22: 368–78.

Kreckhoff, A.; and K. Davis. (1962). Value consensus and need complementarity in mate selection. *American Sociological Review* 17: 295–303.

Kurdek, L.A. (1989). Relationship quality in gay and lesbian cohabiting couples: A one-year follow-up study. *Journal of Social and Personal Relationships* 6: 39–59.

Lasswell, M.; and N. Lobsenz. (1980). *Styles of Loving: Why You Love the Way You Do*. New York: Ballantine.

Lauer, J.; and R. Lauer. (1985). Marriages made to last. *Psychology Today* 19 (June): 22–26.

Lazarus, R. (1984). *Psychological Stress and the Coping Process*. New York: McGraw-Hill.

Lazarus, R.; and S. Folkman. (1984). *Stress Appraisal and Coping*. New York: Springer.

Lederer, W.; and D. Jackson. (1968). *The Mirages of Marriage*. New York: Norton.

Leiter, M.P.; D. Clark; and J. Durup. (1994). Distinct models of burnout and commitment among males and females in the military. *Journal of Applied Behavioral Science* 1: 63–82.

Lerner, G.H. (1988). *Women in Therapy*. New York: Harper.

Liem, R.; and P. Rayman. (1982). Health and social costs of unemployment: Research and policy considerations. *American Psychologist* 37: 1116–23.

Locke, K.D.; and L.M. Horowitz. (1990). Satisfaction in interpersonal interactions as a function of similarity in level of dysphoria. *Journal of Personality and Social Psychology* 58: 823–31.

Malanowski, J.R.; and P.H. Wood. (1984). Burnout and self actualization in public school teachers. *Journal of Psychology* 117 (1): 23–26.

Martin, T.W.; K.J. Berry; and R.B. Jacobsen. (1975). The impact of dual-career marriages on female professional careers. Paper presented at the annual meeting of the National Council on Family Relations, Salt Lake City, Utah, August.

Maslach C.; and S. Jackson. (1985). The role of sex and family variables in burnout. *Sex Roles* 12: 837–51.

———. (1986). *Maslach Burnout Inventory Manual*. Palo Alto, CA: Consulting Psychologists Press.

Maslow, A. (1962). *Toward A Psychology of Being*. New York: Van Nostrand.

May, J.L.; and P.A. Hamilton. (1980). Effects of musically evoked affect on women's interpersonal attraction and perceptual judgments of physical attractiveness of men. *Motivation and Emotion* 4: 217–28.

May, R. (1969). *Love and Will*. New York: Dell.

Mehrabian, A. (1989). Marital choice and compatibility as a function of trait similarity-dissimilarity. *Psychology Reports* 5: 1202.

265

Meissner, W. (1978). The conceptualization of marriage and family dynamics from a psychoanalytic perspective. In *Marriage and Marital Therapy: Psychoanalytic, Behavioral, and Systems Therapy Perspectives,* edited by T. Paolino and B. McCrady, 25–88. New York: Brunner/Mazel.

Merikangas, K.R.; M.M. Weissman; B.A. Prusoff; and K. John. (1988). Assortative mating and affective disorders: Psychopathology in offspring. *Psychiatry* 51: 48–57.

Miller, J.B. (1976). *Toward a New Psychology of Women.* Boston: Beacon Press.

Minuchin, S. (1974). *Families and Family Therapy.* Cambridge: Harvard University Press.

Mittelman, B. (1948). The concurrent analysis of married couples. *Psychoanalytic Quarterly* 17: 182–97.

Money J. (1986). *Lovemaps: Clinical Concepts of Sexual/Erotic Health and Pathology, Paraphilia, and Gender Transposition in Childhood, Adolescence and Maturity.* New York: Irvington.

Murstein, B. (1976). *Who Will Marry Whom?* New York: Springer.

Nadelson, C. (1978). Marital therapy from a psychoanalytic perspective. In *Marriage and Marital Therapy: Psychoanalytic, Behavioral, and Systems Therapy Perspectives,* edited by T. Paolino and B. McCrady, 89–164. New York: Brunner/Mazel.

Nadelson, C.C.; and T. Nadelson. (1980). Dual-career marriages: Benefits and costs. In *Dual-career Couples,* edited by F. Pepitone-Rockwell. Beverly Hills, CA: Sage.

Nagoshi, C.T.; R.C. Johnson; and F.M. Ahern. (1987). Phenotype assortative mating vs. social homogamy among Japanese and Chinese parents. *Behavior Genetics* 17: 477–85.

Neimeyer, G.J. (1984). Cognitive complexity and marital satisfaction. *Journal of Social and Clinical Psychology* 2: 258–63.

Newcomb, T.M. (1961). *The Acquaintance Process.* New York: Holt, Reinhart and Winston.

Nicholson, J. (1984). *Men and Women: How Different Are They?* Oxford: Oxford University Press.

Norton A.J.; and P.C. Glick. (1976). Marital instability past and future. *Journal of Social Issues* 32: 5–20.

Norvell, N.K.; H.A. Hills; and M.R. Murrin. (1993). Understanding burnout in male and female law enforcement officers. *Psychology of Women Quarterly* 3: 289–301.

Nye, I.; and L. Hoffman (eds.) (1963). *The Employed Mother in America.* Chicago: Rand McNally.

Oates, W. (1971). *Confessions of a Workaholic.* Nashville, TN: Abingdon Press.

O'Leary, D.; H. Turkewitz. (1978). Marital therapy from a behavioral perspective. In *Marriage and Marital Therapy: Psychoanalytic, Behavioral and Systems Therapy Perspectives,* edited by T. Paolino and B. McCrady. 240–97. New York: Brunner/Mazel.

Paolino, T.; and B. McCrady (eds.) (1978). *Marriage and Marital Therapy: Psychoanalytic, Behavioral and Systems Therapy Perspectives.* New York: Brunner/Mazel.

Papp, P. (1990). The use of structured fantasy in couple therapy. In *One Couple Four Realities: Multiple Perspectives on Couple Therapy,* edited by C. Chasin, H. Grunebaum, and M. Herzig. New York: Guilford Press.

Parnas, J. (1988). Assortative mating in schizophrenia. *Psychiatry* 51: 58–64.

Paul, J.; and M. Paul. (1983). *Do I Have to Give Up Being Able to Be Loved by You?* Minneapolis, MN: Compcare.

Peck, S.M. (1978). *The Road Less Traveled.* New York: Simon & Schuster.

Pepitone-Rockwell, F. (1980). *Dual-career Couples.* Beverly Hills, CA: Sage.

Phillips, K.; D.W. Fulker; G. Carey; and C.T. Nagoshi. (1988). Direct marital assortment for cognitive and personality variables. *Behavior Genetics* 18: 347–56.

Pines, A. (1979). The influence of goals on people's perceptions of a competent woman. *Sex Roles* 5: 71–76.

———. (1982a). On burnout and the buffering effects of social support. In *Stress and Burnout in the Human Service Professions,* edited by B. Farber. New York: Pergamon Press.

———. (1982b). Changing organizations: Is a work environment without burnout an impossible goal? In *Job Stress and Burnout,* edited by W.S. Pain. Beverly Hills, CA: Sage.

———. (1982c). Helpers' motivation and the burnout syndrome. In *Basic Process in Helping Relationships,* edited by T.A. Wills, 453–464. New York: Academic Press.

———. (August 1983). "Sexual Jealousy as a Cause of Violence." Paper presented at the annual convention of the American Psychological Association, Anaheim, California.

———. (1985). Who is to blame for a helper's burnout? In *Self Care for Health-Care Providers,* edited by C. Scott. New York: William Morrow,

———. (1986). Marriage burnout from women's perspective. In *Everywoman's Emotional Well Being,* edited by C. Tavris. New York: Doubleday.

———. (1987a). Marriage burnout: A new conceptual framework for working with couples. *Psychology in Private Practice* 5: 31–44.

———. (1987b). Polyfidelity: An alternative to monogamous marriage?" in *Communal Life,* edited by Y. Gorni, Y. Oven, and I. Paz, 622–26. Yad Tabenkin Efal, Israel: Transaction Books.

———. (1989). Sex differences in marriage burnout. *Israel Social Science Research* 5: 60–75.

———. (1992). *Romantic Jealousy: Understanding and Conquering the Shadow of Love.* New York: St. Martin's Press.

———. (1992). A burnout workshop: Design and rationale. In *Handbook of Organizational Consultation,* edited by R. Golembiewski. New York: Marcel Dekker 82: 605–13.

———. (1993). Burnout: An existential perspective. In *Professional Burnout: Recent Developments in Theory and Research,* edited by W. Schaufeli, C. Maslach, and T. Marek. Washington, DC: Taylor and Francis 3: 33–52.

Pines, A.; and E. Aronson. (1981). Polyfidelity: An alternative lifestyle without jealousy. *Alternative Lifestyles* 4: 323–92.

———. (1983). The antecedents, correlates and consequences of sexual jealousy. *Journal of Personality* 54: 108–35.

————. (1988). *Career Burnout: Causes and Cures*. 2d ed. New York: Free Press.

Pines, A.; and D. Kafry. (1981a). Coping with burnout. In *The Burnout Syndrome*, edited by J. Jones, 139–150. Park Ridge, IL: London House Press.

————. (1981b). Tedium in the life and work of professional women as compared with men. *Sex Roles* 7: 963–77.

Prochaska, J.; and J. Prochaska. (1978). Twentieth century trends in marriage and marital therapy. In *Marriage and Marital Therapy: Psychoanalytic, Behavioral and Systems Therapy Perspectives*, edited by T. Paolino and B. McCrady, 1–24. New York: Brunner/Mazel.

Rank, O. (1945). *Will Therapy and Truth and Reality*. New York: Knopf.

————. (1958). *Beyond Psychology*. New York: Dover Books.

————. (1961). *Psychology and the Soul*. New York: Perpetual Books Edition.

Rapoport, R.; and R. Rapoport. (1969). The dual career family, *Human Relations* 22: 3–30.

Reik, T. (1964). *The Need to Be Loved*. New York: Bantam.

Rogers, C. (1961). *On Becoming a Person*. Boston: Houghton Mifflin.

Rubin, L. (1983). *Intimate Strangers*. New York: Harper & Row.

Rushton, P. (1988). Genetic similarity, mate choice, and fecundity in humans. *Ethology and Sociobiology* 9: 329–34.

Rushton, J.; and P.I.R. Nicholson. (1988). Genetic similarity theory, intelligence, and human mate choice. *Ethology and Sociobiology* 9, 45–58.

Safir, M.P.; Y. Peres; M. Lichtenstein; Z. Hoch; and J. Shepher. (1982). Psychological androgyny and sexual adequacy. *Journal of Sex and Marital Therapy* 8: 228–40.

Sager, C. (1976). *Marriage Contracts and Couple Therapy*. New York: Brunner/Mazel.

Scarf, M. (1979). The more sorrowful sex. *Psychology Today* 12: 44–52.

Schachter, S. (1964). The Interaction of cognitive and physiological determinants of emotional state. In *Advances in Experimental Social Psychology*, edited by L. Berkowitz. New York: Academic Press.

Schachter, S. ; and J. Singer. (1962). Cognitive, social and physiological determinants of emotional state. *Psychological review* 69: 379–99.

Schafer, R.B.; and P.M. Keith. (1990). Matching by weight in married couples: A life cycle perspective. *Journal of Social Psychology* 130: 657–64.

Segal, M.W. (1974). Alphabet and attraction: Unobtrusive measure of the effect of propinquity in a field setting. *Journal of Personality and Social Psychology* 30: 654–57.

Segraves, R.T. (1982). *Marital Therapy: A Combined Psychodynamic Behavioral Approach*. New York: Plenum Medical Book Company.

Smith, J.E.; V.A. Waldorf; and D.L. Trembath. (1990). Single white male looking for thin, very attractive . . . *Sex Roles* 23: 675–85.

Snyder, M. (1979) When belief creates reality: The self fulfilling impact of first impressions on social interaction. In *Experiencing Social Psychology*, edited by A. Pines and C. Maslach. New York: Random House.

Sprecher, S.; Q. Sullivan; and E. Hatfield. (1994). Male selection preferences: Gender differences examined in a national sample. *Journal of Personality and Social Psychology* 66: 1074–80.

Stephan, W.A.; E. Berscheid; and E.H. Walster. (1971). Sexual arousal and interpersonal perception. *Journal of Personality and Social Psychology* 20: 93–101.

Stuart, R.B. (1969). Operant-interpersonal treatment for marital discord. *Journal of Consulting and Clinical Psychology* 33: 675–82.

Stuart, R.B. (1980). *Helping Couples Change: A Social Learning Approach to Marital Therapy*. New York: Guilford Press.

Suyin, H. (1960). *A Many Splendoured Thing*. New York: Penguin.

Tannen, D. (1990). *You Just Don't Understand*. New York: William Morrow.

Taylor, M.; and S.G. Vandenberg. (1988) Assortative mating for IQ and personality due to propinquity and personal preference. *Behavior Genetics* 18: 339–45.

Tennov, D. (1979). *Love and Limerence: The Experience of Being in Love*. New York: Stein and Day.

Thelen, T. (1988). Effect of late familiarization on human mating preferences. *Social Biology* 35: 251–66.

U.S. Bureau of the Census (1981). *Current Population Report*. Washington, DC: U.S. GPO.

Valins, S. (1966). Cognitive effects of false heart rate feedback. *Journal of Personality and Social Psychology* 4: 400–408.

Veitch, R.; and W. Griffitt. (1976). Good news, bad news: Affective and interpersonal effects. *Journal of Applied Social Psychology* 6: 69–75.

Wallerstein, J.S.; and S. Blakeslee. (1995). *The Good Marriage: How and Why Love Lasts*. Boston: Houghton Mifflin.

Walster E.; and E. Berscheid. (1971). Adrenalin makes the heart grow fonder. *Psychology Today* (June): 47–62.

———. (1969). *Interpersonal Attraction*. Menlo Park, CA: Addison-Wesley.

Walster, E.; and W.G. Walster. (1978). *A New Look at Love*. Reading, MA: Addison Wesley.

Walters, M.; B. Carter, B.; P. Papp; and O. Silverstein. (1991). *The Invisible Web: Gender Patterns in Family Relationships*. New York: Guilford Press.

Watts, A. (1985). Divine madness. In *Challenge of the Heart*, edited by John Welwood. Boston: Shambhala.

Watzlawick, P.; J.H. Weakland; and R. Fisch. (1974). *Change: Principles of Problem Formation and Problem Resolution*. New York: Norton.

Weiderman, M.W.; and E.R. Allgeier. (1992). Gender differences in mate selection criteria: Sociobiological or socioeconomic explanation? *Ethology and Sociobiology* 13: 115–24.

Weinberg, S.; G. Edwards; and W.E. Garove. (1983) Burnout among employees of state residential facilities serving developmentally disabled persons. *Children and Youth Services Review* 5: 239–53.

Weissman, M.; and Klerman, G. (1981). Sex differences and the epidemiology of depression. In *Women and Mental Health*, edited by E. Howell and M. Bay. New York: Basic Books.

Westman, M.; and D. Etzion. (1990). Job stress and burnout: The moderating effect of social support and sense of control. Paper presented at the first European Network of Organizational Psychologists conference on Professional Burnout. Cracow, Poland, September 24–27.

White, G.L. (1980). Physical attractiveness and courtship progress. *Journal of Personality and Social Psychology* 39: 660–68.

Whitaker, C.; and D.V. Keith. (1977). Counseling the dissolving marriage. In *Klemer's Counseling: Marital and Sexual Problems*, edited by R.F. Stahmann and W.J. Hiebert. Baltimore, MD: William and Wilkins.

White, G.L.; S. Fishbein; and J. Rutstein. (1981). Passionate love: The misattribution of arousal. *Journal of Personality and Social Psychology* 41: 56–62.

White, G.L.; and D. Shapiro. (1989). Don't I know you? Antecedents and social consequences of perceived familiarity. *Journal of Experimental Social psychology* 23: 75–92.

White, M.; and D. Epston. (1990). *Narrative Means to Therapeutic Ends*. New York: W.W. Norton.

Wile, D. (1981). *Couple Therapy*. New York: Wiley

———. (1995). The ego analytic approach to couple therapy. In *Clinical Theory of Couple Therapy*, edited by Neil Jackobson and Alan Gurman. New York: Guilford Press.

Wilson, W. (1989). Brief resolution of the issue of similarity versus complementarity in mate selection using height preference as a model. *Psychological Reports* 65: 387–93.

Winch, R. (1958). *Mate selection: A study of complementary needs* New York: Harper & Row.

Wolman, B. (1973). *Dictionary of Behavioral Science*. New York: Van Nostrand.

Yalom, I.D. (1980). *Existential Psychotherapy*. New York: Basic Books.

Zajonc, R.B. (1968). Attitudinal effects of mere exposure. *Journal of Personality and Social Psychology*. Monograph supplement 9, part 2, 1–27.

Zajonc, R.B.; P.K. Adelmann; S.T. Murphy; and P.M. Niedenthal. (1987). Convergence in physical appearance of spouses. *Motivation and Emotion* 11: 335–46.

Zilbergeld, B. (1992). *The New Male Sexuality*. New York: Bantam.

Zimbardo, P.; C. Haney; W.C. Banks; and D.A. Jaffe. (1973). Pirandellian prison: The mind is a formidable jailer. *New York Times Magazine* (April 8): 38–60.

About the Author

Ayala Malach Pines is the head of the Division of Psychology and Behavioral Sciences at the Institute of Arts, Sciences, and Technology in Israel, as well as Senior Researcher and Codirector of a graduate program of Women Therapy, both at Tel-Aviv University. She is also a couple therapist in Israel and California, and the author of nine books, twenty book chapters, and fifty research articles. Among her other books are *Romantic Jealousy: Understanding and Conquering the Shadow of Love* (1992), *Career Burnout: Causes and Cures* (1988) coauthored with Elliot Aronson, and *Experiencing Social Psychology* (third edition, 1992) coauthored with Christina Maslach. Three of these books were translated into other languages including German, French, Hebrew, and Japanese.